THANK YOU LT. DREW T. BROWN III FOR MAKING US BELIEVERS!

From a Relieved Parent:
"I was looking for a miracle. Thank God I didn't have to wait that long. Lt. Drew Brown came along at precisely the right time with the guidance that would enable my children to become successful, functional members of society. In Lt. Brown we all saw the American Dream come alive. He's proof that the system works!"

From an Inspired Kid:
"What you said helped my friends. That night after they left school they went home and got all of the drugs out of their cars and threw them in the dumpster. They said they were never going to touch the stuff again because they didn't want to kill themselves."

From a Grateful Government:
"I want you to know how important I feel the role Lt. Drew Brown is playing to help us in the serious health threat of drug abuse. He is able to reach out and touch the very ones who must be educated and informed about this issue. His presentation is so well received by each audience that its impact is bound to continue having significant effect in the months and years to come."
Robert E. Windom, M.D., Asst. U.S. Secretary for Health

DREW T. BROWN III is a lieutenant in the U.S. Naval Reserve and a pilot for Federal Express. He has been awarded the Meritorious Service Medal and the U.S. Chamber of Commerce Special Salute for his **AMERICAN DREAM** campaign with today's youth.

You Gotta BELIEVE!

THE INSPIRING LIFE STORY OF A TRUE AMERICAN HERO

DREW T. BROWN III

AVON BOOKS NEW YORK

Grateful acknowledgment is made to the following publishers and individuals for permission to reprint from the following:

The Color Purple. Copyright © 1985 by Warner Bros., Inc. Based on the novel by Alice Walker. Screenplay by Menno Meyjes.

Jet magazine, "Navy 'A Family Affair' for Ali's Ex-Aide Bundini Brown and Jet Pilot Son." Copyright © 1983. Reprinted by permission of the publisher.

Kingsborough Community College *Scepter*, "Drew Brown Takes on New York." Copyright © 1974. Reprinted by permission of the publisher.

Loser and Still Champion: Muhammad Ali by Budd Schulberg. Copyright © 1972. Reprinted by permission of Random House.

Muhammad Ali, Who Once Was Cassius Clay by John Cottrell. Copyright © 1967 by John Cottrell. Reprinted by permission of HarperCollins Publishers, Inc.

Shaft. Copyright © 1971 by Metro-Goldwyn-Mayer, Inc. Screenplay by Ernest Tidyman and John D.F. Black.

AVON BOOKS
A division of
The Hearst Corporation
1350 Avenue of the Americas
New York, New York 10019

Copyright © 1991 by Drew Brown III
Published by arrangement with the author
Library of Congress Catalog Card Number: 90-45976
ISBN: 0-380-71007-2

Published in hardcover by William Morrow and Company, Inc.; for information address Permissions Department, William Morrow and Company, Inc., 1350 Avenue of the Americas, New York, New York 10019.

The William Morrow and Company edition contains the following Library of Congress Cataloging in Publication Data:

Brown, Drew T.
    You gotta believe : education + hard work – drugs = the American dream / Drew T. Brown III.— 1st ed.
        p.   cm.
    Includes bibliographical references.
    1. Brown, Drew T. 2. Afro-Americans—Biography 3. Afro-American youth—Social conditions. 4. Drug abuse—Social aspects—United States. 5. Success—United States. I. Title.
    E185.97.B865A3   1990
    362.29′092—dc20
    [B]   90-45976
    A GREENE *Communications*® Book   CIP

First Avon Books Trade Printing: February 1992

AVON TRADEMARK REG. U.S. PAT. OFF. AND IN OTHER COUNTRIES, MARCA REGISTRADA, HECHO EN U.S.A.

Printed in the U.S.A.

OPM   10   9   8   7   6   5   4   3   2   1

To my mother, Rhoda, my father, Drew Jr., and my
grandparents,
Bubba and Poppa Jack,
who made me feel special;
To my loving wife, Laurie Ann,
who truly makes me special;
To our children, Taryn Christine and Drew Jacques IV,
whom we've made and are special;
To God (Shorty),
who has made us all special.

Contents

PART ONE: I'm Bad, and Kickin' Live

1

Everybody here—white, black, fat, skinny, tall, short, old, and young— wakes up for one reason, and one reason only.

That's why some people pump so much Jheri Curl juice in their hair that it drips all over the place. That's why you have girls who wear sixteen earrings in their ears. They have so many holes in their heads that when the wind blows, it sounds like they're whistlin' "Dixie." You know 'em.

And that's also why they have this new hairstyle, which is my favorite, called the "High Top Fade." You know the style them brothers wear that looks like they have Wheaties boxes on their heads.

But people wear these different styles, and you dress the way you do, because everybody wakes up for one reason, and one reason only: That reason is to be happy and have fun, and that's what life is all about. . . .

During my high school years, Florida was *the* place to spend Easter break. So in 1971 when we were juniors, Danny "Rap" Rappaport, Ricky "Cubby" Katz, Gary "Princey" Prince, and I couldn't wait to escape Brooklyn's Abraham Lincoln High School. We left as soon as we could that weekend in April. All of us are Jewish, but that didn't prevent us from using a Christian holiday as an excuse to exit our Brighton Beach neighborhood. The Boardwalk was deader than a Liberace record. But Fort Lauderdale, we all knew, was *happening*. Like Jimi Hendrix's guitar at the time, it was *jammin'*.

Rap, the adventurer in our gang, was from a wealthy family. (Years later, he would become the youngest member on the board of directors of the New York Commodities Exchange.) He also owned *the* car, so we took it south. We had to. All of us loved the big metal "feet" that he had installed to replace the blue Impala's gas and brake pedals.

Once we reached Miami Beach, Princey (who worked hard at everything) got swept up in the partying and the girls—the stuff that guys always do on Easter breaks. But it was important to Rap, Cubby, and me that we were sixteen. The big one-six. We wanted real excitement this year. So the three of us took a boat to the Bahamas where, we had been told, they were celebrating Goombay Summer—the season of low prices and high spirits on the islands.

Partying appears to be second nature to the Bahamians. From the dock to Bay Street, colorful banners hung from every lamppost and rooftop in Nassau. Rhythm bands rocked on corner platforms, and people everywhere were dancing in the streets. It's an island of all black people, and they were doing nothing but jamming.

I loved it because, unlike my friends, who are white, I'm black, and back in all-white Brighton Beach, I had always been the obvious minority. A black Jew. In addition, my white Jewish buddies never went with me to Harlem, where I spent my childhood and where they would have been minorities. So for once in our friendship, the tables were turned in Nassau.

To emphasize the point and to join the festival fun, I persuaded Rap and Cubby that we needed a gimmick. So I put them on a string, and they played along, acting like trained monkeys. Then I led them through the streets, and like a barker at the entrance to a circus tent, I yelled, "Come on up. Look at the white boys. They can walk. They can talk. They sing and dance. So come one, come all, and see the amazing white boys."

Maybe it was the prevalence of rum, or the unstoppable lightheartedness of the festival, but we drew large crowds with our act. People laughed with us, applauded, and some threw money.

It was better than any bar mitzvah reception we had ever attended.

Then sometime that afternoon Rap met a man who said his name was Cowboy. An ebony-skinned Bahamian, Cowboy ran a banana-boat-like shuttle between the islands of Nassau and Andros. His clothes and flesh and breath reeked of rum, but he told great stories. And the best of them centered around scuba diving. That convinced Rap that the grandest adventure we could have would be diving off the Andros coast. Unfortunately, Cubby got sick. But I was game, so Rap and I made arrangements to leave the next morning on Cowboy's boat.

When we reached Andros, our new friend took us to his home—a hut that looked like it was thrown together out of grass, concrete, and tin. It was barely furnished, and it also reeked of rum and the stale odors embedded in the hut's dirt floor. But somehow I knew these putrid odors could not be as bad as I thought, because Cowboy lived here. He was a human being too. And he had befriended us.

Later that day, Cowboy told us about The Cut. At the time, this reef was one of the ten best places in the world for scuba diving. A constant current moved through it, allowing divers to travel rapidly amid treacherous beauty. Rap, who had his diving certification, was thrilled and asked Cowboy to take us to the dive shop nearest The Cut. I agreed. But I also pulled Rap aside and reminded him that I had never put on a mask or tanks, much less been certified.

"Cool out," Rap said. "I can guide you through the diving. But the real problem will be getting past the shop owner. He won't rent us gear unless we both have certification." So that night we came up with a plan.

The next morning at the shop, the owner immediately asked for our cards. As planned, I searched confidently through my wallet. Then I stopped, feigning a sudden expression of shock, and began yelling, "I can't believe it. I've lost my card."

At that, Rap tripped out, and we launched into a rehearsed argument, complete with lingo that only certified scuba divers would understand. Other divers were there, donning their rented gear and waiting for the boat to leave. They quickly became impatient and joined the argument too. Then just before Rap and I started hitting one another—which was Scene

Two of our scheme—the shop owner intervened. As we had hoped, he settled the dispute by renting the gear to us.

Scene Three, however, was beyond anything that we had imagined.

Among the other divers were several professional photographers, and as the boat headed toward the first dropoff point along The Cut, they busied themselves in checking and preparing their gear. I complained loudly about my shoulder, which I said had been hurt in an old basketball injury. This gave Rap an excuse to help me get into my gear, and to whisper a few last-minute instructions. But we reached the dropoff point much sooner than I expected. So I was still fumbling with my mask when the boat stopped and all the divers stood. Everyone joined hands, so I did the same. And within a second, *Boom,* I was in the water.

As we sank hand in hand, the water pressure immediately got to me. I couldn't see straight. Like a watermelon hurled onto concrete, my head felt as though it was going to split open. My lungs ached, and I couldn't breathe. And I panicked when, beyond the pain, I realized that I could not control my body. Meanwhile, the weight of my gear pulled me downward, and the powerful current kept thrusting me forward. I felt as though I were floating in *The Twilight Zone,* with my only link to reality being the tight grip that I maintained on Rap's hand. But instinctively, I knew that if I descended as fast as the other divers were, I would die in a matter of seconds. So I did the unthinkable: I let go of Rap's hand.

Suddenly, through the flood of water and bubbles that separated us, I saw his eyes bulge from behind his mask. They looked big and white, like baseballs in a jar, and they seemed to scream, "Come back, come back. You can't do this without me!" But in that same instant, they also said a pitiful good-bye. Then more silent than clouds racing across the sky, he and the other divers drifted. Their suspended bodies sank rapidly like a team of masked angels on a mission into oblivion.

Within seconds, they disappeared from my sight, and I felt an overwhelming sense of aloneness. I also began to hyperventilate, because I didn't know how to breathe through the diver's mask. The tighter my chest felt, the harder I inhaled. But I still couldn't get enough air from the tank. That's when all that I had learned on the streets of New York seemed to hit me at once. And this knowledge was, quite simply, my common street sense.

The primary rule of the streets is: *Whatever you must do to survive, do it fast.* Clearly, I had to breathe. So I tried to relax, hoping that grace under pressure would help me breathe better through the tank. I knew that I couldn't stop hyperventilation, but I did believe that I could slow down its rate. I forced myself to breathe softly. The softer I inhaled, the more air I drew from the tank. *Aaah.* And the more air I took in, the calmer I became. *All right.* My Harlem maxims were working.

The street brother's voice in my head agreed. He said calmly, "Problem one solved, home boy. You won't die. Not yet, anyway."

Then I looked down and saw gray. I looked to the sides and saw gray. And I looked up. More gray. No matter where I looked there was nothing but gray matter all around, so I couldn't really determine directions. But even if that had not been the case, I wouldn't have surfaced, because the second rule of the streets is: *Don't quit.*

I let the forces take me. As I relaxed in the water, the weight of my gear gradually pulled me deeper while the current continued to drive me forward. But being out of control was not new to me. Over the years I had run with the brothers into many hostile situations. Junkies don't hang out by the rules of *Mister Rogers' Neighborhood.*

As a result, I knew that other street rules applied here, too: *If you don't live in the neighborhood, and you don't know what you're doing, then travel like a smart stranger. Don't bother anybody. And don't look at anybody too long.* After all, street-smart people don't stare at strangers in New York. Because if a stranger yells, "Whatchu lookin' at?" then you know *that* dude is not asking you to dance.

So I played by street rules until I had dropped nearly ninety feet below the surface. Suddenly, this dark gray realm opened into a bright, gleaming one. It was as if the sun only cared about this single spot on the ocean floor. And to my surprise, I started hearing music. It was like an orchestra featuring violins and flutes, and in that era of psychedelic acid trips, it was the ultimate high. I saw big lobsters and crabs crawling through coral of the most brilliant reds and greens imaginable. And I saw fish as big as walls, with light reflecting off them like mirrors in a disco. But I touched nothing. And I didn't stare too long. The Cut wasn't my neighborhood. It was theirs.

Trying to stay cool, however, my mind still raced a million miles a second. Surrounded by all the beauty in The Cut, I was far, far away from Harlem. But in terms of survival, I was actually strolling down Amsterdam Avenue, and basking in the midnight glow of neon. But ready at any moment for trouble to jump from the next alley.

I drifted with the current and marveled at everything I saw until, *Bingo,* what came to mind would subsequently save my life. Again the street brother's voice whispered, "How do you know when you runnin' out of air? Does a bell go off? Does a sign flash? How the heck will *you* know?"

"I don't," I mumbled into my mouthpiece, and I had to make a choice. Either I continued along The Cut and took my chances, or it was time to head up. But believe me, that decision was easy. *On the streets of Harlem, when questions outnumber answers, then you leave.* So I started kicking against both gravity and current, and immediately, I began to rise.

Suddenly I recalled all those nights that I had watched Lloyd Bridges on *Sea Hunt,* and I remembered the warnings he had given new divers: "If you go up too fast, you'll die from the bends." Well, I didn't know what the bends were, but I hadn't gotten this far simply to die. So I did what I remembered him doing, and I forced myself to rise slowly.

I moved with such slowness that it must have taken me a half hour to go up. I felt like a sleepwalker in an empty world. But as slowly as I was having to move, I didn't mind this stark aloneness. As an only child, I had learned many ways to entertain myself. So I kept my mind alert by chanting, "I won't die. I will survive. I can't die. I will survive." How else would I get to enjoy the envy on Rap, Cubby, and Princey's faces when they heard about my adventure?

Gradually, I got closer to the surface, and it became even more difficult to go slowly. I couldn't wait to pop above the water, rip off my mask, and breathe fresh air. But once I did, and the bright Atlantic sun hit my face, I had barely gotten the mask off and was sucking in air when, *bloop,* the weight of my gear pulled me two feet under. That's when I realized that Lloyd Bridges never showed the viewers how a weighted diver could stay on top. So I bobbed up and down. Each time I surfaced I gasped air, only to be sucked under, again and again.

And whenever my eyes saw sky, I searched for the boat. When I finally spotted it, however, I couldn't believe Rap's expression. It wasn't envy, as I had expected. It wasn't even surprise. Instead, it was total elation and disbelief, all wrapped into one. Rap had thought I died, so he was silently grieving. But seeing me return to life, so to speak, sent Rap's emotions into the psychological equivalent of the bends. He didn't know whether to laugh or cry as the crew hauled me into the boat.

After I settled on board, we both were speechless. For once. Blood was trickling from my ears and nose, and Rap's face was white as snow, as if he were sitting beside a shivering ghost.

"How come you left us?" one of the professional divers yelled loudly, and shook a long pointed finger in my face. "We're supposed to stick together."

"I know," I responded casually. "I just wanted to check some things out by myself."

"Hey, diving on this trip is not done like that, man," another argued. "Haven't you heard about The Cut?"

"Oh," I said in a tone meant to convince them that one of the world's most treacherous reefs hadn't been that big a deal to me. "If you guys can't make it down there alone, then don't ever ride the subway and pop up in Harlem."

Twenty years have passed since that teenage adventure. But this year, as America continues through the 1990s, I'm on another big adventure. Each month I speak to high school, college, and adult audiences around this country, and that's an incredible trip. It's a high because these kids live the way that Rap, Cubby, Princey, and I did. Everybody lives to party. To get high. And like us, today's kids don't hesitate to flirt with death.

It's true for every generation. The young are not afraid of dying. The absence of such fear is so prevalent that the United States Navy coined the acronym, NAFOD, that stands for No APPARENT FEAR OF DEATH. They seek that trait in young recruits. In fact, naval jet pilots *must* demonstrate some NAFOD during aviation training, and instructors weed out the ones who don't. I know. At one time I was the only black jet attack pilot among fourteen thousand men in the fleet. Not only had I demonstrated NAFOD when I was sixteen and struggling to survive that reef, but years later I flew 550 miles an hour, fifty feet from the ground, and carried twenty-two five-hundred-pound bombs under the wings of my all-weather, "anytime baby" attack jet known as the A-6 Intruder. Tom Cruise only pretended to be a "top gun." I *was* one.

So, yes, today's kids party, and get high, and take risks just as we did. Ask them. They'll admit it. But they differ from us, too. And that difference disturbs me. You see, an increasing number of today's kids no longer dream. I call it TAFOD, or TEENS AFRAID OF DREAMING. But whatever your term, it's as prevalent across this nation as their inability to fear death. For example, when I stand before a teenage audience and talk about The American Dream, their expressions usually go blank. They know the words, of course. Some even understand the concept. But most are afraid to dream about their futures. And their reasons are legion.

"Why reach beyond my grasp?" a pretty seventeen-year-old girl asked me in Ohio. Immediately, I remembered the Funkadelic lyric that this black rock group had coined: "To each his reach. And if you can't cop, it's not yours to have." So I knew where she was coming from. But she had personal reasons, too.

The bulge around the waist of her New Kids on the Block T-shirt revealed the early months of a pregnancy. And when she saw me notice, this perky, blond-haired girl added, "You can see, college ain't in my future, man. I can't even read!" Then tiny tears streaked the makeup on her soft, white face, and she whispered, "So tell me now why I should dream? Please tell me."

A member of the Crips gang argued with me for an hour on the streets of Los Angeles. I knew that, by reputation, he sold drugs. He said that he had all the guns and knives, crack and cash that he needed. The same, he said, was true for women. He also bragged about killing people. The Bloods. And he acted bad—no, *knew* he was bad—because he had his colors. "We are your worst nightmare," he boasted. "We have no conscience. We ain't gonna make it no way." And he said that he was nineteen. But I could see by his smooth, black complexion that he had not yet needed to shave. Not once. He was only fourteen.

In Manhattan, a young teenage girl, apparently a runaway, stopped me along Broadway just off 42nd Street. "I saw you on TV in some motel," she said. Her round, pretty face looked Native American. Her eyes, glazed by drugs, were dark and disinterested. But her voice was practiced. "You said that if kids take drugs they're gonna die," she said with a laugh, then flipped a wave of long black hair from her brow, and added, "I'm a kid, too, mister. Come on, you wanna do me? After all, I might be dead tomorrow."

Because that pregnant, illiterate girl asked. Because that member of the Crips boasted. Because that runaway laughed. And because millions of seemingly "typical" American kids are also afraid of dreaming, I now write my story.

Like my adventure along The Cut, it's a story that will first plunge into the dark, dangerous realms that I experienced as a child, a boy unprepared for a Drew's lot in the city. During my teenage years, there were moments of promise and hope, though our family was no *Brady Bunch* scene. Then this story entangles in a series of wrong turns that I took as a young man, repeatedly flirting with death and defeat. Fortunately, I found love along the way. But I also came close to losing it. And in the process, I learned the real meanings of fear and dreams. By proving worthy of love, I truly became a man. And only after that did I achieve success and The American Dream.

The U.S. Navy played its part. And in their separate ways, so did my wife, our children, and my parents. So mine is a dramatic story, packed into a few short years. I am only thirty-six. But it's an important story because I represent an *attainable* dream. Mike Tyson, the heavyweight champion of the world, says he's bad. My boy, Michael Jackson, has the *audacity* to say that he's bad. Well, guess what? They're not bad. *I'm* bad. Why? Because Martin Luther King, Jr., died for me. Rosa Parks refused to get off a Montgomery bus for me. And millions of Jews died in Nazi death camps for me. They all paved the way to freedom, and made my opportunities possible.

I'm so bad and kickin' live that, after active duty in the U.S. Navy, I am now a lieutenant in the United States Naval Reserve and a pilot for Federal Express. In 1988 I founded, and am president of, The American Dream—a program to combat the use of illegal drugs and to confront the education issues that currently threaten our nation. This organization is my vehicle for igniting students with low levels of self-confidence and self-esteem to get smoked. Not on drugs or mediocrity. But on this nation's time-proven values. My formula is simple: *Education* + Hard Work − *Drugs* = *Success and The American Dream.*

But that's too simple, you say?

Then sit back. Relax. And take a ride in my long black Cadillac. Travel with me, first to Seminole County, Florida, where my father grew up under segregation; then north to the streets of Harlem, New York, where as a boy I knew the pimps and hustlers by name. And they knew me. But near the Apollo Theatre, let's pull the car over and stop beside a homeless black woman. She is wrapped in a blanket and asleep above the steaming grate in the sidewalk. We walk toward her, until the stench of warm urine stops us flat. But even without speaking to her, we understand that, far more than her body, her mind has been wasted by drugs and alcohol.

I do not recognize her, but I know her. She is my street sister. And if I had not escaped these New York streets, I could be curled up beside her. You don't believe me? Then without a doubt, this story must begin where my life as "a Drew" got its start.

PART TWO: Education

2

How did they keep black people down two hundred years ago? You think it was with some whips, or with chains, or by making us pick cotton? No. They kept a whole nation of people slaves—some who used to be kings and queens—just 'cause they wouldn't let us read.

On the other hand, how come every time you watch Dallas, Dynasty, *or* Falcon Crest—*or when you ring the doorbell at the admiral's house, the governor's mansion, or at some big estate home belonging to the president of a large corporation—how come somebody always comes to the door and says, "They will meet you in the library"? How come everybody in this country who has something has a library? Yet they kept a whole nation of people slaves, just 'cause they wouldn't let us read.*

So you better wake up, and get to this. If you don't plan on learning how to read, and you don't further your education, you're gonna be a slave. Accept it now.

But if you do read, and get a college education, you can be anything that you wanna be in this country.

You see, I'm gonna be your worst nightmare. I'm your conscience. And either you listen to me now, or I promise you one thing in life, you're gonna listen to me later. But you will listen. . . .

My genes come from people who were always looking for The American Dream. My mother's parents and grandparents were Jews who struggled to find freedom in Russia. Ultimately, they escaped to America so they could have free religious choices. But on my father's side there was something much different. My paternal roots came out of Africa when my black ancestors were brought to America—not by their own will, but on slave ships. So all of my genes know the search and the struggle for freedom, though only in my generation has this been possible.

Back in the 1920s and '30s, the first "Drew"—my grandfather, Drew Brown—was an angry young man because black people in this country were literally *inferior* to whites by law. The American court system upheld poll taxes and literacy tests that kept blacks like my illiterate granddaddy from voting. And other laws, inhuman and unwritten laws, dictated that when white people walked down the sidewalk, blacks like my educated grandmother, Elizabeth White Brown, had to step aside. Blacks always had to answer whites with a "Yes, sir," or a "Yes, ma'am," while they demeaned us with greetings like "Hey, boy," or "Hey, girl."

No wonder theirs was a generation of bitter men and women. A whole society made them feel inadequate and worthless. Blacks in the South couldn't even drink from the same public fountains as whites. This meant that when Granddaddy Drew was thirsty in his hometown of Sanford, Florida, he had to find a "For Colored Only" sign scribbled above a dirty porcelain fountain.

Such injustices started something bad in my Brown family— the conflict between loved ones. You see, when he and my grandmother were young and living in Florida's Seminole County, they had The American Dream in their hearts, too. Elizabeth was a schoolteacher who believed that she could achieve that dream through education and by working *within* the system to change people. In her, Granddaddy Drew saw a fiery spirit, another black person determined to create a different type of world for the next generation of blacks. He courted her, he married her, and then they started a family.

But during the early decades of this century, the Emancipation Proclamation and the Union victory in the Civil War were already ancient history, as far as my grandparents were concerned. They could look around and see that these great events in American history had failed to end the system that kept black people in ignorance. Why? Because after the first ten years of Reconstruction in the 1800s, this nation had settled into more than half a century during which the means of keeping southern and many northern blacks enslaved grew even harsher. America's white power system—stripped of legal authority to own human beings and to deny them any form of human rights—had chosen other means. Blacks were systematically humiliated, deprived of protection under the law, and when all else failed, they were terrorized.

That's what made Granddaddy Drew buck the system. He despised the racist segregation that denied blacks opportunities, not only to eat in all-white restaurants, but to live in white neighborhoods or to attend white schools. He resented poll taxes and literacy tests because they not only denied blacks the right to vote, but through that, these injustices excluded blacks from the right to hold any office or to shape the laws that left them with unequal protection. A white committing a crime against a black was almost certain to be acquitted, if not applauded. Yet a black accused of a crime against a white was almost certain to end up on a chain gang, or worse, to be hanged.

Worse still, if the law didn't get blacks, the Ku Klux Klan did. Their favorite punishment for men like Granddaddy Drew was the tar-and-feather method. Klansmen would hold blacks to the ground, pour boiling tar over their bodies, and then shower these tortured people with mounds of feathers—perhaps the most painful form of burning ever devised by man. Fortunately for him, my grandfather escaped this; some of his friends, however, could not.

So as in earlier years, blacks responded to such persecution the way persecuted people have always done. The great majority just gave up and accepted what they could not change. But the few who refused to surrender became divided into two camps: those, like Elizabeth White Brown, remaining determined to work within the system to make life better for the next generation; and those, like Drew Brown, remaining equally determined to fight that system. And inevitably, such opposing views created a civil war within my twentieth-century family. Granddaddy Drew bucked the system that Elizabeth labored within. His enemy was her cause. And that difference would make their marriage impossible.

Granddaddy Drew Brown was indomitable. He would not bow down. He would not be ruled by fear of man or fear of beast. He was a Brown of Sanford, Florida, and they were a mean bunch. They didn't take any nonsense. During his lifetime, they became a renegade power in Seminole County. Not financially, of course, because they had no money, but they were still a family to be reckoned with. A Brown man and wife represented male power and female integrity. The Brown men were feared for their abilities to fight, and the women, for their churchgoing righteousness. The men regularly went crazy with alcohol and anger, but the women brought them back into the fold. The family always had the final say. With every Brown, that is, except my granddaddy.

Somehow, Granddaddy Drew proved himself the meanest of them all. A short, wiry man, he had a strange and fearful presence about him. When he spoke, his voice growled with a lisp through his teeth, his jaw remaining stiff, locked, and forceful. His was the low, commanding voice of a renegade among renegades. He supplemented his paycheck as a railroad worker by hunting alligators and selling their hides. He mastered the silent kill—hunting alone, at night, with only a knife. Africa was thick in his blood. Yet he always wore starched, white, stiff-collared shirts, and he habitually smoked Prince Albert cigars. In the swamps. At the crossroads store. Or on his day job along the rails.

Long statements annoyed him, so he didn't waste words. He said what he wanted, and he usually got it—though more often, he preferred to speak through his actions. Most particularly, with his knife. He boiled with a certain anger, which explained many of his actions, because he not only hated white men, but he also abhorred what the white system had done to his spirit. The same determination that drove him to hunt alligators alone in the dark also made him refuse to shuffle his feet during the white man's day. In their midst, he walked tall like a man, and with his hands, he fought both the system and the men themselves. And anytime his fists proved insufficient for these brawls, he didn't hesitate to produce a knife or a gun.

Elizabeth bore him two sons, and was as powerful as the other Brown women. Educated, driven by reason, a teacher at the county's black school, she embodied respectability. So she hated the fact that, in an era when black men did not retaliate against whites, her husband regularly fought out his disagreements with white men. To her, it was little consolation that he usually won these bar brawls—at the scene, anyway—because she knew that he could not prevail against the white system's law. Repeatedly, the Seminole County sheriff arrested him on warrants signed by white men, and this humiliated her.

But more than humiliation, she feared the violence that erupted from within Granddaddy Drew when he came home drunk and frustrated from fighting so hard. I'm sure that he loved his wife and sons, but alcohol-propelled anger caused him to abuse and beat them. Society's injustices had cut too deep, and something within would not allow him to quit striking out, even after he was back home with the people who loved him.

Elizabeth took this abuse for a few years, and protected her sons when she could; but when it became obvious that the line between love and hate was too finely drawn in her husband's soul, she had to act. So before my father finished the third grade, Elizabeth announced that she was leaving. Granddaddy Drew's only response was that she could not take him, their eldest son, with her. He was a Drew.

It was a horrible choice: She could win freedom from the marriage by giving up a son; or she could stay, endure increasing abuse, and watch those sons grow up to be like him. But she had to choose. The following day, she left with their son Elbert, and did not return. My father remembered waiting, day after day, beside the mailbox where he last saw the two figures disappear, the day his momma walked away. He waited, either for her to come walking back, or for her letter to arrive, telling him how to come and find her. But neither came. It was Elizabeth White Brown's price to pay, in order to gain freedom.

But all of Granddaddy Drew's resistance actually changed nothing. All the years of his life, the system stayed the same. No matter how hard he fought, he couldn't make the world any fairer for his sons, and that ate at him like an alligator gnawing at his guts. Proud he was, and brave he was, and indomitable he was, but to these traits his frustration added violence and alcohol. He went wrong, fighting for all that was right. And his behavior had been more than the gentle Elizabeth could stand. Just as determined as he, she had been more patient and practical. She had believed that if they raised their sons to be better educated and better mannered, then the boys would be accepted. Time would change things.

The tragedy is, both my grandparents were wrong. Neither resistance nor self-improvement would offer their sons any hope, unless they fled the area in which they were born and raised. And even that was a fearsome journey north, because America was trapped in the dark days of the 1930s when many highly skilled whites could not find decent jobs, even in Chicago or New York City.

The divorce did not change Granddaddy Drew. He continued drinking and fighting. But the divorce did mean that there was now no one (except Aunt Jane) to keep his son while the father went out. If Granddaddy left little Drew alone, the boy followed his father into the night. Once, Granddaddy Drew was halfway into the swamps on an alligator hunt when he spied the boy in barefooted pursuit after him. So Granddaddy Drew devised a severe form of baby-sitting: He beat and then tied my father to a vent on the rooftop, so the boy couldn't follow. That was Granddaddy Drew's way of protecting his son. Certain men, if they can't speak with their minds, must always resort to communicating with their fists.

But for all of his faults, Granddaddy Drew never stopped being a man whose word was his honor. One day, for example, not long after Elizabeth left, he was bathing my father in a big gray metal tub in the yard. They kept the tub there so that the water could be heated by the sun, since the house lacked indoor plumbing.

Moments later, however, Granddaddy Drew heard the sheriff's car approaching, but my grandfather never looked up from his task. He wanted the sheriff to come to him.

When the official reached the tub, he said, "Come on, Drew. It's time for you to go down to jail. You know what you did last night."

Without even looking up from the tub, and without missing a stroke while smoothing oil on my father's naked body, Granddaddy Drew told the white sheriff, "You get the hell off my land right now. I'll be down to the jail. But first I need to tend to my boy."

The sheriff knew that my grandfather might do anything at any time, and that he hated white people with a passion. So the official returned to his car and drove away.

Later that evening, after Granddaddy Drew had put his son to bed, he walked to town. He wore a freshly ironed white shirt, his sheathed knife glistened at his waist, and a cigar hung from his lips. Without saying a word, he entered the jail, laid his knife and cigar on the sheriff's desk, and surrendered to serve his time. He was demonstrating that, even to people he hated, a Drew's word was his bond.

But in 1938, a strange and wonderful event momentarily united black and white Americans in a way that nothing else could accomplish. The Joe Louis–Max Schmeling prize fight promised to be more than black versus white. It was America versus Hitler's champion, and both the *Führer* and his boxer had boasted relentlessly that no one could stand up to the Aryan might. In reaction to that bragging, probably nothing else before Pearl Harbor so united the American people.

And that amazed my father, who was only nine at the time. All of a sudden, it wasn't black and white anymore in this country. For a few weeks anyway, it was who would win, democracy or a dictatorship, America or Nazi Germany? Two men fighting one another became a symbol of ignorance versus intelligence. The democratic intelligence of the American people as a whole wanted to beat the racist ignorance of the Nazi German regime. And in the process, the American people—and my young father in particular—got their first lesson in a hard-to-master subject: There is no black and white.

Down in Sanford, Florida, on the night of that fight, all the Browns gathered around the radio at one of the few crossroads stores that welcomed blacks as customers. Among them were my father, his uncles Alonzo, Willie, Johnnie, and Coley, and my father's aunt Sadie. The grown men bragged and took turns buying rounds of scotch or beer while they placed bets from that week's pay. The children wagered marbles and pennies, or jabbed at one another in fancy boxer stances. Excitement in the room was like a disease, spreading from one to the other. No night had been like this. In minutes, the "Brown Bomber" from Alabama, big Joe Louis, would defend his world heavyweight title against Max Schmeling, Nazi Germany's "White Hope."

Far to the north in Yankee Stadium, white sportscasters at the microphone praised Louis's record, but cautioned that he had lost to Schmeling before. Back at the store near Lake Monroe, however, Louis remained the favorite. Then the bell sounded.

When the crowd in New York saw Louis leap toward Schmeling, they roared. But in Florida, the Brown men were silent for the first time that night. They wanted to hear every blow. And there were plenty during the next one hundred seconds— almost all of them against the German.

At the end of two minutes, when the New York announcer said that Schmeling was hit, a low rumbling laugh began to shake the windows at the crossroads store. But above the Brown boys' laughter—even above the radio voice of the surprised announcer that echoed the stadium crowd's roar—a chilling scream rang out.

"What happened?" my father yelled at the radio speaker.

Instantly, Granddaddy Drew smacked his taut hand across his son's mouth, held tight, and grumbled, "Listen, boy."

Then the answer from Yankee Stadium sent emotional shock waves not only to Florida, but also to Roosevelt beside his radio at the White House, and to Hitler in Berlin. Louis's right to Schmeling's head had caused the German to scream, then collapse. After the count, the announcer said that the American had knocked the German out cold.

Immediately, the silence in the crossroads store vanished. My grandfather even let go of Daddy's mouth so that the boy could scream, too.

But in a soft voice, my father asked, "You mean it's over?"

"That's right. The Brown Bomber kicked Max's butt."

"Good," my daddy said with a grin. Then he hustled around the store to collect the marbles and pennies that he had won.

But the radio stayed on. While the Brown boys drank and celebrated in Florida, Joe Louis left Yankee Stadium and rode

7273

in a police-escorted caravan to Harlem. There, in the lobby of the Hotel Theresa on 125th Street, he held court, and a radio announcer broadcast a "live" interview with the champ. Back at the crossroads store, my father was mesmerized by what he heard.

I don't know what was said in that interview. My father didn't remember details. But Budd Schulberg was on the streets of Harlem that night, and years later he would write: "We attended a democratic carnival in Harlem. Behind a coffin draped with a Nazi flag, tens of thousands big-appled and cakewalked. It was a spontaneous political demonstration. Joe Louis had gone forth to do battle for all of us, and everyone was rejoicing, from Wendell Wi[l]lkie to the black number[s] runner who pulled out a roll and set up drinks for the house at a corner bar we wandered into on Amsterdam Avenue. . . . Everybody laughed, and we hugged each other, and the closest thing to it I would ever know was VE Night in London. The two victory street operas overlap in my memory—marking the beginning and ending of the long war. . . ."[1]

But whatever my father heard on the radio that night, he never forgot how the sounds from Harlem made him feel. He promised himself that one day he, too, would live in that magic-sounding realm where a black boxer could be the honored guest at a hotel, where black people could dance in the streets, and where no white man could make a black man feel out of place. It sounded like paradise—a village of black people where Drew Brown, Jr., could wear a long, black coat and a stylish hat, and celebrate freedom as he strolled along Harlem's sidewalks.

The problem today is that I see children acting the same way that my granddaddy did. Back then, my formula of "Education + Hard Work − Drugs = Success and The American Dream" didn't work. But now after people have died for these rights, the formula does work. Children today have no reason to act the way they do. And not just the kids, but the adults today as well. There is no longer a reason for blacks to drink and fight, as Granddaddy Drew did, because today, with education and determination and belief in one's self, blacks can be anything in this country. Anything. It's a new day, and time for us to wake up.

Times have changed. Wake up!

3

You were not put on this earth to be dropouts, drug addicts, derelicts, gang bangers and prostitutes, alcoholics or bums.

You were put here on this earth to be better than your parents, and to make this world a better place for your children. You were put here to carry your family name from now on, with pride, dignity, and class.

You better listen to me now, or you're gonna listen to me later. But God forbid that it's later, because that just might be too late. . . .

At the age of twenty, my father rented a white-owned hall and became the first black man to promote a professional boxing match in Seminole County. With the money he made from that 1949 event, he moved north to Harlem, New York. But by then, he had acquired much more than dollars to prepare him for the streets of New York City. He was handsome, stood just over six feet tall, and despite the fact that he was slender, his muscles were well toned and powerful.

"He would stand there with a grin on his odd half-moon face. . . . And even though he told you, you still wondered where he came from, and how he got here," a best-selling book would describe my father, twenty-six years after he moved into his first apartment on 114th Street in Harlem. "He had papers showing that he had been [in the navy] at the age of thirteen, [and] that he had grown up in . . . Florida. 'I've been paying my own rent since I was nine years old,' he said, and he'd been out on his own since he was eleven; been in sea camps, reform schools, prison; been around the world a dozen times; was a hustler who hustled the hustlers. . . . [But whatever the origins, Drew Brown, Jr.] had a way of throwing his whole life and soul into every project he believed in."[1]

As a naval steward, my father had been the ship's boy who shined shoes for the officers. He told me that at a port in India, he acquired the nickname "Bundini" when a group of girls followed him back to the boat and repeatedly yelled the word while the ship pulled out of port. My father, barely a teenager, told his shipmates that *bundini* meant "lover." After that, the nickname stuck.

Seven years later, Bundini became a "player" on the streets of Harlem. During the early fifties, some players were pimps or drug dealers; others ran scams or con games. But since all the best players survived by their wits, my father was a natural. Granddaddy Drew had not given him much of a childhood, but he had raised his son to be a Drew. So Bundini was well prepared to hustle. His nickname, he told the players, meant "Fastblack."

By 1952, however, the name *Bundini* had assumed yet another meaning, "The Black Prince," because my father had quickly become a leading player on Harlem's streets. As proof of this status, he rented the front apartment above Sugar Ray's Bar on Amsterdam near 123rd Street. This address enabled Bundini to operate out of what was then the heart of Harlem's nightlife.

It was the hub because Sugar Ray Robinson reigned as the king of boxers. He had won both the welterweight and middleweight championships, and was past his prime. But because television was new, and because each week it aired championship boxing matches—including Sugar Ray's hard-fought victories and comebacks—his name began rivaling Joe Louis's as the champ most admired by black Americans.

During the daytime, my father sometimes worked at conventional jobs, like being a restaurant cook, yet his nights remained dedicated to hustling. And the sign beneath his apartment windows—*Sugar Ray's* displayed in glittering neon script— attracted easy money.

There, jazz musicians and neighborhood singers elbowed with record producers. Pimps, prostitutes, and old boxers sized up the young hopefuls. White couples came from downtown to soak up the dark atmosphere that centered around a plush leather bar with stools. But they also came for drugs and sex. And once hooked, many glamorous white babes returned to walk alone under the nightclub's covered-wagon canopy. White women going with black men was in vogue. Drugs were plentiful. And in Harlem, both were status symbols that held as much meaning as Sugar Ray's pink convertible Cadillac, which he kept parked in front of his bar.

My mother was born Rhoda Palestine—the beautiful, fun-loving daughter of white Russian Jews who came to America from Rogachor, a small village thirty miles from Kiev in the 1920s. They reared her and a brother, Herbert, first in Brooklyn, and then the Bronx, before settling back into the all-white neighborhood of Brighton Beach. After this final move, their apartment building, the Waldorf, was one lot from the Boardwalk's southern end. At the other end, Coney Island stretched out for acres. Except for being parts of Greater New York City, however, Momma's Brighton and Daddy's Harlem were worlds apart.

She describes her girlhood personality as "aggressive, gregarious, and outgoing with a positive nature. Nothing could stop me, and there wasn't anything that I wouldn't have done." But Momma was a dreamer, too, and those dreams evolved during her school years. "I kept looking for a way to save the world," she said, remembering that, in order, she had wanted to be a teacher, a dancer, an actress, and a nurse. By the time she entered junior high school in 1943, she decided that journalism would be her career. So her parents, Mildred and Zeda Jack Palestine, bought an Underwood typewriter, and Momma began to write.

But when God made my mother, bless her, He threw away

the mold. She was an excellent student in high school, but sometimes she demonstrated theatrical emotions, or danced in the halls. For the era, that behavior was considered outrageous. And if teachers or peers protested, Momma had a pat response: "So what? I'm the reincarnation of Genghis Khan and Sitting Bull."

None of that sat well at school, or in Momma's Orthodox Jewish home. But her bubbly personality did find admirers at USO centers, or during Coast Guard dances at the Maritime in Manhattan Beach. World War II was in full swing, then; the Maritime was crowded with sailors; and enlisted men filled the USO Centers. So these weekly dances were a magnet for Brooklyn girls, Momma included.

She found her niche while working the monitor board at a USO center near her home. That job enabled her to know the guys by name, and to talk. She preferred talking. That feminine art, she recalls, had been perfected during late nights on the Boardwalk with guys in her neighborhood. "It was a time when we all grew up fast," she said. "We had to."

Even though Momma was only seventeen in 1947 when she graduated from high school—and underage to do so—she got jobs at several nightclubs, mostly as the camera girl. This meant that, for a fee, she took pictures of patrons and, later in the evening, presented them with the finished prints. The following year when she was eighteen, she left New York—moving first to California, then back to the East Coast. While in Florida, she was the only woman on staff at Leon and Eddie's—a popular nightclub that featured female impersonators as entertainment.

But Momma is a true New Yorker, so she couldn't stay away long. Upon her return, she went from job to job in several nightclubs, though there was one constant in her life. She started going each week to a beauty school across from the Times Tower on 42nd Street. "Because of the texture of my hair," she said, "the teacher always worked on me. I got special treatment. And I would come away with fantastic bouffants—the latest styles laced with waves and sprinkles. It was marvelous. So every Thursday night I looked like a queen, felt like a queen. And from there, I would go directly to Birdland."

At the time, Birdland was a popular jazz club north of Times Square. And since Momma loved to sing Billie Holiday songs, and dance, Birdland became Momma's hangout. "If you didn't sit at the bar or reserve one of the main tables, which were expensive, you were ushered into the *bullpen*," she recalls. "I always headed for the bullpen, because it was near bands like Count Basie's, Charlie Parker's, and Lester Young's. But I'll never forget the group that played the Birdland when I first started going. The Three Flames was their name, and how I loved their lead number, which was a hot jazz tune called 'Open the Door, Richard.' I stayed many nights, all night, drinking in the bullpen and interpreting the Three Flames' songs with my dances."

Even though harsh conservatism swept across America at the time, Momma was a wonderful free spirit. So nightclubs like Birdland became her haven. Getting high on the music, the partying, and the booze, nobody in those clubs worried that McCarthyism was halting free expression of ideas, or that a coalition of antiblack Republicans and Democrats in the Deep South was supporting Ike for president.

"Being with black guys was not unusual," she said, "because my friends were artists and musicians. So nobody in our world had any concept of, you know, racial inequalities. Who cared about religious inequalities? Nobody cared if you were fat or short or whatever. It was talent that each one responded to."

By the summer of '52, Momma was the camera girl at the Village Vanguard. But that famous Greenwich Village jazz club had temporarily switched its bookings to folk music, in step with the sudden popularity of groups like Pete Seeger and The Weavers. Momma hated this music, and so did most of the Vanguard's regulars. So the business waned, and she got laid off.

"But that didn't bother me," she remembers. "We all belonged to the 'Fifty-two/Twenty Club.' Twenty dollars' unemployment for fifty-two weeks." So she collected her unemployment, and went to a jazz club on West 54th Street called The French Quarter. And it was there, that night, that Rhoda Palestine met Drew Bundini Brown.

"I went to hear Miles Davis. Sweet Miles. Ole sweet Miles," she recalls. "But it was still a question whether Miles would show up for the gig, 'cause he didn't always. Yet this particular night, right, I sat down to the bar. I had on a black dress and high-heeled shoes. I looked nice. And I ordered myself a Johnny Walker Black Label, with a glass of ice water on the side, then drank it down. But even though I had a twenty stuck in my bra, I didn't pay. The place was full, so I figured some guy would treat me. And before I ordered the next drink, me still listening to Miles, that's what happened.

"I heard this very charming, sweet voice say, 'Young lady, may I buy you a drink?' I swear I never heard Drew talk in that tone again. But it was sure in his voice that night. So I turned around, and I saw these flashing eyes, and a shining happy face with bright flashing teeth—a beautiful black handsome face. He was wearing a pearl gray jacket with a black shirt and a white satin tie. There was just something about him, an immediate attraction. So I said, 'Yes, thank you.' Then he ordered another Johnny Walker for me, but a vermouth for himself. Well, I thought, this guy's no drinker. But that was it, nonetheless. That was it.

"That night I went with him to Harlem, and I stayed with him. He had this Japanese figurine of a woman on a large mirrored vanity, and he called her 'Twala, Twala.' I could see that this was a really neat guy. Except, he had a drawer full of dirty socks and pawnshop tickets; so the next day, I washed out his socks, already. That was his only shortcoming. That, and the fact that when I woke up, he was gone, and so was my twenty dollars."

After a couple of nights in Harlem, Momma went back home to her parents in Brighton. A few days later, however, my father arrived on the Boardwalk, and telephoned the Palestine residence. "Either you come down and meet me," he told Momma, "or I'm coming up to the house." So she went down.

Walking together, he told her, "I want to come meet your family. That's all."

"Please, my father's a sick man," she responded, quickly considering how her white family would react to this resolute black man. Brighton Beach, she knew, was nothing like Harlem, or even the permissive Birdland.

"My mother, I knew, could handle it," Momma recalls. "She had no qualms. Bubba would tell you just what she thought. She was a strong woman. She'd tell you the truth. But I just didn't know what to do. I was frustrated. Then I figured, all right a'ready, my mother is home. Let him come up.'"

So Momma phoned my grandmother and prepared Bubba, then took my father to the Waldorf Apartments. "And Drew comes in, charming, oh Mister Charming, saying 'Mrs. Palestine, this,' and 'Please, Mrs. Palestine, that,'" Momma remembers. "Well in a second, Bubba was putty in his hands. But she warned him, 'My husband's already sick. And if he comes, this will make him worse. So won't you please leave, Mister Brown.'"

"But, no," Momma recalls, "your father was determined that we were going to be together. And I was caught up in the undertow, you see.

"Well, Drew stayed in the house until my father came home. And Bubba introduced him as a plumber. But Poppa Jack understood everything, and he tried to use his powers of persuasion. He sat Drew down, treated him like a gentleman, and said, 'Look. A marriage like this is not going to work.'

"But Drew Brown was a persuader among persuaders. So he said, 'Mister Palestine. God made green pears and brown pears. He made red apples and yellow apples. . . .' And the way he was talking, he just mesmerized them."

Yet Bubba and Poppa Jack failed to interject what Momma describes as "the first and foremost questions that Jewish families ask: What do you do for a living? And how are you going to support my daughter?" The truth was, neither Bundini nor Rhoda had a conventional job at the time.

Nonetheless, a few weeks later, Bubba did take my father to visit Cousin Seymour, the relative who always settled family differences. By then, my parents were living together, and Bundini claimed to have changed his mind. "I no longer want to get married," he said, and that upset Bubba more than the racial issues had. She insisted that, like it or not, Bundini now *had* to marry Rhoda, since the couple already shared his Harlem apartment.

"But whatever Drew decides, I'm not going to relinquish the

right to live with him," Momma told Bubba. "Certainly not on grounds of race." So with Bubba, Poppa Jack, and my parents all in disagreement, Cousin Seymour's services were clearly needed.

During the train ride to Seymour's house, however, Bundini charmed Bubba once again. They talked about boxing, and she confided that her first love had been a boxer, Harry Galfund though she quickly reminded Bundini that she had chosen Poppa Jack over Harry, "because a boxer is rarely a provider."

"Why, Mrs. Palestine, I'm not a boxer," Bundini protested. "I'm a promoter. And a motivator. That's where the money is."

So Bubba liked him, in spite of her suspicions. But during the train ride, she wore dark sunglasses and held an issue of *Life* magazine in front of her face—hoping that the other passengers would not think that she and Bundini were together. Bubba intended for the meeting with Cousin Seymour to result in a Harlem wedding. To accomplish that, however, she knew that she had to keep Bundini off guard until he said yes.

Momma remembers the events that followed that meeting with Cousin Seymour so clearly, I'll let her tell what happened:

We went down, took the Wasserman, and got the marriage license. But we couldn't agree on the wedding itself. Well, thirty days elapsed on the blood test, so it was no good. And we had to take another one.

Drew just didn't want the responsibility of being married. And I realized that he had no happy memories of any marriage. His mother had left his father because Granddaddy Drew was a difficult man. And even though Elizabeth had promised to come back for him, she didn't. So from that day, Drew had an inner hatred of women.

I tried to explain that it was just the times. That even though his mother had been a teacher, which was a great accomplishment for black women back then, his mother really had few options. But his father had made Drew quit school in the third grade when she left, and Drew blamed her for that.

So we talked, and talked, and we discovered that what we really had in common was a love of humanity. Your father was intelligent, and had common sense. He believed as passionately as I did that people are people. And we saw through the sham of the world. We were two human beings, a man and a woman, who thought we'd make it, in spite of the crap that people had invented.

When Bundini did consent to get married, he brought a Pentecostal preacher, dressed in a royal purple robe, to perform the ceremony in his Harlem apartment. But when Bubba arrived, she sized up the situation—including the fact that Bundini was obviously having second thoughts.

"Don't worry," my savvy Jewish grandmother whispered to him. "A marriage like *this* doesn't really matter. You don't have to get it that legal, requiring a divorce or whatever. Just get *married,* a'ready!"

But standing in front of the preacher, Bundini asked, "Is this a legal, you know, tyin' of the knot?"

"Yes, my son, it is," the minister responded.

"Well I'm not getting married, Bubba," Bundini yelled. "You *lied* to me." Nothing angered my father more than a lie.

"So that was it for me," Momma recalls. "Now *I* was offended. So I took the marriage license, tore it in a hundred pieces, then I said 'So long' and left with my mother. The next day, I came back to get my clothes. He wasn't home, and Bubba was waiting in a cab, so I went up to pack the suitcase. But while I was there, I found the license. I don't know how Drew did it, but that thing was Scotch-taped back in perfect order. I was so hurt, though, that I didn't care, and I made it halfway back down the stairs when who should walk up? He did.

" 'Rosebud,' he said, using his favorite nickname for me. And in that sweet voice, saying, 'Where you goin'? We're gettin' married!'

" 'Forget about it,' I said. 'It's over.'

"But meanwhile, Bubba had seen him come in, so she left the cab. And by the time she reached the stairs, he was pulling the suitcase upstairs. So with me in the middle, she started pulling in the other direction. This went on for a while until I yelled, 'Please. I'm hungry. Let's stop, a'ready, get something to eat, and discuss this.' My head was splitting.

"So after we ate, he brought back the same Pentecostal preacher, and handed him the taped-up license. But gone was the royal robe. This time the preacher wore a suit with its collar turned up, like Drew had shoved the coat on him. And the minister looked at us all very suspiciously. Drew was silent. Bubba was silent, so I didn't know what to think. It just wasn't the same.

"And if you ever saw a black man turn green, Drew Bundini Brown did, the moment he said, 'I do.' Then he fainted back in a chair, and that was that. It was October 29, 1952, and we were legally married. That made Bubba happy. And for a while, we were, too."

4

Listen to me. I'm kickin' live, and I like to have fun, too. Since I went to college, my level of fun has risen to new heights. When I party, I party in Paris. When I jam, I jam in Jamaica. I do the cabbage patch in Monte Carlo. Since I went to college, I'm so bad, I do the butt in the Bahamas. . . .

When I was sixteen, my father appeared as Willy in the movie *Shaft*. It was a minor role—but at least he had a part in a hit movie that affected millions of American blacks during the early seventies. I'm proud of that accomplishment. In fact, the following scene was tailor-made for Daddy. He understood the character. He had lived it.

[WILLY and BUMPY, two players from Harlem, walk down the corridor toward SHAFT's office near Times Square. At the door. WILLY knocks, but there is no answer.]

WILLY

Cat say he gonna be here, he should be here.

BUMPY

Open it up.

[WILLY and BUMPY enter SHAFT's one-room office, its window and door still damaged after the fight.]

WILLY

Cat say he gonna be here, and he ain't. It ain't right . . . Boss.

BUMPY

We'll wait.

WILLY

You take crap off of 'im, he'll give you some more crap.

BUMPY

We'll wait.

WILLY

That's some cold shit—throwin' my man Leroy out th' window. Jus' pick my man up, and threw 'im out th' goddam' window—

[SHAFT enters, unnoticed by WILLY]

WILLY

—Then got us standin' around. Waitin' to say, 'Thank you.'

SHAFT

Glad you let yourself in, Bumpy. Give me a bad name, have you hangin' around in th' hall.

WILLY

Look. If the man ever come down here . . . Again to see you, you make sure you be here. Waitin'.[1]

Within the story, Willy serves as the mouthpiece for Bumpy Jones—a self-made lord over prostitution, drugs, and the numbers racket. Their territory is Harlem; and their main turf, the 125th Street neighborhood that surrounds the Apollo Theatre, the Hotel Theresa, and even the Amsterdam strip in front of Sugar Ray's. The money and power are Bumpy's, of course. But keeping tabs on the Boss's *image* was Willy's job. Exclusively. And that, too, was Daddy's specialty.

However, as a young child in the fifties, I didn't know what my daddy did to make money. And that troubled me. Other kids in the ghetto could at least say *something* about the man living with their mothers—that he was a cabby, a cook, a waiter, or maybe a bartender who worked for some downtown establishment. We understood those jobs. We also knew that their mothers did other people's floors or laundry. We could watch their mothers catch buses each morning to work as maids in fancy apartments. Those jobs were normal enough to us. And since these adults went downtown to work, we quickly learned that ghetto families relied on downtown money in order to live.

But most days, it was obvious that my parents stayed uptown, or at home. Even on nights when they left me with Aunt Fannie while they went out, I still knew that they were somewhere in uptown Harlem, and that didn't seem normal.

The real problem for me came when my friends began asking, "Yo, Drew, what does your ole man do?" At first I made up an answer, like "None of your business. What are you writing— a book?" But as I got older, I learned to dodge the question with more effective strokes, like "At least I know *who* my daddy is." That always cut the talk short, because most street kids had no idea who their biological fathers were. Yet they all knew mine, and more important, they all knew that he had given me his name. My daddy's presence, and that name, *Drew Brown,* became my distinctions. I was somebody, in spite of whatever my daddy did or did not do. I had a home—my mother made sure of that. And clearly, I belonged.

Not knowing the facts, I imagined glamorous, mysterious lives for my parents. For instance, when Momma first told me that I had been conceived after hours, above Sugar Ray's bar, I was too young to understand what the words meant. But I liked the sound of her voice when she said it. So I imagined my parents literally *making* a little Drew above a bar—a kind of unexplainable, but loving and careful deed that my mind associated with the way Momma *made* gingerbread men on a counter in the kitchen.

They also told me about the events leading up to the January 20 morning when I was born in 1955. As the story goes, my mother tried repeatedly that night to drag Daddy away from the TV. She was in labor, and he needed to take her to the hospital. "I think it's time, Drew," she pleaded, "it's time." But he kept stalling by saying, "One more round, Rosebud. Just hold on for one more round. The big fight's almost over," because he was mesmerized by Sugar Ray fighting Dick "Tiger" Jones in one of the early *Gillette Friday Night at the Fights.*

Later, in the early morning hours at Harlem's Sydenham Hospital, the doctor discovered that the umbilical cord had wrapped around my neck. But amid all the confusion in the delivery room, I astonished them all by miraculously untangling myself, and emerging unharmed, from what could have been a stillbirth.

Because I was a boy, my daddy boasted about his son's birth to his friends. And the Harlem players presented me with a special gift—miniature boxing gloves that hung as ornaments on my crib. Each glove bore the authentic autographs of champs like Louis, Robinson, and Jack Dempsey, and I still have those ornaments, thirty-six years later.

So stories like these made me, the young boy, imagine that my parents lived the high life among Harlem's boxing elite. I envisioned Daddy, who was twenty-six when I was born, being so admired by famous black men that *they* paid all our bills—just because they liked Bundini, and wanted him around. And I saw Momma as a beautiful white woman who made all the street brothers jealous whenever my parents entered a room. To me, they were the perfect couple: Momma, two years younger than he, and hip, fun-loving, a bit exotic, but always vivacious; and Daddy, a dashing, handsome, streetwise, legendary young buck to be feared. All of this combined, in my mind at least, to make Drew and Rhoda Brown the one man and his woman who could party and jam better than anyone.

Momma enhanced these images when she talked about the three of us, often in an idealized way. "Your father and I have similar ways of thinking about life and people," she would explain. "So in spite of the differences you can see—who's black and who's white—we will make it. And because of what we do, somehow, somewhere along the way, we'll make this world a better place for others to live in, and to enjoy."

Her enthusiasm even spread to Bubba, my white Jewish grandmother, who had been less than excited about the interracial marriage. The day my parents first brought me to see her and Poppa Jack, we pulled up in a big, brand-new, shining yellow Checker Cab, and there was nothing but bright sunshine in the sky. Bubba pulled back the baby blanket, stared at me for several seconds, then said with a giggle in her voice, "He's not so bad. A little baby powder on his face, and my first grandson'll be all fixed up! He's all mine and I love him."

*   *   *

Momma's actual details about her and Daddy's nights in Harlem—the few that she confided in me as a boy—were nearly as exciting as my imagination. For example, I remember her describing an all-night landmark: "Right on Amsterdam is the Golden Gloves Barber Shop. Sugar Ray owns that place, too, and it has this wide, open window. Inside are brightly colored lights and mirrors. But you should see the way the men fight over the manicurists! And how they look, these flashy fellows, while having their hair straightened, or waves put in—big, grown guys just sitting there, acting cool, with shiny pink nets over their heads!"

Back then, my daddy wore his hair in what was called the "Five-Finger Curl." This meant that Momma could put her hand on his head, and between each of her dainty fingers would lay one of his waves. In fact, his wavy conk was so distinctive that the barbershop displayed Daddy's picture in the Golden Gloves window. So every time my parents left me to stay over with Aunt Fannie, the image that kept me from missing them more was Bundini's handsome Five-Finger Curl being featured right there on the strip, for all the Harlem couples to envy and admire.

I did not have to imagine, however, that my parents made me feel special. During those early years, they demonstrated openly. "You're a wanted child, son. It was necessary for you to be born," Momma always reminded me. And Daddy wrestled with me, and told me jokes. It was as if the three of us were an island away from the world, a breed set apart; and I, the first-born of that new realm.

One of my dearest, and earliest, memories is of Momma singing me to sleep. Her lullaby's words were a simple "Loo-loo, loo-loo, loo-loo" that she sang in groups of threes. Its tune was Jewish and Old World, but also mystical. Yet somehow her soft, raspy voice, usually in the key of E-flat minor, shaped it all into a chantlike melody that never failed to soothe me.

That song, I now know, is probably an ancient lullaby from Yiddish-speaking ghettos in Russia. And because its powers proved enchanting to babies over time, it calmed Bubba and Momma when they were children. Then my turn came. And since then, one after the other, my children's turns have also come. Our family sings this lullaby because it symbolizes a basic truth: To make sure that a child survives, somebody must make that little one feel wanted, and necessary, and special.

But what I imagined was not what had happened.

When I was a young teen, Momma drank frequently, and heavily; and in these drunken states, she began telling me the real details about her early relationship with my father. At the time, I didn't really want to know facts. What I had imagined all those years seemed far better, and much less painful.

Since I've become a man, however, I'm glad that Momma told me the truth. I love her more now, because of the honest, direct way in which she told me about my beginnings. "I may con people, but I don't lie," Moses Gunn as Bumpy says in *Shaft,* and my parents lived by that street code, too. They shielded me from the facts for years, but they never lied to me.

This, then, is what Momma remembers.

"At first, there were happy moments when your father and I would go out," she told me. "We both loved jazz, so we went places, listened to music, drank together, and got high. Just like the night we first met.

"But we had very little money after we married. So more and more, we just stayed in Harlem, and went to Sugar Ray's. Or across Amsterdam to a club called the Shalimar. It had a jukebox, and the owners also brought in 'live' singers each week. So we would go there because, now that I think of it, the Shalimar *was* a nice place.

"I guess, in those days, I believed that *life* was religion. And I showed it by caring more about others, and less about myself. Your father cared about other people, too. But as time went on, he just didn't care about *me.* Yet even when Drew Brown wasn't good to me, I could see a goodness in that man. I always said, 'He's going to be different. He's gonna change.'

"But neither of us did change. Drew went his way, and did his thing, hanging out with friends. And I went by myself to bars and after-hours places. Most nights, I'd stay out until I had too much to drink. And wherever I ended up, I kind of took over. Forgot that other people were sitting there, I guess. So there isn't a place I went that didn't eventually ask me, like,

'Tootle-loo, Rhoda. It's time to leave.' And the reason, Sonny Boy, was that I was a working girl."

The first time she said this, I refused to believe it. *Not Momma*, I said to myself. Not this sweet, eccentric woman who makes me laugh, and who used to hold me when I cried. Not the woman who sang me to sleep with lullabies, or entertained me with Freddy Fox stories that always had a moral. As I got older, however, I believed her because Momma never lied. But by then, I was old enough that I had to know the reasons behind the facts. And when I asked, Momma was, once again, just as frank and honest.

"Back then in Harlem, your father brought very little money home, if any, and we had to eat and live," she said. "But you mustn't believe, son, that he was the cause. He wasn't, really. Not entirely, that is, because there were others before him. I was never jealous about your father being with other women. For his thirtieth birthday, I paid for a gal to be with him. And he wasn't jealous of me. We weren't like that— back then, anyway.

"So when Drew said we had to hustle, I took it on as a role, and really as a learning experience. I didn't care to make that much money. Just enough. And I never really went in for the clothing bit, or whatever. So I guess I said okay, because I believed that, one day, I could use the experience, somewhere in my life. Maybe as an actress, or to write a book—who knows what you think when you're young? And I *was* young—twenty-two—so I believed that nothing could get in our way. Nothing could harm us.

"But I also did it because I knew the conventional life, and I wanted to see what the other side of life was like. Back in high school, my friends and I were always talking about Freudian psychology, or about how much we hated our parents because we thought *they* were the cause of all our problems. It seemed to me that adults in those days never spoke truthfully about what sex was. In the beginning, I mean. And what little they did say seemed like some cover-up. Like sex was this bad thing."

Few men want to hear their mothers talk about sex, and I certainly didn't. So even though I had asked, I interrupted. "But what about *me*, Momma?" I asked. "Didn't you think about the future? About you and Daddy making a family with children?"

"Growing up," she responded, "I really wanted to be a virgin for my husband—whoever he might be. All of us girls felt that way to some extent, but I was serious. I dreamed about that special thing where I would fall in love, right, and be a virgin." At that moment, her voice sounded sincere, and soft, giving me a glimpse of the teenager she must have been: a bright-eyed, idealistic, Jewish darling, just like Bubba had been before her.

"But when I saw married people who weren't really happy," Momma added, "I wanted to cut through all the crap. Girls my age only seemed to care about gossip and clothes. But talking to guys was different. They seemed to be brighter than girls. They had ideas and dreams, and that's what they shared with me. So I came to believe that a woman's role in life was a combination of, like a Jewish mother and a geisha girl. That became my ideal, because I believed that I *could* be both. I thought that to give a man a great deal of pleasure was a woman's role. So I did that. I gave your father a great deal of pleasure. And for a while, that was the future to me."

Listening to Momma, I could not help thinking about my father. If she understood, and accepted what she had done, that was one thing. But how could he have accepted, and understood? Then it sank in that, according to her, he had asked her to do it. "How *could* you?" I wanted to ask him. But, as was true for much of my life, he wasn't there. So I directed this question for him to Momma, and she answered. After all, she knew him longer than anyone.

"During those years, Drew was about as half-hearted a pimp with me as I was with working," she said. "He never forced me to go out, or do anything I didn't agree to. And sometimes, I met guys on my own. We'd have a couple of drinks, and chat about what they did with their lives, and their wives, or whatever. But then I'd end up asking, 'So why are *you* here? And why look for a girl?' Often, that would lead to the kind of dialogue where they'd end up giving me fifteen or twenty dollars, just for talking, and then they'd go back home to their wives. Sometimes, I felt like a marriage counselor or a psychiatrist."

I looked across the table at my wisp of a mother. Her eyes still held their natural sparkle, even though time and experience had wrinkled her smooth skin. Somehow, I couldn't imagine this beautiful, energetic white woman coping, alone in Harlem, with the dangers of street life. So I asked how she protected herself when Daddy wasn't there.

"My friends used to ask the same thing," she replied. " 'Damn, Rhoda,' they would say, 'suppose somebody bothers you. Who'll come to your rescue?' And I'd say, 'Nobody's gonna bother me. I talk myself out of trouble. And if I can't beat 'em with my tongue, then neither a knife nor a .357 Magnum is gonna help.' Then I would always grin, and add, 'But if you ever hear me say, PLEH. . . .' And they would look puzzled, and ask, 'PLEH? What's PLEH?' Then I'd say, 'That's H-E-L-P spelled backwards. So if I say PLEH in a certain way, then you'll know Rhoda is in really deep trouble."

"I did this, on and off, up until the time you were two years old," Momma explained. This meant that from the summer of 1952 when my parents met, through the early part of 1957, she made most of our family's money, uptown, on the streets, and in the bars and hotels of Harlem's nights.

But I remembered what had happened in 1957. Even though I was little, I knew that Momma had become pregnant. At the time, all that meant to me was that I'd have a brother. Until then, I had pretended that my cousins Larry, Butch, and Mona (Aunt Fannie's children) were my brothers and sister. But with Momma expecting, I'd finally have somebody to talk to, and to share my pain with. Yet months passed, nobody talked about my mother being pregnant anymore, and the new brother never came. Years later, I learned that she had had an abortion.

"That's when I realized, hey, this is not playing games anymore," she explained. "I had a mind to earn a living, and the time had come. It *had* to be over. Working like that is *not* something that's fun. And by then, Sonny, you were getting old enough that you would be asking questions. Such a bright child, you were. So I quit. I never wanted you to ask, 'Hey, Mom, where you goin'?' and me having to lie to you."

It mattered to me what my daddy thought then, so I asked

her. "Your father really couldn't see it," she said. "He was not prepared to go out and work. The only kind of job I ever knew him to have back then—a *real* job, that is—was when I was pregnant with you. During those months, he worked as the night manager at Shelton's Rib House. So I told him I was going on welfare to take care of you.

"Well, there was some discussion, though he didn't really say anything. But I knew that he wasn't going to stay with me. And as for work, there was nothing he could do. He wasn't going to take a ship and go to sea, like he did as a boy. No. He was going to continue into the night, and the high life of Harlem. 'But not me,' I warned him, 'Go back to that, and you'll go without Rhoda.'"

One reason Daddy hustled, and would not give it up, was because *there was nothing* that he could do. He couldn't read well enough to study a manual and learn a skill. He couldn't read a magazine with sufficient insight to see how other people lived, and aspire to another kind of life for himself. He was his father's son. A Drew. The street was their curriculum. And people's weaknesses their textbook. So hustling had not been something that Daddy tried, for the experience, the way Momma did. A hustler was what he had been raised to be.

The swamps of Florida breed rare predators, not saints.

My mother and I went on welfare, but its rules were strict. We could not have a telephone, and no man could live with us. "Every month, when they came to inspect, I had to hide the telephone, and your father's stuff," she recalls. "They'd go through my kitchen to see what kind of food I kept. And they'd look under the bed and in the closet to hunt for men's clothing. But what I hated the most: They never told me when they were coming."

Yet whether we liked it or not, welfare was the only way Momma could stay home, and provide for me. And by hiding my father's things, she made it possible, when he would be there, for the three of us to have a few more good times.

All along, I knew so little about what was going on. Yet I could see that, while there was something beautiful about the three of us, there was also something very strange in my house. And that strangeness came to a climax when I was three years old.

One morning I walked into my parents' room, and Daddy was sitting on the edge of the bed. I sensed that he was troubled, so I went to the dresser. Its light oak vanity section was my favorite spot in the room, because under its glass top were pictures of my black father and my white mother; my white grandparents, and my black grandfather; my white relatives and my black ones; and all these snapshots surrounded several pictures of me.

When I got enough courage to look back at Daddy, I saw that he was putting on, and tying, his alligator shoes. But what caught my eye were suitcases, behind him on the bed. So I said, "Daddy, Daddy, what are you doing?"

"Son," he said in a soft voice. "It's time for me to go."

It didn't occur to me that he was leaving, because he was my father, and I knew my father wouldn't leave. So I decided that he was going on a trip, and I got excited. "Where are you going, and when will you be back?" I asked in a tone filled with enough eagerness to mask my apprehension.

"I'm leaving, Sneezer. And I'll always be your daddy," he said. "But I won't be able to live at home anymore." (He had given me the nickname, "Sneezer," because he said whenever anybody sneezed, somebody would always say, "God bless you.")

My mind didn't know how to say what I felt. I wanted to say, *It's okay if you and Momma fight and argue. But that's no reason to leave. Because even if you two fight, you've always got to come home. That's what daddies do. I love you, and you're* my *daddy.*

"You'll be better off if I leave," he said, as if he understood what I couldn't express. "But I'll come visit you, from time to time." Then he picked up his leather suitcases, and I watched him walk away.

That was over thirty years ago, but as I write this, I can see that moment as clearly as if it were yesterday. And his big alligator shoes seem as real to me now as the ache that moved into my heart in 1958.

Even though my parents divorced that same year, Daddy would continue to move in and out of our apartments, and our lives, until 1971. "I accepted your father back many times," Momma explained recently, "because I always believed that we could be a well-adjusted, happy family. I dreamed of having a good family. And I always knew that, one day, he would make it big, and be a success in some way. But I really thought that he would then share that success with me and you. That's what I wanted more than anything else in this world.

"And that's one thing I'll never take away from your father. He was really one of the world's finest trainers that boxing has ever seen. He was *my* American Dream."

In a peculiar sense, then, what I didn't know affected my life as much as what I did know. And learning, years later, the truth about my beginnings has helped me understand why I went through what I did. It helped me make sense of the feelings I had as a teenager and a young man—why I wanted to experiment and to take risks—long before I ever knew what my parents did. *Experimental* is as much in my blood as being black or Jewish.

I must admit, though, that telling these stories about my mother is very hard. She is the *real* reason for my success. As you'll see in subsequent chapters, when I was growing up she loved me; she read to me; and most important of all, she believed in me. I love her with all my heart and respect her even more.

But no one is perfect, and kids need to know the truth. So today, when I speak to young audiences and students ask questions about premarital sex, I often hear my mother's voice whisper about her painful experiences, saying, "I don't understand."

So my answers reflect that. I want young people to know that they don't have to experiment or go through needless pain. I want them to realize that the old values still hold true. That's why I tell them:

> *You guys know what it's like to be next to a girl. And to think that you're gonna do it. Then she pushes you back, and you don't do it, but you get this unexplainable feeling in your chest, anyway. Well, that's ten times the excitement you'll ever have, once you start having sex. And one more thing: A sexual experience is the worst thing that you can ever have as a child. Not only because of AIDS runnin' around, but also because sex is God's gift.*

You're supposed to have a baby with sex, and if you have sex with your wife, then that's fine. God made sex pleasurable, because having a baby is one of life's greatest miracles.

But if you ever, ever exploit a gift that is "a real God-given high," like having a baby, then that's a sin. If you have a child out of wedlock, that will then become your (both parents') lifelong responsibility, and if you don't take on that responsibility, then without a doubt, you will pay for that sin.

Listen to me now, or listen to me later. I'm your worst nightmare. I'm your conscience. You will listen.

By the sound of my voice, and the earnestness of my expressions, these kids understand. They know *more* than the facts that society gives them. They see through the crap, and they get the message. Drew Timothy Brown III knows what he's talking about.

My life is the story that no child in America *has* to live.

5

"Everything you done to me,
you already done to you.

[Miss Celie Harris Johnson—as she leaves the man who had abused her
for years—in The Color Purple.[1]]

Everybody in this room right now lives by a certain theory. It's called
"The Drew Brown Circle Theory of Life," and all of you live by it, right
now.

Every single thing you do in life—no matter how small, no matter
how large—every single thing you do in life is coming back to you.

You steal a quarter for lunch from that girl over there? Next week,
you're going to look for that dollar your mother gave you. "What happened to that dollar?" you'll ask.

It's gone. The universe has taken it.

If you have the nerve to disrespect your friends in here? Keep disrespecting them. 'Cause one day, I promise you, you won't have any
friends. And the worst thing to be in this world is lonely.

Or you disrespect your parents, and the people that bring you up?
And I don't just mean your biological parents. I mean anybody who
gives you love. Well, keep disrespecting them.

'Cause ninety-nine percent of you kids in here, one day, are going to have children. And if you disrespected your parents, then as your kids are growing up, they're gonna wear your little butts out!

You see, either you listen to me now, or you listen to me later. That's right, because stuff that goes around, comes around.

It's as certain as a circle. . . .

For years after the divorce, I pushed hard to get my parents back together. At first, Momma resisted, but I continued to force both of them into circumstances that would restore our threesome. I kept the hope alive. I wanted a normal family, *The Brady Bunch*. And my parent's didn't just listen to appease me. They understood, and believed in, what I said because—like my father—I was born a persuader. So they compromised. Daddy came in and out of our apartment as he pleased. To me, that was okay, because it made it seem as though we all still lived together.

But my parents couldn't shield me from the violence and abusive behavior that persisted, even after they divorced. Inside a family, trouble needs no introduction. Yet I could also see the love between them that the divorce had not destroyed, and that's another reason I wanted us to stay together. United, and happy, we were the most blissful family you could imagine. The divorce did not change the best moments. To me, it was only a paper divorce—not God's.

Sometimes, we even argued well. When Momma and Daddy got into a hot disagreement, I'd bring them into the kitchen, and act like the judge. Even though I was just old enough to go to school, being the judge transformed me into a little man. I'd sit on a stool so that I towered above them. And I'd let one adult speak, then the other one speak, until the argument was settled. These momentary victories, however, only added to my hurt—because no matter how hard I tried, I could never make the perfect times last.

In fairness to Daddy, he made his own good times for me during those first few years. When I could stand in the car seat and barely peer over the convertible's door, he took me for day rides along Harlem's streets—just us two Drews, cruising in his

Chevy. He had nicknamed it "The Blue Goose," and he explained the name by noting that "she's always running."

I liked it that Daddy named, and explained, things to me, because everything and everybody had nicknames in Harlem. Like "Fats," the chili vendor, who worked 125th Street. Or "Sweet Potato," the manicurist who did Daddy's nails at a shop next door to the Shalimar. Whenever my daddy arrived with me in his arms, the players always got excited. They shouted greetings to him, "Hey, Bundini, Bundini! The Black Prince is here with his boy!" But their loud voices were frightening, and made me cry. So Sweet Potato assumed the responsibility of calming me with lollipops. And this became a ritual of sorts, those greetings, my tears, and the manicurist's candy.

On these trips, too, I called all the players "uncle." And they also had nicknames, like "Uncle Youngblood," "Uncle Speckie," and "Uncle Shelton." I loved to spy Uncle Speckie's face, because the bright-skinned black man had red freckles all over it, and his full smile disarmed the brothers and charmed the ladies. Uncle Shelton was a thin, dark-skinned black man with a sharp conk and a soft-spoken voice. Like my father, Shelton had married a white woman. But she was the opposite of my mother, because Shelton's fragile, nervous wife still suffered from the childhood trauma of having been raped by the Nazis. She became a beautiful model, but she swore never to be with another white man. In contrast, Uncle Blood was a warm, brown-skinned, weary-looking man whose smile rivaled even Speckie's. Blood's grin was a toothy, broad gleam beneath dark, penetrating eyes and a shining scalp that was balding prematurely. In later years, I would come to love Uncle Blood the most, because I knew him the longest. In the sixties and seventies, he assumed the Black Muslim name of Wali Muhammad and worked with my father as a boxing trainer.

And whenever these three uncles gathered around Bundini, they always drew a crowd. One man who regularly showed up was "Cheeko," the pimp, hustler, and drug dealer who was a midget. Sometimes, he rode in the back of his long, green Cadillac, and always kept a pistol on the seat beside him. But what truly made Uncle Cheeko memorable was that, in order to drive the Caddy, he had to sit on two Manhattan phone books.

Other players soon stopped on the street corner, exchanged loud greetings and handshakes, and then broke into rapid-fire conversations, all going at once. But even with all the uncles talking right in front of my face, I couldn't understand a word they said. They spoke Harlemese, a language unto itself. It was street lingo, I understood later, and it enabled them to do business without being understood by outsiders. Sometimes, they even altered its vocabulary from week to week. That was their security system against eavesdroppers, rival players, and the vice squad.

But I didn't go with Daddy often enough to the streets to penetrate the code. Like most boys, I would have to pick up the slang as I got older. During the years when I put in my own street time.

"Mrs. Fox had planned a surprise birthday party for Freddy. So when he got up, she didn't say 'Good Morning,' or 'Happy birthday, son.' Well, Freddy was surprised, and hurt. His mother had never forgotten a special day, before now. But he crawled out of bed, anyway, walked unsteadily toward the bathroom, and thought, 'My goodness, Mother forgot my birthday.' "

That was how Momma began the first of many Freddy Fox stories that she told me over the years. Like us, Freddy and his mother lived alone. And Mr. Fox? According to mother's invention, he had been killed in a hunting accident, so there was never a father in these stories. Momma was clever. She told these stories for a reason. And from the night that she told me this first one, I loved them, and would beg for a Freddy Fox story every evening before I'd go to sleep.

I now understand that this was Momma's way of filling the void that Daddy's leaving had created. And because of her deep unconditional love for me, she created one story after another.

"On his way to school, Freddy got worried," that first story continues, "because for weeks, he'd been telling all his friends that his birthday was coming up. But when Freddy reached the playground, this particular birthday morning, neither Ollie the octopus or Harry the horse said anything. And boy, did Freddy Fox feel bad!

"Throughout the day, no matter how much Freddy hinted,

neither his friends nor his teachers indicated that today was anything more than just another day. So by the time the last bell rang, Freddy said good-bye to everyone, and walked dejectedly toward home.

"But as soon as Freddy walked inside his tree house, there were all his friends and teachers. Harry the horse wore a party hat, and colored balloons were tied to all of Ollie the octopus's arms. And they all screamed at once, 'Happy Birthday, Freddy Fox!'

" 'Oh, gee,' Freddy cried, as he ran to his mother. 'I just knew everybody wouldn't forget my birthday.'

" 'Of course not,' Mrs. Fox said. 'Everything that happened today was planned, my son—from me not telling you good morning, to the kids not mentioning the party.' Then Mrs. Fox pulled her little boy close to her side, and said, 'Surprises mean more when you *really* want them, Sonny Boy. So don't ever take anything for granted. Not when friends and family love you.' "

With stories like these, Momma was also trying to teach me about our new life. By then, she was working full-time at a legitimate, daytime job as a bookkeeper, and with the help of money from Bubba she had enrolled me in nursery school. In every way, Momma was struggling to change, and to raise me the way she had been. Her days of experimenting—she wanted both of us to believe—were over. And like Mrs. Fox and Freddy, we were living a normal, conventional life. On that, Momma was focused. She had given up her marriage and her life for me.

But gradually, Daddy did spend less and less time with us. My day trips with him to visit the Amsterdam uncles became less frequent, too, because he had moved Dolores, a white woman, into his apartment. On the sly, Sweet Potato tried to explain it all to me, but I hated the loneliness and wouldn't listen. I shut the truth out of my mind, and continued to live as if Daddy were still dropping by. *The divorce did not happen,* I told myself. *Everything is the same. Just different.*

Momma despised the loneliness, too, and once in a while she brought men home with her at nights. But I was five years old, and my happiness seemed to be vanishing, the way smoke from the tenement chimneys disappears, silently, and without warning, into the gray Manhattan sky. I felt betrayed on all sides.

And I *had* to do something. With other men in my daddy's place, what did it matter that I was a Drew, too?

Then one night, I heard noises coming from Momma's bedroom. I tiptoed down the narrow hall, slowly opened her closed door, and in the glow of city lights shining through her window, I saw her making love with a strange man who was in Daddy's position. So I eased the door closed again, then found the telephone where she kept it hidden from welfare inspectors, and I dialed my daddy's number.

I knew that all of them would be angry once I betrayed what I had seen; but I also believed that Daddy would, somehow, be the saving prince who would sweep me up, out of this misery.

Then, while I watched from behind the couch, the strange man ran naked into the bathroom, dressed, and quickly left. Moments later, there was a loud banging on the green metal front door. And in burst my daddy, dressed in a long leather coat. But he did not look like the prince that I expected. Instead, he was a raging dragon with tears in his eyes. He said nothing, even though Momma was screaming questions, one after the other. He just threw her to the floor.

I couldn't believe what I was seeing, so I rushed to her rescue. But my daddy's eyes turned on me, and in his glare, I saw an evil and vengeance that I had never experienced. "Go to your room, boy," he yelled. "Stand by the window, and don't you look anywhere but out."

I did what he said. Then I heard screaming and yelling in the other room, and more than once, the breaking of glass. Throughout, my father's powerful voice punctuated the chaos with "How could you do that? Oh, Rhoda, how could you do that to my boy?" Isolated in my room, I didn't know whether to feel saved, guilty, or betrayed. My call for help had conjured up a monster, not a knight, because the daddy that was beating my mother was as much a stranger to me as the man who had been in her bedroom.

Several times, when Mamma's screams were the worst, I ran back toward the living room. But every time, my father's wild eyes burned in my direction, and his terrifying voice halted me with "You listen to your daddy, boy. Go back in that room. And stare out that window. You hear?" So I went back. I went to the window and I cried. I cried until I started shivering. And then I cried and shivered and screamed, all at the same time, just to make my voice drown out my mother's screams.

Standing there, screaming too, I lost track of time, so I don't know how long I kept crying after Momma's voice had fallen silent. But finally I grew hoarse and stopped. After that, the apartment was deathly quiet. I stood there, scared, and puzzled. Was the order to stay in my room still in effect? It seemed as though hours passed, but then I heard the front door slam, so I ran to my mother.

The living room still smelled of leather from Daddy's coat, even though he had gone. Momma lay curled on the floor. Her face was bruised and swollen, her eyes blackened, and blood trickled from her nose. Then as my glance met hers, she cried, "Why did you tell him, my little Drew? Why?"

I had to look away, because Momma knew that *I* was responsible for this. In my selfishness to bring my parents back together, I had caused the only person who was taking care of me to be brutalized. And that's when something clicked in my brain. I swore to myself that, when I got big enough, I would never let my daddy hurt my mother again.

Like Granddaddy Drew, my father had a battle raging within him. The deepest emotions, such as love for women who truly loved them, were the hardest for the Drews to express, except through sex, anger, and violence. Yet both were deep-feeling men. So they ended up hurting the people they loved, while at the same time, misunderstanding why we felt hurt or betrayed by their violence and excessive anger.

Having a raw, raging soul, however, is an advantage in boxing circles. Many champions also harbor an inarticulate rage within their personalities, and that attracted Bundini to them, and they to him.

Johnny Bratton, for example, died in a mental institution. But when he was in his prime as a boxer, my daddy was one of his best friends. And I considered Sugar Ray one of my Harlem uncles, because he and Daddy were so close. But at one of the training sessions I attended as a boy, I witnessed Sugar Ray's calculated rage in action. He's the only fighter I ever saw who could work a speed bag so hard that the screws gradually turned on its mount. Then at will, Sugar Ray would deal the bag one last, furious blow that sent it flying twenty feet across the room.

Audiences back then loved Sugar Ray and Johnny Bratton; and years later, boxing fans would love my daddy, too, once national publicity revealed his extraordinary talents as a trainer. But the public rarely saw how much hurt-become-anger there was behind the virtues, and even the genuine love, in such men. Daddy was a street angel and a home devil.

Though his beating of Momma after my telephone call was my initial glimpse of this rage, it was hardly her first encounter. Before they met, she had gotten a black afghan hound that she named Pasha. "It meant royal son of the dame of Palestine," she said, and she grew very attached to it. Then after my parents married, both of them enjoyed the dog's companionship.

Daddy liked to walk Pasha, Momma recalls, "because he could meet women walking their dogs and have some groovy conversations." And that *was* my daddy. No matter how much he loved Momma, other women appealed to him, too. (In a cameo appearance in *The Color Purple*, he played a "jook joint patron" who is mesmerized by "Shug Avery" singing a hot jazz tune. And there, captured in film at the joint named Harpo's, is Bundini's best smile, and his woman-loving gaze, as he growls his only line, "You can catch a fish without a hook, girl."[2])

"But your father was jealous of my love for Pasha," Momma recalls. "There was no doubt about that."

Then one day, Daddy accidentally stepped on Pasha's tail. In pain, the afghan howled, jumped up, and sank one of his canine teeth into Daddy's lip. Momma remembers that my father did not immediately react. Instead, he went to the bathroom mirror and examined the cut, which was small but bleeding. "But looking at how his handsome beauty had been altered, he got so angry that he ran to the kitchen, grabbed a knife, and slit Pasha's throat," she said.

"Right away, I wrapped a towel around Pasha's neck," she explained, "and I looked at your father's face. 'Why hurt my Pasha?' I moaned, but he was still crazy with anger.

"Bubba was visiting with us that day, so she took Drew to the hospital, and I took Pasha to the ASPCA on East 92nd Street. They fixed the dog up, and it survived. But after that, I knew that there was no more living with the two of them in the same apartment."

Underlying the pain and violence in our family, there was also poverty during my early years. We were poor. But as a child, I never felt that we were, because we seemed to live better than most ghetto families in Manhattan. This was particularly the case each December.

No matter how bad things got, there was always a holiday truce from fighting in our house. Both of my parents celebrated Christmas, not in a religious sense, but in a festive one. And I can still see Momma and me, every year, dragging a tree from 105th Street to the projects, and all the apartment windows glowing with colored lights as we hauled through the snow the biggest tree that she could find. My mother and her parents also celebrated Hanukkah as the religious holiday, and that's when Bubba and Poppa Jack gave me gifts. So at least once a year, I doubled up on presents, and what an experience! Momma couldn't afford expensive things, so she concentrated on quantity. And she always wrapped all of them in layers of colored tissue paper, so that I had to rip and tear to get at every surprise. Opening her gifts was as much fun as getting what was inside. Momma was no fool!

And if, as the years progressed, Bundini could be described as a "Christmas father," at least he was the best one in town. During any given year, he might never come through with anything else, but my daddy always came through for Christmas. It might be midnight before he arrived, but he never failed to show up, laughing, joking, and brandishing an armload of packages. And since I was an only child, I got it all. (That was the only time I didn't miss the brother that I almost had.) One year, Daddy even had to borrow money from Sugar Ray on Christmas Eve, just so he could buy a set of toy six-shooters. But late that night, he made it all right. On time, and guns in hand.

So Christmas was always the happiest day of the year for me, because the good times that we had were the best. And because of these memories, right up to today, this Jewish boy *loves* Christmas—if only for the tree, the gifts, and the sense of family that it fosters. And my sweet memories.

In reality, however, the divorce had divided not much money in half—zero divided by zero is still zero—so we all suffered financially. Daddy shared his small apartment on West 96th Street with a series of girlfriends, while Momma and I lived a fifty-five-cent cab ride away in Spanish Harlem. Rent on our eleventh-floor two-bedroom unit was $44.85 a month. That was the cost for a single mother with one child to live in the Carver House, a government-subsidized housing project at 60 East 102nd Street, between Park and Madison. And that place, apartment 11-F, was the first one I remember that felt like home.

But Momma didn't let our lack of money stand in the way of opportunities for me. Every summer for four years, she made certain that I went to summer camp, like the middle-class New York kid she wanted me to be. The first two years, Bubba helped her with the tuition at Broadview Farm in Barnstead, New Hampshire. Then Momma worked the next two summers on staff at Twin Link Camp—a nonsectarian, interracial, coed institution sponsored by the United Community Centers, Inc.— so that my tuition would be paid, and I could go to the Catskills. Like other Jewish boys.

I blocked Daddy's absence so completely out of my mind that I didn't consider seeing him to be *visits*. But I distinctly remember one visit. Momma had bought a tan trench coat for me that matched my father's London Fog. And when he came to pick me up, I remember her watching us—the two Drews dressed alike—leave the projects and go for a walk along the East River.

"You walk like me," he said softly, the first words between us in blocks, after we had walked out of Momma's sight. In fact, we were approaching the ASPCA building, and momentarily, I thought about Pasha.

"I know," I responded, clasping my hands behind my back the way Daddy did, pacing my stride to match his. No matter who he was, or what he did, I loved being like my father, and being with him. That's why I asked, "So when are you comin' home?"

"I won't be," he said, not talking to me like a child. Instead, he talked to me like a *mensch* (meaning *a man* in Yiddish). "I can't sit in that living room, and cross my legs, and watch TV with you. Not anymore, son. That's Shorty's job, now."

I knew that *Shorty* was my father's name for God. ("God is not the big, bearded guy on a throne," he would say. "God is the short guy on every street corner. The one being ignored, and scorned, and ridiculed. But he's also the one who's always watchin', takin' notes—and unknown to everybody—the one who's makin' things happen.") And that delighted me. Because Daddy wasn't talking to me about stupid things, like circuses or games. Even though I was only seven, he was talking to me about life! It was honest, open talk, and he could see that I accepted him. Not just as Daddy, but as a friend, too.

"I'll never talk to you like a boy again," he said, when we came back within sight of the projects. "You're here on this earth for a purpose, son. Shorty made you to be a prophet." At the time, that was very hard to hear; but I knew that if Daddy said it, there must be a reason.

Then he stuck his broad palm toward me for a handshake. But when I extended all five of my fingers, he protested. "No, no. Give me the little one," he said. "The big ones take care of themselves."

I laughed, understanding that he was making a point. If you listened, he always did. Then I turned back all but my little finger, and only then did Daddy take my smallest finger in his big hand. And with that grip in place, he said, "Remember. Shorty knows. And he'll make you a prophet."

After that visit, it didn't matter so much that my daddy didn't come around often. I couldn't hold all that pain inside forever. I was a rubber kid who learned quickly how to bounce back. And Daddy knew that. So he gave me his heart, the handshake, and the assurance of Shorty's watchful eyes. The rest, with time, would take care of itself.

In 1963, when I was eight years old, my father's luck changed dramatically. Cassius Clay, a controversial twenty-one-year-old boxer from Kentucky, had been attracting national attention.

His prowess in the ring dazzled fans, but his personality shocked them even more. Clay was street-smart, unpredictable, and brash, but poetic in a comic way, and powerful when he strapped on the gloves. Daddy always said, "Cassius Clay could kick Muhammad Ali's ass." But most Harlem players were wary of Clay, and bet against him in the early fights. Not my father, though. He spotted potential in Clay, and went after the young contender.

Years later Daddy would tell me about his first meeting with Cassius Clay. But it occurred, according to the Champ's memoir, because earlier Clay had asked Sugar Ray Robinson how to become a champion. Then, according to Daddy's version, Sugar Ray told Clay that the only thing he lacked was having people around who truly believed in him; and when Clay asked, "Who should I get?" Sugar Ray told him about my daddy.

At the first meeting between Clay and Bundini, then, as the Champ's memoir details, Daddy's first words were, "You're either a phony or Shorty's in your corner!" (This was because, as Daddy told me, he didn't believe that anybody could predict the rounds in which they're going to knock somebody out.) Then my father recalled adding, "And tell me why you have such a *big* mouth!"

Sugar Ray's influence apparently caused the Champ to be very frank, because according to the memoir, he said: "The truth is, every time I go into the ring I'm scared to death." Then according to my father, Clay added, "I know there's a whole lotta people out there who want to see me get my butt kicked. So I fool them by talking and predicting so much."

When Daddy heard this he started to cry because, as he told me, he knew the answer. "You got the power and I got the spirit," the Champ records Daddy as saying. Then my father remembered adding, "With me in your corner, they can never whip us both."

But from both accounts one thing is certain: Shorty was truly there that night, and from then on, Daddy would train and love the Champ. The rest is history.[3]

But my father's new money made no real difference in life at apartment 11-F. No Cassius Clay cash came to us. And the limelight that immediately enveloped the Champ and my daddy only cast Momma and me into even darker shadows. We could read about, and see pictures of, Drew Bundini Brown in the newspapers. But there was no mention of us. Daddy had made it. But for whatever reasons, he forgot to bring the success home, as he had promised Momma. And that broke our hearts. Especially hers.

6

I come from the ghetto, the projects of Harlem in New York City. Now I don't know about you, but if you think you got it bad in your area, let me tell you, the rats in my school were so big, the cats carried assault weapons.

That's right, I come from the streets. And in the streets, we used to play this little game. It's called "Fifty-two." And you know what "Fifty-two" meant? It simply meant that any game you played, if you quit that game, everybody punched you fifty-two times in the chest. So I learned from a little boy: I don't quit nothin'.

Because when you quit, you start hanging out with quitters, and then you start growing up with quitters. Then one day you'll marry a quitter, and then when you have your own children, they'll be called the quit-tets!

So there's no difference between me and any of you in this room—except that I believe in myself, and I never quit. . . .

No matter where kids lived in the Carver Housing Authority projects, we didn't think in terms of neighbors; we were all just friends on the streets. In fact, I never met the people who lived next to our apartment. I just heard them banging on the walls whenever Momma and Daddy would fight. And except for Carl Fuller, Bud, and me, my Harlem friends had interesting Spanish names, like Ricardo or Rivera. But it was Harlem, after all, so we also needed the street identity that nicknames gave us. A kid from the fifteenth floor was called Carl "Footie," which was short for *football*, because his head looked like one. A guy on the eighth floor we called "Girdle," because he was fat and looked as though he needed one; Bud, my friend from the fifth floor, had his nickname because he was so short; and "Buttons," my friend from across the street, kept outgrowing his clothes, causing his buttons to pop off. But the toughest kid on the block we called "White Johnnie," because he was from the only other white family we knew in Harlem.

Beyond the street friendships, however, our most basic common link was that we all were *latchkey kids*—long before that term became popular—since our parents were either gone, or divorced, or working. So most of the time we lived outside, because no one was home in our apartments. Central Park became our front yard; and the subway tunnel between 102nd and 96th streets was our playground. But the public sections of the red-bricked project buildings were ours exclusively, as surely as if we had owned them.

In those project elevators, for example, I vividly recall the funky, pungent, ammonialike stench of urine, and I hated how slowly the elevators moved up the fifteen-story buildings, because I usually had to stand on tiptoes, straddling the yellow liquid on the floor. We endured this, though, because we were all scared of using the project stairways. They had been painted in green and gray, which made them dark and spooky. The older kids usually punched out the lights, and the junkies hung out there. Plus, with all the filth, the graffiti, the bloody hypodermic needles hanging by rubber bands from the fire hoses, and the broken glass, those stairwells seemed like seething haunted houses, more terrifying than at any carnival because the dangers along the project stairs were real. So whenever possible, we used the elevators to get from our apartments to the streets. The pavement was *our* world.

A courtyard separated the two project buildings, and that's where we played competitive and dangerous games like *hot peas and butter*. In this, the flag pole was our "free zone," or home base. And to play, one of us took off his belt and hid it (usually Girdle's, since he was so big and had a big brass buckle) while the rest of us waited at home base. Once he returned, we scurried in all directions to find the belt, because whoever did got to use the buckle end of the belt to beat anyone who had not yet made it back to base. For street-smart skills, then, H.P. and B. taught us a basic rule of survival: *Always be looking—particularly at what's behind you.*

This courtyard was also where we built homemade scooters and skateboards. I made mine by attaching a wooden milk crate to a two-by-four; then I shared a pair of skates with Footie, and attached my set of wheels under the two-by-four. But my scooter was special (I always felt that my things should be better than the others'), because it also contained *the* toolbox. Inside it were the nails, hammer, pliers, and screwdriver that we used for pit stops when wrecks, or normal wear and tear, broke down a scooter in action.

For me, what we *did* as kids defined *time* itself in the city. There was no distinguishable autumn or spring in Harlem. You needed flowers to recognize those changes. So we defined seasons on the streets by our games. When it snowed, we piled seven deep on sleds in Central Park, or we had snowball fights—except that some punk always put rocks in the middle of his. That defined winter. And when it was hot, we enjoyed the season of waterguns, H.P. and B., or *shoot the pump.* That was a game in which we used tin cans to direct the force of water flowing out of fire hydrants. Then before the heat gave way to snow, once again, we had *scully* season. Scully was a form of checkers that we played with bottle caps that we filled with wax on checkerboards that the project builders had painted on the cement in the courtyard. Between the snow and the return of heat, we also had baseball and skateboard seasons. But 365 days a year, the real season was basketball; we played it in the snow and in the heat. Even when the rain turned our red-brick buildings a light pink, we were B-ball junkies.

And because we played during the days, nighttime on the streets always seemed to come too quickly. In contrast, the game seasons came regular and even, just as summer, autumn, fall, and spring do, outside the maze of our city. But to us latchkeys, landlocked in one small section of Manhattan Island, what we knew was all there was. That's how we found happiness, right where we were.

Maybe it was these limitations that made me imagine more. But whatever the cause, I did. When my father talked in a mystical and mysterious way about us being *Drews,* I perceived it as a type of black knighthood. Yet Daddy could also hurl this *Drewism* against me. If he wanted me to do something, and I refused, the most persuasive words that my father could say were "A real Drew would have done that," or "You're not a real Drew." That devastated me. Like most sons, I needed my father to be proud of me, and I knew that proving myself a real Drew was the ultimate test.

Yet somehow, I always seemed to be failing that test. One sunny day at P.S. 171, all of my friends were gathered around the flagpole on the school playground. They all knew that I had challenged Richie Baron to "meet me at the flagpole," which meant that we would fight during the lunch break. So when Richie and I arrived, the ceremony began.

We started by "sounding on each other"—that is, exchanging put-downs designed to divide the crowd into supporters. My best shot was "I went to your house, stepped on a roach, and your mother yelled, 'Save me the white meat!' " He fired back a comparable insult, and this continued until all the Puerto Rican kids were cheering him on, and all the blacks were rooting for me. Then the girls came, and the sounding intensified. Richie and I removed our jackets, appointed our best friends as corner men, and then began striking our best fighting poses—because it was more important in New York to look good than to be good.

I chose the dancing/jabbing/shuffling moves that my daddy was instilling in Cassius Clay. But Richie stood steady, staring me down. In response, the majority of the kids began screaming, "Drew, Drew, Drew," which pumped me up even more.

I started shuffling my feet and biting down on my lip, to give off good facial expressions, when—*whap*—Richie hit me with an open-handed right that sent my teeth through the skin. Blood gushed out, and the kids went crazy, "Ooooh, yeah. He got you, Drew."

In defense, I came back with what would have been a beautiful right hook, certain to even the score. But it never reached Richie's jaw. My teacher, Mr. Garcia, had broken through the crowd, and when I swung my revenge punch, the teacher caught it with both his hands. That ended the noontime fight.

Even though I had looked better, Richie won because the blood was on *my* face. Nobody cared that Richie had drawn blood with nothing more than a slap, and I was more humiliated and embarrassed than if I had gotten my butt kicked.

To make matters worse, that afternoon, the school nurse made me wear a big bandage on my lip. This badge of shame made the kids tease me about the loss, and it motivated a dark-skinned guy whom we called "Black" Albert. He had failed several grades, and was older and bigger than the rest of us, and he held the unchallenged title as the number-one bully of P.S. 171. "You shuffle like Cassius Clay," Black Albert yelled across the hall, "but you fight like his *mother*."

I stopped, my bandaged lip quivering, and I yelled back, "Get outta my face, man."

Black Albert just laughed and said, "If you're so bad, punk, then make sure you're at the flagpole at three." But no way was I going to be there. Another beating was the last thing that I needed. Plus, Black Albert had the rep that he always carried a knife or a gun, and my stomach churned. My busted lip was embarrassment enough, without the prospect of being dead by three-fifteen.

Richie Baron may have been my bitter enemy in the morning, but everybody hated and feared Black Albert, so by the time school dismissed that afternoon, Richie sided with me, and we had a plan. We stayed in the after-school center from three until nearly five o'clock, and only then did we leave the building. We just knew that, during the two-hour wait, Black Albert had lost patience and left.

A tall chain-link fence separated the schoolyard from the sidewalk, and Richie and I walked arm in arm along the fence. We were whistling and laughing nervously, so proud that we had outsmarted Black Albert. Suddenly, our delight in the rhythm of the streets fell silent as Black Albert emerged from behind a van parked beside the sidewalk.

At the sight of his fierce eyes, both Richie and I spun around to run. Then—*pow*—Black Albert punched me in the back, so I stopped. Just then a car screeched to a halt on Madison Avenue, but I turned to face Black Albert. To my surprise, however, he was running, and in a second I saw why.

Out of the halted car emerged my daddy and a friend. They jumped between me and the fleeing bully. "What happened, boy? What happened?" my daddy yelled, and he seemed to want to chase after Black Albert.

I was stunned. I hadn't seen my father in weeks. Yet at the worst moment of the worst possible day, here he emerged like Superman from a passing car. And when he saw that I was speechless, he persisted, "Why didn't you fight him, Drew? Why? Why?"

At that, I was really lost for words. Clearly, I had failed to prove my manhood, right in front of my father. How could I ever make that up? Even though Daddy never mentioned the incident again, I couldn't forget it. I was humiliated, and left wanting. I had to prove myself. I had to win a fight, and my daddy *had* to be there.

More and more, my daddy's pride was being directed, not at me, but at Cassius Clay. Writers at the time called Bundini the "guru-in-residence" in Miami's Fifth Street Gym, where he and Angelo Dundee were preparing Clay for his February 25, 1964, fight against world heavyweight champion Sonny "The Bear" Liston.[1] As the guru, my daddy was formulating Clay's "psychological warfare" against Liston. In fact, it was during one prefight sparring match that my daddy coined the camp slogan "Float like a butterfly, sting like a bee," which would become Clay's career-long motto.[2]

Liston hated the Clay-Bundini tauntings, and that fed the psychological warfare even more. Day after day in the projects, I read newspaper accounts of how my daddy and Clay unleashed new verbal assaults. "He's a tramp; I'm the champ," Clay yelled repeatedly on one such occasion outside Liston's training quarters. Then he and my daddy screamed chants like "We're predicting as true as fate—that the big tramp will fall in eight!" until Liston called the police to remove them.[3] By the night of the fight's official weigh-in, the psyching of Sonny reached peak proportions. He not only faced Clay's speed and power in the ring, but also my daddy's relentless screams from the challenger's corner. It was a two-to-one combo designed to combat Liston's eight-to-one prefight odds advantage from the sportscasters. And it worked.[4]

The next morning, I saw my daddy on every front page of papers at every newsstand. One picture was the seventh-round shot of Daddy bearhugging Clay—the boxer's arms upstretched in the V-gesture—after Liston refused to fight, causing Clay to win his first world heavyweight championship. In another picture, my father's eyes seemed blinded by victory tears as he escorted Clay to the dressing room.[5] What the world saw in those photos was two black men bonded by challenge, friendship, and victory. But at the time, what I saw was my daddy adoring Clay, like a father loves a son, instead of adoring me—his real son, yearning to be hugged.

The day after the Clay-Liston fight, the victor from Lousiville announced his conversation to Islam, changed his name to Muhammad Ali, and took some time off from boxing to visit Africa and the Middle East. During these tours, Ali was interviewed by the major papers of the world, and reports appeared regularly on American television. Within weeks, many who were not boxing fans became familiar with Ali.[6] And they either loved or hated what they saw.

But these events held a personal irony for my daddy. Just as suddenly as the Clay/Ali phenomenon had distanced my father from Momma and me, Ali's sabbatical from boxing sent Daddy back to Harlem. Until the Ali-Liston rematch scheduled for the spring of 1965, my father was once again out of work. He had helped Clay win boxing's most prized title, but in the process, another Harlem faction had won Ali's ear.

The most famous of these other gurus was Malcolm X, then the rising star of black militancy. Just a few years earlier, he had been the Harlem player known as "Big Red"—the thief, dope peddler, and pimp who, through the teaching of Elijah Muhammad, had transformed his life of ghetto hustling into a new role as liberator of more than twenty million brothers suffering white America's suppression.[7] Clay had named his tour bus "Big Red," and all along, Malcolm X had been a member of Clay's entourage. But after Ali seized the championship, no black man in the world possessed so much power and charisma. So the followers of Elijah Muhammad and those of Malcolm X vied bitterly for Ali's allegiance, and my daddy was caught in the religious and political crossfires. Shorty was his god, and the Champ was his cause, so my father refused to join either faction of Islam. As a result, he was temporarily fired because of the Champ's Islamic advisors. And that hurt my daddy as much as his not including Momma and me in his success had hurt us.

Back in Harlem, he resumed his visits to our apartment in the projects. But he was a different man. At the age of thirty-five, he had struggled for decades with boxing as his only real dream. Then he had seized that dream. But just as suddenly it had slipped away again. And Momma was different, too. In the interim, she had married a Greek guy from Brighton who was an alcoholic and an unemployed mechanic. He called her "Sputnik," and moved into the projects with us. But his drinking only drained our finances more, and she was attempting to have the marriage annulled when, one night, he died of a heart attack on the Boardwalk.

After that, nothing seemed to work in her life. She went from one bookkeeping job, back to unemployment, then on to other bookkeeping jobs just long enough to draw more unemployment. But to her credit, I never knew as a child when she was unemployed. Momma got up every morning and dressed for office work, then saw me off to school—even if she had nothing more to do that day than to collect welfare or unemployment checks, or look for a new job.

Looking back, I realize that in remarrying, then in her second husband's death, and even in the drinking that followed, Momma was struggling. She loved my father, but he kept breaking her heart. She couldn't stop loving him, yet he kept leaving and coming back to her. It was a cycle. And she hung on to this spinning life-style in order, quite simply, to take care of her son, and to get her man back.

At the time, however, all that mattered to me was that Daddy was with us once again. It did not trouble me when he came home high from alcohol or drugs. That's what a daddy did, and at least mine didn't stay home alone and get high in front of me. My parents were still shielding me from that. Even Momma did her drinking elsewhere. She had mastered the art of hiding what she didn't want me to know. Nor did it impress me that my daddy was becoming famous, because Uncle Sugar Ray and Uncle Cassius were famous, and that didn't make me love them any more than I did my other Harlem uncles. To me, it was a given: Boxing meant fame and big money, the way being a player meant glamor and money on the sly. And since boxers fascinated Daddy, I wanted him to direct that gleam in his eyes at me. I longed to hear him say, "Now you're a real Drew, boy."

One afternoon my father came in, and slammed our apartment's green, thick metal door. He was wearing a new leather coat, and when he hugged me, I could smell whiskey on his breath. Despite my enthusiasm at seeing him, he said little as we went to the kitchen to make sandwiches. Back then, all the project kitchens were yellow. But this particular afternoon, that shiny paint reflected pale light from the project's green, wire-reinforced windows into the otherwise dim area. To me, it seemed like the dingy atmosphere of a boxing gym. So I said, "Come on, Daddy. Let's box, let's box," without explaining that I might want to grow up to be a fighter.

But he could see that I was testing him, so his face locked in that characteristic Bundini expression—mouth tight, teeth exposed, lower jaw thrust forward, and eyes glaring in fascination. I responded by getting in my Sugar Ray stance, ready to throw the jabs and make the faces that stylish boxers executed on the televised matches. Then the father-son sparring began.

After the first few punches, however, my daddy turned his back on me and growled, "I don't wantchu to be no fighter, boy."

I was too psyched up to listen, so I persisted. "Aw, come on, Dad. Box me," I challenged. "Betcha can't stop me, I'm *soooo* fast."

Once again, my father's voice boomed. "Boy! I said, I don't want you to be no fighter. Shorty's plans don't call for you to learn with your hands."

But I had seen fathers and sons box playfully on TV shows, so I kept egging my daddy on until he squared up. His massive shoulders hunched over in a boxing position that—to my surprise—was not stylish, but awkward and determined. Then he started throwing punches at me.

At first, they were light, but they immediately penetrated my light, little defenses. So I tried to throw a couple of strong punches back, and then—*bam*—he hit me in the chest.

My ribs and lungs could not have ached more if the refrigerator had fallen on me. But it wasn't just the force of his fists. Those hands had spanked me before. Yet this was the first time he had ever hurt me without being angry and yelling. Instead, he was cool, deliberate, and silent, as if to say by his actions, and his demeanor: *You wanna be a boxer? Then come on and fight.*

At that, his punches battered me in the arms, the shoulders, and back in my chest. I fought them off as best I could, and wondered if he would soon start working on my face. His fists were closed, like a man meaning business, and no matter how hard I fought back, I couldn't box. I could not stop his onslaught of power.

But still, he kept hitting me. Even when frustration, more than pain, brought tears to my eyes, Daddy persisted. There was no easing up. No breaks. I couldn't match his punches, or beat him, and I felt that he wasn't playing fair, because he wasn't hitting me the way a father hits his little boy. Instead, he was hitting me man to man.

Yet blow by blow, my daddy seemed to beat out of me the desire to become a fighter. And when I fell, defeated, into his arms, he whispered, "Son, you've got a dreamer's head and a prophet's soul. But boxing ain't in your heart. So don't you ever lie to yourself, boy. And don't *ever* lie to God. Shorty made you to be the *educated* Drew."

Most Friday afternoons after school, I had been taking the train to visit my grandparents in Brighton Beach. There, Poppa Jack met me at the station and took me directly to Jack's, the barbershop. It was a transition ritual between all-black Harlem and all-white Brighton. Invariably, my grandfather would carry out Bubba's orders and make me get what I called "a Floyd Patterson haircut"—that is, a pompadour in the front, with the rest of my hair shaved close to the scalp. Even though I hated that style—preferring to keep the longer Afro that I selected between visits to Brighton—I always walked away from Jack's swirling candystick barber pole with the fresh cut of my grandmother's choosing.

Poppa Jack was a man's man, and the epitome of a *mensch*. I remember him as the only person in my life who didn't use his ego against others. You did what he wanted, not based on what he said, but because of who he was. "Poppa Jack was the *honest* man that Diogenes couldn't find," my mother once said. "They missed each other by just over two thousand years."

In school, or at home and on the streets in Harlem, curse words were as common as baseball cards. But the strongest language that I ever heard Poppa Jack use was *goshdarnit,* which he said in a habitual, soft-spoken manner whenever I failed to wash my hands before a meal. He was such a strong man that he never *needed* to curse. He looked like Dick Powell; but in terms of being kind and nice, he acted like Kris Kringle in *Miracle on 34th Street.* And because he had such a perfect physique, I once asked if he had boxed when he was young.

"Sure, I did," he replied with a smile. "I used to box oranges"—meaning that he had worked as a crater in a fruit company.

My earliest memories of Poppa Jack were of him pushing me in a blue stroller along the Boardwalk. Every day, we went from Brighton to Coney Island and back. When people stared, it never seemed to occur to him that they might be having racist thoughts. He just believed that I was the best-looking grandson in the world, so he expected us to be noticed. Poppa Jack was like that. He accepted me. And that feeling of acceptance meant so much that I begged him to take me out, and push me in that stroller, long after my legs had outgrown its infant-size seat.

He also watched over me while I played for hours in the Second Street Park near their apartment. Whenever I looked up, Poppa Jack would be on a bench along the Boardwalk that overlooked the park, just watching me. Never interfering, and always at a distance, but watching nonetheless. Like my guardian angel. He was the father I didn't think that I had, because my own daddy didn't do for me what Poppa Jack did; but looking back, I now realize that Poppa Jack *was* a real father to me. It was he who had a special pole that we used to fish off the Boardwalk pier. And it was Poppa Jack who loved me, and others, no matter what the color of our skins were. He was a biblical-type character, but alive, and all mine.

*   *   *

If Poppa Jack was the salt of the earth, then Bubba was pepper. Before I was born, he suffered serious injuries in an accident at the fruit company. His body was jammed between two trucks in the loading dock. Later, at the hospital, Bubba and Momma and her brother Herbie were gathered around Poppa Jack's bed when the rabbi arrived. Immediately, Uncle Herbie started acting religious, holding up the Bible and saying *mitzvahs* (prayers) while the rabbi spoke with the physician. Then when the rabbi pulled Bubba aside and whispered, "'Mildred Palestine. Go and get a new suit. This is it," Momma began crying. Death was in the room.

But Bubba said nothing to the rabbi. Instead, she walked over to the bed where Poppa Jack was sleeping. Then she leaned down, and yelled into his ear, "Get up, goddammit, get up! What-the-hell do you think you're doing, Jack Palestine? You can't leave me with these two kids. Oh, no. I won't stand for it. So just get yourself up, right this minute. And don't you even think about dying. You hear me, Jack?"

Well, Poppa Jack opened his eyes, and lived. Uncle Herbie, Momma, the doctors, and the rabbi—they were all surprised, and shocked. But not Bubba. She had *kvetched* (argued) her husband back to life, and they would stay together another forty years.

In many ways, then, my Bubba was our entire family's life-blood. It was she who nicknamed me *Beryl David*, which is Hebrew for "Buddy Drew," and that nickname stuck, both in Brighton and on the streets of Harlem. In fact, I still answer to Buddy Drew, because nobody contradicted my grandmother. Not even my father.

Years before, when my parents' divorce papers had to be served, the police wouldn't do it. So Bubba took the train to Manhattan, then wandered alone through the streets of Harlem until she found my father hanging out with his friends on a street corner. While these black brothers watched, and laughed, Bubba smacked my father dead in the face, stuffed the papers in his suit pocket, and then kissed him good-bye. That was Bubba's way. She was feisty enough, and steady to the core, so that even the toughest Harlem player loved her.

And as long as she was able, Bubba worked for the Loews Corporation. She's the only person in our family who consistently had a job. Though she was short and stocky, she bore her weight well, and always dressed neatly. I particularly recall what gorgeous legs she had, and they always seemed to be in motion. Bubba loved to work, and walk. And she was the only punctual person I knew. Every day at ten minutes past five, Bubba came striding from the train station. She was a person you could count on.

Wherever Bubba went, she carried two shopping bags. Always two, never one. Daddy used to joke when she visited us—her shopping bags in tow—"Came light, but leavin' heavy, hey, Bubba. You better weigh her, Rosebud!" The truth was, however, that Bubba always brought us food or other necessities when she came. And she had bought all the furniture in our apartment.

Because my grandmother worked, and managed money well, anything I ever wanted she got for me. If I went to the sidewalk in front of their building and yelled up, Bubba always stuck her head out the window and tossed down coins in her handkerchief for me to get ice cream or go to a movie. I guess I ran to Bubba so many times in those early years that I got to the point where I wasn't running anymore. I just went. Bubba was my anchor. If Bundini became Momma's American Dream, nobody ever believed that I would succeed the way my grandmother did. I was Bubba's immigrant dream of what America could offer.

Because I enjoyed such love and acceptance with my grandparents in Brighton, I also wanted to be friends with the white kids who lived in the neighborhood. They had names like Hoffstein, Goldberg, Biederman, and Fogle, but no Ricardos or Riveras. Yet from the beginning, these kids demonstrated bitterness toward me, and they did it in the hurtful ways that only children can: lying to me, hiding when I came around the corner, or running from me on the playground. But the more they ran, the more I wanted to run to them.

I finally realized that their bitterness was because of my color, and not because of my personality. Brighton was a close-knit community. Everyone knew that my father and I were black, and that my mother was white. So my being black and Jewish, complete with white grandparents, created a resentment in Brighton's kids that shocked me.

"What are you? Black? Or white?" one boy yelled at me one afternoon. "Or are you a *zebra?*" His saying this in front of all the other Jewish boys devastated me. Back in Harlem, I never felt bitterness or prejudice from my friends toward Momma or Bubba or me. In fact, my black and Hispanic friends adored them. Why, then, I wondered, was the reverse not true? Why would white kids treat me differently from black kids?

But it wasn't just the kids in Brighton. One day I watched from Bubba's window while all the guys ran up the street and into the door leading to Richard Goldberg's apartment. They lived on the sixth floor. Well, I figured that I'd join them, so I ran downstairs and across the street. Inside the slow-rising elevator in their building, I prayed that they would accept me. Then when it reached the sixth floor, I ran down the hallway and knocked on the Goldbergs' door. Soon, my friend's nice mother opened it, stepped out into the hallway, and pulled the door behind her as she said, "Hi, Buddy, how're you doing?"

"Fine, Mrs. Goldberg. Can I play with the guys today?"

She looked me straight in the eyes and said, "I'm sorry, Buddy, but they're not here. And I don't know where they went."

I didn't take the elevator. Instead, I walked down the six flights of stairs. I was numb. For the first time, I realized that grownups would lie, and be racist, just like their kids. I never felt so rejected in my life. It was clear. Adults were part of this white game, too.

Once I reached the street, I went across to Bubba's stoop and sat, waiting. I watched for almost an hour until, finally, all four boys left the Goldbergs' building, and they were laughing. From then on, I felt a vengeance. *I'll show them,* I said to myself. *I don't have to be their friend. But one day, they're gonna have to be mine.*

7

I don't know what the big deal is about getting high. I get high! I do. I get high when they shoot me from zero to 140 miles per hour in 2.3 seconds, off the front end of an aircraft carrier. BOOM. I'm overdosin'.

I get high. You got to get high! But if you use drugs, you're gonna die. Why do you think they call it dope, DOPE? . . .

In the projects the older dudes (meaning guys in their late teens or early twenties) always drank brown-bagged cans of beer, or smoked pot, while they sat on the benches along the right side of the courtyard. Those of us who were younger weren't allowed there. But we could sit on the benches along the opposite side and watch them. To us, these older guys were cool. They were our heroes—just because they played basketball better than we could—so we studied every move they made. How they laughed; how they drank beer through a straw to get higher, quicker; how they held their smokes, tight-fingered and never far from their lips; how they made high-pitched sounds when they inhaled; and how the girls were attracted to them. We wanted to be just like these dudes.

So one night my boys and I gave a wino on 102nd Street a dollar to buy a six-pack of Colt 45 malt liquor and some straws for us from the Met Food Store. Then we took our brew to the corner of Central Park along Fifth Avenue, and there we hid along the gray stone walls—out of sight, but close enough to the streetlights in case we needed to escape.

The moon was full, and the windows gleamed on the high-priced apartment buildings that, ironically, were just a block from our ghetto. It was a gorgeous hideaway, and the four of us were so proud of ourselves, hiding and drinking and admiring the big city lights. The only problem was, the malt liquor tasted gross, almost like acid.

Like the others, I drank it anyway, and acted cool. But I couldn't imagine how the older guys could drink something this horrible on a regular basis, and still smile, laugh, and be cool.

We couldn't. As soon as we finished off the six-pack, we headed back to the projects. When I entered the elevator, which reeked of fresh urine, I was so sick to my stomach that I could hardly breathe. So entering my apartment, I avoided Momma, who was asleep on the couch, then rushed to my room. There, stretched out on my bed, my head felt as though it was spinning. And that spinning kept getting faster and faster, until I tried to stop this dizziness by imagining that the room was spinning in the *other* direction. That did it. I spent the next half hour throwing up in the commode.

The next day, my friends and I broke the projects' rule of perpetual coolness and discussed our experiment. "How can they drink that garbage?" one guy asked. "It's not even as good as 7UP." The rest of us laughed, delighted that someone had *said* what we all felt.

"Yeah," another guy said, "and Coca-Cola never made me throw up!" At that, we broke out in laughter. Then one by one, everybody confessed to have gotten sick—which was why, the night before, we had all silently agreed to leave the park so quickly.

After that experiment, we lost interest in drinking booze. We were too young to buy it. We hated the taste. And worse, we despised throwing up. But more important, we lost some of our admiration for the older dudes. Their coolness after drinking suddenly seemed hollow, once we knew for ourselves that what they sucked through their straws was liquid garbage that tasted like acid, led to vomiting, and certainly did nothing for their game of basketball.

In late 1964, my popularity with the black kids of P.S. 171 in Manhattan got an enormous boost. At the time, Ali had returned from his tours abroad to train for the May 25, 1965, rematch with Liston. And against the wishes of his Islamic advisors, Ali had rehired Daddy to work with him in Harlem and Miami gyms. (Over the years, the champ would hire my father eight times, and fire him seven times—all because Ali needed Daddy for the fights, but between matches, the conflicts between my father and Ali's other advisors were unending.) So I didn't really expect my daddy to come and see me in a play at school. Only mothers did that. And anyway, I knew that Daddy had a championship title to protect.

The day of the play, when our class entered the auditorium, I spotted Bubba and Momma seated together in the audience. But as the time came for the play to begin, I looked at every face in the crowd, and none of them was my father's. Minutes later, however, as I walked center stage to deliver my lines as an old English statesman, white wig and all, the auditorium's rear door flew open. I gasped in midsentence, and everyone turned around to see what I saw. Then all the fourth, fifth, and sixth graders seemed to gasp at once, because through the doorway strutted Muhammad Ali. The Champ was dressed in a tailored black suit, a white shirt, but no necktie, and he wielded a well-polished walking cane.

I smiled. The Champ grinned wider. Then from behind his massive shoulders stepped my daddy, making me grin from ear to ear. Suddenly, the six hundred or so students jumped to their feet and began screaming, "Cassius Clay, Muhammad Ali! Cassius Clay, Muhammad Ali!"

I didn't know what to do. Should I continue my lines, or let the Champ speak? But Ali and my daddy calmed the crowd, moved to a pair of empty seats in the front row, and then nodded to me to continue.

Needless to say, I couldn't concentrate. The lines slipped through my mind like water down the sewer, but I persisted. I babbled along in a British accent until my part ended, and the curtain closed. Then the principal, Mrs. Veronica Flynn, went to the microphone and introduced the Champ.

As Ali got up, I looked from the wings of the stage and saw my daddy's gaze connect with mine. "See, son, I told you," his happy eyes seemed to say. "I'll never let you down. I'll always come through for you." In response, I stuck my little finger in the air, as a gesture to symbolize my daddy's handshake.

Meanwhile Ali was reciting his poems to the kids, and the entire school was laughing and cheering. Then I watched while the Champ gradually turned their amusement to serious listening. He switched topics and told the kids to get an education, because there would never be another Muhammad Ali, so they shouldn't grow up the way he had.

Then he allowed the students to ask questions, and one boy stood up and yelled, "Hey, Clay. How come you have such a *big* mouth?"

That sent the place into an uproar. My father chuckled, and Ali laughed back. We all understood it was *put-down time,* another street ritual. Everybody in Harlem—particularly the successful dudes—had to react to put-downs, because they were the spontaneous test of wits that proved you were as smooth as your reputation.

So the Champ responded, "You're right, son. I *do* have a big mouth. But I've got *big* fists to back it up." And everybody cheered. We all understood that Ali handled the put-down just right. The kid had tried to score on the Champ, but the Champ came right back and scored on the rebound.

That was the first motivational speech I ever heard that talked about the importance of kids' getting an education. But what impressed me was that Ali also mixed his message with street humor, jive talk, and put-downs. Who would have thought that, years later, I would be the one talking to kids about education and The American Dream? Yet that day, within seconds after Ali came to sit with me and my daddy, I saw how effective the speech had really been. The principal dismissed us, and immediately, hundreds of kids gathered around Ali, my daddy, and me to get the Champ's autograph. Ali was kind and patient with the kids, but he was particularly kind to me. He made it clear to all my friends that he, the Champ, was my big brother. From that day on, I did feel as though Ali and I were brothers—two young guys being guided in the world by Bundini, our common psychological father.

But Ali could be vain and unpredictable. At twenty-two, he was still a boy in many ways, and still growing, too. Since the 1964 fight with Liston, Ali's height had increased a half inch to six feet three, and he was in excellent shape. "I'm so beautiful, I should be chiseled in gold," he boasted to reporters.[1] But this self-admiration could just as quickly turn to jealousy and racism.

Later that year, for example, I was visiting at the Champ's house, and we got into an argument. There was a playful side to him that made it difficult to tell when he was genuinely angry, so I persisted in arguing until we had gone too far.

"You're just a nappyheaded little Jew," he snapped. That hurt me so much that, even though I was just a boy, I went after him, swinging my fists and trying to kill him. But he held me at bay with his long right arm, and danced about the room with a quickness that I couldn't match. To him, it was only a joke, and the Champ laughed it off. To me, however, it was a betrayal. My brother had demeaned me with racism, and I would not forget it.

That same spring, Ali's racial views caused a rift between him and my father. Traveling on "Big Red" from Miami to Massachusetts for the second Ali-Liston fight, they stopped at a restaurant in the South. But when my daddy led the entourage inside, he was directed by the manager to the "BLACKS ONLY" section in the rear. Daddy refused, and was arguing the absurdity of treating the world heavyweight champion like this, when Ali interrupted.

"You fool, what's the matter with you?" the Champ yelled in front of all the patrons. ". . . I told you, you ought to be a Muslim; then you don't go places where you're not wanted. You clear out of this place, nigger. You ain't wanted here. . . ." Then he grabbed my father and pushed him outside.

There Ali continued his verbal assaults. "I'm glad, Bundini. I'm glad you got showed."

"Leave me alone," my father said. "I'm good enough to eat here. I'm a free man. God made me—not Henry Ford."

Later, as the bus headed north once again, Ali began calling my father an "Uncle Tom," and the Champ boasted, "This teach you a lesson, Bundini."

"My head don't belong between my knees," my father replied. "It's up in the stars. I'm free. I keep trying. If I find a water hole is dry, I go on and find another. . . . That man, that manager—he'll sleep on it. He may be no better, but he'll think on it, and he'll be ashamed. I dropped a little medicine in that place."[2]

But the damage was done. My father believed that all men were created equal, while Ali held just as resolutely to Black Muslim beliefs, and the ideals of black separation and liberation. My father viewed Ali's career as something mystical and spiritual, while the Champ was rapidly becoming the "angry gloved messenger of the black revolution."[3]

Events like these also created a tension between me and Ali that made our brotherly bond bittersweet for many years. We were vying for attention from the same father figure. Daddy loved each of us passionately, but he also loved us differently. And that difference was painful, because the Champ was definitely jealous of the love that my father and I shared. And to be loved by Bundini was like an addiction. Once you had it, you wanted it all to yourself.

Tensions aside, 1965 through 1967 proved momentous years for Ali and my father. In May 1965, Liston once again fell victim to their boxing prowess, as did Floyd Patterson in November. By 1966, twenty-four-year-old Ali seemed unbeatable. These victories had pushed his total career earnings above the $2 million mark, with another $1.2 million coming in 1967 alone.[4] But more significantly, Ali's emergence as a bona fide celebrity came at a critical moment when millions of blacks were hungry for our own heroes, from Nat Turner to Stokely Carmichael. Earlier in 1965, Malcolm X had been gunned down in the Audubon Ballroom where Harlemites had gathered to hear his plans for black nationalism. So to most of us, outspoken Muhammad Ali fit the bill perfectly. He said what we dared not think, and he had the power to be heard. He was our new folk hero.[5]

In the wake of Ali's success, my father prospered for the first time in his life. Though Mamma and I still lived in the projects,

Daddy rented a nice apartment for himself on the Upper East Side. He bought a long black Cadillac, and in that posh neighborhood he opened a bar called Bundini's World, located on Second Avenue and 81st Street. What I remember most distinctly was that he started carrying business cards that listed himself as the bar's president, and he gave me one for my scrapbook.

For a while, Momma worked as the bar's bookkeeper, and the business flourished. Ali would come there, and he attracted other celebrities like Norman Mailer and George Plimpton. As a result, Bundini's World became, almost overnight, a melting pot of boxing insiders and famous writers, but also a chic nook in the white establishment from which Harlem's best pimps and prostitutes could work a new clientele. In short, it was an East Side Sugar Ray's, only classier.

Sometimes during this period, Daddy took me to churches, synagogues, and little chapels all over Manhattan. We would slip in, just the two of us, find a pew near the back, and pray—no matter what type of service was actually being held. But when the priest or minister approached us and asked if we wanted to join, my daddy always responded, "No, thank you. We belong."

About this same time, two gangsters held up my daddy's bar one night. He resisted, but they overcame him and left him with a six-inch scar on his right cheek. The robbers got away, not only with all his cash but also with an original LeRoy Neiman painting of me. Afterward, Daddy assured me, "Don't worry, son. The Circle Theory will take care of them," and two weeks later, it did. These same robbers were both killed during another hold-up attempt.

At heart, my daddy was an idea man, a preacher of the motivational gospel. As my parents had done earlier in their relationship, my father began sharing ideas again with Momma, and she wrote them down. Collaborating on these writings was something positive that they could still do together, and it gave him a new means to express his beliefs. More than a dozen years earlier, he had shaved his head and had actually preached from a soapbox on the streets of Harlem. But by the mid-sixties, his gospel had become secularized. The bar was his assembly, these writings were his epistles, and famous men like Plimpton began circulating Daddy's street-philosophy manuscripts among various Manhattan publishers. So for a season at least, it looked as though Bundini and Rhoda Brown were finally making their way into the legitimate high life.

Back in the projects, however, I realized that a strange evolution had been taking place in the courtyard. Instead of the older dudes singing, laughing, yelling, playing music, and talking to girls, the way they used to do, by 1967 a gray cloud had settled above the benches on the righthand side. The dudes' smiles had been replaced by sullen expressions, and all of them were nodding—their heads jerking slowly, up and down, into strange positions, We younger guys knew why. They were sleeping away their days on the benches, because the dudes were using heroin. Our heroes had become junkies.

As before, we studied their moves. We hid in the stairwells and spied as the poorer dudes paid two dollars to dealers who provided smack in cellophane packets. To get a discount, though, the tough dudes would buy a bundle of twenty-five packets. That really impressed us. And after the buys, we saw the older dudes duck around corners and snort the packets, or gather in circles so that the one in the middle could shoot up. To us, the whole process looked stupid, but because of all the secrecy, it also seemed cool. So I decided to try. That was my nature. I was twelve years old, and I wanted to be part of everything that happened.

I saved up two dollars, and I studied a particular dealer's moves. Then when I thought I was ready, I stopped him on the street and said, "Yo, I want to cop a deuce bag."

The dealer, who was in his twenties, looked at me, the boy, as if to say, "What, are you crazy?"

I knew that, messing with dealers, you better *look* like you know what you were doing, so I tried to be real smooth as I repeated, "I said, I need to cop a deuce."

"Cool," he said. "Meet me in the first-floor hallway. On the *even* side."

"You got it," I responded with confidence, even though I knew something was wrong. The project buildings had two sets of elevators. One set stopped at all the even-numbered floors, while the other stopped at the odd-numbered ones. Living in 11-F, I was familiar with the odd set, and everybody knew who used which elevators. Yet the dealer insisted on meeting me *outside* my territory.

Despite my suspicions, I told all my friends. They were impressed, and that motivated me to go to the basement of the even elevators and wait for the dealer. It also persuaded me to comply when the dealer showed up, asked for my two dollars, and then promised. "You wait here, and I'll be back in ten with the dope."

Well, I waited in that basement for half an hour, and the longer I waited the clearer it became that the dealer had beat me. But on the streets, getting beat was worse than not copping dope at all. Empty-handed, I couldn't face my friends.

So I devised a plan. I took the even elevator to the twelfth floor, walked down the stairs to my floor, and in my apartment, I went through all the motions of scoring a packet. I cut paper to the exact size of a packet. I poured onto the paper the proper amount of salt that I thought a deuce bag would hold. Next, using the shell of a ballpoint pen, the way I had seen the toughest dudes do, I pretended to snort a bit of it at a time, though I actually scraped the salt into an ashtray. Then I threw all the paraphernalia into the trash, and sat for five minutes. I had to get in character, if I was going to act high. Remember: On the streets, you could con your friends, but you dared not lie to them. So I had to go through the motions of scoring smack. Otherwise, my con would be a betrayal.

When I had conjured up what I considered a convincing high, I went back to our bench, started nodding, my friends bought the act, and that did it. None of us actually tried drugs, as long as I lived in the projects. We were too poor to buy. And watching our heroes become dope fiends was very disillusioning. They even lost interest in girls. So we wanted no part of something, no matter how cool, that turned dudes off to the babes.

But during these years I also saw the beginnings of what drugs can do to a whole person, because I witnessed the early phase of my daddy's addiction to alcohol and cocaine. By then, he had the money to afford it, so he lived to get high. He had bought into the sixties' myth that cocaine was the safe, nonaddictive, recreational drug of the elite. Yet within a few short years, I would see how cocaine began deteriorating his mind, his body, his soul—everything that he lived for. My mother estimates that within the five-year period of 1963–1968, he went through over $250,000 in earnings, with most of that money going for drugs.

There's never been a man who made it, unscathed, through a cocaine addiction; and as great a man as my father was, he would never be the same after that. Instead of building on his success as a boxing trainer, cocaine seized his mind when my father was at his peak. That's the tragedy. Drugs stole half a lifetime of knowledge from my daddy's brain; but he would live another twenty years before his body gave way to the loss that his brain and soul had already suffered.

By my seventh-grade year in school, I could no longer tolerate the arguing and fighting that characterized our home life when both my parents were around. Running a bar was the worst thing that a mother prone to drinking and a father on drugs could do. They lost themselves in it. And I could not cope with the extended periods when I didn't know where either of my parents were. Ali and Bundini's World had become their lives. That left me alone—the kid back in the projects who was theirs, when either or both of them had no place else to go.

In addition, the lure from the streets of drugs and alcohol, and the possibility of getting involved in criminal activities, were too close to me. I could go either way, so I knew that the time had come to decide. One night I went to the Spanish theater near the projects, and sitting by myself in the dark auditorium, I stared at the screen. The movie was *Goldfinger,* but the subtitles were in English and the dialogue was in Spanish. Hearing James Bond sound like Desi Arnaz, I realized that there were many worlds beyond Harlem. There were languages to learn, and other cultures that I'd never know if I stayed where I was. So that night I decided to move in with my grandparents in Brighton Beach, and to enroll in P.S. 43, James J. Reynolds Junior High in Sheepshead Bay, Brooklyn.

Across the East River from the Harlem that I understood,

Brighton promised to be both a challenge and a haven. I would be the only black Jewish boy in a white Jewish community, but I would also be the only little boy in Bubba and Poppa Jack's life. And with them, I believed that I'd finally have a family, a stable home, and a chance at a better education and a real life.

8

In the Jewish calendar the year is 5728. In the Gregorian calendar the year is 1968. It is a time of chaos, confusion, and insecurity in the world. But today, I stand here ready and willing to accept the first responsibilities of manhood.

I sincerely give my gratitude with all my heart and soul to the people who made this day possible: my dearest mother, Rhoda; my great father, Drew Jr.; my wonderful grandparents, Zeda "Poppa" Jack Palestine and Mildred "Bubba" Palestine; and all of my relatives and friends.

I would like to give recognition also to Rabbi Lazar and Rabbi Fuller, who helped guide me spiritually to become a man who will respect all mankind through understanding, love, and respect.

My prayer for the world of today is that man should find peace and harmony within himself, in order that he may be able to get along with all mankind. God will not destroy the world! But man will, if he doesn't find peace, love, and understanding with his fellow man. The price of a free world is respect, love, and peace for each other. Shabot Shalom.

My bar mitzvah speech[1]

Moving into apartment 4-K at 3121 Brighton Fifth Street, I immediately felt like a Brighton Beacher. Visiting there over the years had not done that. But moving in with my grandparents had. I also began seeing things differently. Instead of feeling prejudices, I found beauty in this thoroughly Jewish and white community. In contrast to Manhattan's high rises, buildings in Brighton were rarely more than six stories tall; my new neighborhood seemed cozier, and scaled down to a size that was less threatening to a boy. So compared to life on the other side of the tracks, Brighton seemed like a resort by the sea.

Another difference was the subway trains. They traveled above ground in Brooklyn, and their vibrations along the rusted steel tracks were louder than the commuter trains that rushed past Harlem. In fact, noises along the elevated rails (the "El") could be heard for blocks. But to me, that made the train sounds at the Brighton Fifth Street stop function like chimes on a clock. I could tell which one was bringing Bubba home from work each day, and by the frequency of the trains I could tell what time it was, even on an overcast day. There was a routineness in Brighton that felt stable and supportive, and I had no family routines in Harlem.

Under the El were dozens of small, family-owned Jewish shops along Brighton Avenue—the tailors and dry cleaners and pizza parlors, the delis and fish or food stands, the bakeries, the fruit and vegetable markets, the trinket shops, and many, many kosher meat markets. Unlike the store clerks in Harlem, these shopkeepers were friendly and trusting, and they cared about their customers. In heavy Jewish accents, they greeted children on a first-name basis, and they all called me Buddy Drew; but adults were "Mr." and "Mrs." It was a warm, personal, and respectful way to do business.

Walking down the residential streets was just as friendly, but somehow exotic. The old people yelled down from their windows to others who sat on benches or stoops along the sidewalk. They were *yentering* (gossiping) about this one, and that one, in Yiddish or German or Russian or a dozen other languages that I didn't know. It felt as though I had been dropped into a European village, even though, from the El, I could still see the top of Manhattan's Empire State Building. So I was in a different world, but I was still at home in New York City, too.

Some of that gossip was about me. Other than a local wino's and the building superintendents', mine was the only black face on these streets. And though I could not yet understand the languages of this yentering, their expressions told me everyone knew that I now belonged. I was a resident. Somehow, that softened their expressions, and made the old people smile at me, or pat me on the head as I walked by. It was as if, suddenly, they all seemed to adore me; as if I was the missing link that allowed them to say, "That's right. I always knew that I wanted to like black kids, and this one is the epitome, because he's such a good Jewish boy."

All of this made Brighton seem like one huge, extended family, and having a sense of family was of the utmost importance to me and this community. When people didn't have a family, they were lonely, and you knew it. They suffered from emptiness. In fact, there were many mentally disturbed people roaming the streets each day, and they demonstrated this vividly.

There was the Cat Lady who fed the hundreds of felines that prowled the empty lots and alleys in Brighton. They were her family. But there was also Rosie the Witch, whose lover had left her when she was a beautiful, twenty-year-old teacher. By the time I first saw Rosie, however, she was an old, haggard woman who always wore black hats and dresses, accented only by a pair of yellow socks. She never spoke to, or bothered, anyone; but if we kids taunted her, she would chase us away with broken English and Yiddish curses. Yet even then, she always ran with her purse in front of her face, because Rosie the Witch never looked anyone in the eyes. She was alone and ashamed of having no family, and she publicly mourned her loss.

Or there was Hymie, a heavyset man whose head was bald, except for a few patches of gray stubble. Yet his tongue was the real distinction. It was so long and curved that he could—and did—lick the end of his nose in a type of nervous habit that was incredibly disgusting. In spite of his repulsiveness, we pitied poor Hymie. Years earlier, his only child had died as an infant; so by my time in Brighton, Hymie spent his days talking to an expensive, empty baby carriage that he pushed along the sidewalks. He was mourning too.

There was even the lady who went in every phone booth along Brighton Beach Avenue, picked up the receiver, pretended to put a dime in the slot, then dialed a number, and started cursing. "You sonuvabitch, I can't believe you didn't pick me up tonight. . . ." Everyone knew that her boyfriend had left her thirty years before. Yet when that "call" was over, she would leave the booth, slam the door, then rush to the next phone booth and repeat the process.

But my favorite was a wino named Shorty. This old black gentleman hung out on the corner of Brighton Fifth Street where, every day, he sang the same song, "Sweet Georgia Brown." It was his gift, his contribution, to the community; and though his clothes were tattered, his bloodshot eyes always twinkled—especially when he saw me. He alone seemed to notice when my white buddies ran away from me, or tried to make me feel inferior. They made fun of him, too, but I never did, because Shorty made me feel special. "You go to school, and don't end up like me," he would whisper, his stale breath making me cringe, " 'Cause one day, you gonna stand out among men. You hear?" Shorty was a bum, but he was the best bum I ever knew.

Such, then, were their jobs—Cat Lady, Rosie, Hymie, the phone-booth fanatic, and Shorty—and they performed these tasks every day. They were people without a family. But I understood them. I was in Brighton because I desperately needed my grandparents to give me a family.

In sharp contrast to the project's dullish-brown tile floors and its musty yellow walls, Bubba's building had shiny black-and-white tile and beige walls, ornamented with sculptured designs that had been trimmed in gold paint. These features gave the building its Old World flavor and warmth. In sharp contrast to the filth in the projects, in Bubba's building the super regularly kept the floors polished and the walls clean. More remarkable to me, though, were the stairways. Unlike the dark, scary stairwells in the projects, the Waldorf had open-air stairs that led up to our fourth-floor apartment. And its elevators did not reek of urine; nor did they rattle, or creep slowly from floor to floor. These elevators moved smoothly, and were swept clean each day. It was all so wonderful that I took a knife, and in tiny letters that were virtually unnoticeable, I carved my first graffiti. I wrote BUDDY into the elevator's polished paneling. That was my Harlem way of saying, "This is my building. Buddy Drew belongs here."

Bubba's door proclaimed the same message. Instead of the green metal doors of the projects, Bubba's was a polished wooden door. On the door frame there was a *mazuzah* (an ornament that blessed the house each time someone kissed it), just as on all the others in the building, But our door also contained my Buy Scout emblem, my Little League stickers, and any other award that I brought home—as if everything that I did brought us good luck.

An even subtler difference was the view. Back in Harlem, all that I could see from my bedroom window were row upon row of project buildings, plus the commuter-train tracks that linked Manhattan to Connecticut. But from Bubba's window, I could look to the right and see the train station, and the hustle and bustle of Brighton Beach Avenue; or to the left, I could see and smell the Atlantic Ocean and watch people saunter along the Boardwalk. Her window, however, was not just important for its view. All of our family business was conducted through it. Bubba kept a handsomely covered pillow on its wide sill, and most days, she took time to stand there, leaning on the pillow, while she talked to her neighbors. That's where plans were made, and problems were solved.

It was also where I watched to see where the action was. Unlike the projects, which had the wide courtyard where we played, everything in Brighton was more compact and segmented. Alleys and back alleys snaked among the buildings, and that's where kids hung out. So I would watch from Bubba's window until I spotted a gang gathering. Then I'd rush downstairs to join in the fun. There, beneath the maze of fire escapes in those alleys, we had to learn very exacting skills. For example, since most alleyways were no wider than twenty feet, we had to perfect the art of hitting "Pensy Pinkies" (rubber baseballs) only to center field. Any other hit would veer like bullets off the walls and break windows—making stickball a deadly sport.

Further up the Boardwalk was Coney Island Avenue, and that's where Bubba took me for weekly visits to the Lincoln Savings Bank. There, in the savings account that she had helped me open, we deposited five or ten dollars at a time. Afterward, we stopped at the Forty Thieves newspaper stand, and she bought egg creams in Coca-Cola glasses. But like real special New Yorkers, we only got *vanilla* egg creams. Sometimes, we also went across to the famous Mrs. Stahl's, where Bubba bought delicious homemade cherry-cheese knishes. Yet we had to eat all of this before we got home, because Poppa Jack was a diabetic, and we didn't want to tempt him.

Through all of it—her door displays, her yentering from the window, the savings account, and the egg creams and knishes—Bubba was doing everything she could to make me feel loved. And I was so hungry for such love that I never resisted.

Bubba was also determined to teach me about my Jewish heritage. She and Poppa Jack were orthodox Jews, and over the years, they had taken me to synagogue on the high holidays. During my visits, she had also taught me Yiddish, and some Hebrew. But once I moved in with them, she immediately enrolled me in Hebrew school, and I had to attend classes every day. Rabbi Lazar helped me with the *Torah, Barucha,* and *Haftarah.* He was old, had a long gray beard, and he liked me because I had enthusiasm for learning. Plus, I was his first black pupil, so he seemed fascinated with the whole process.

Yet those lessons were difficult. The good rabbi had a bad habit of picking his ears, and then using that same wax-smeared finger to point out Hebrew words on the scrolls. After that, the wax became *my* problem. When the rabbi would remove his finger, the wax often blurred what I was supposed to recite.

"Vhat is dat vord?" he would say, after I mispronounced what the wax had covered.

"But, rabbi, I can't read it," I would respond.

"Vhat do you mean, you *cannot* read it?"

To that, I could say nothing. I knew that Rabbi Lazar was a holy man whom I dared not embarrass by saying that his ear wax covered the words. So I'd take the back of my pencil, scratch off the wax, and then pray that I could still read the Hebrew.

Four months before my thirteenth birthday in January, the rabbi informed Bubba that we should start preparations for a bar mitzvah. My progress under his guidance, he said, was excellent—though under the circumstances, a better word might have been *remarkable*.

Yet the rabbi's nod was all that Bubba needed. She swung into action. At the kitchen table, she and I addressed invitation envelopes and inserted my picture in each one. Back then, most kids had bar mitzvah pictures made in a fancy Brooklyn studio, but Bubba had taken mine. She dressed me in a new suit that she had bought. Then we took all the pictures off her bedroom wall; she made me stand on her bed; and there in "Bubba's studio," she shot a roll of film for my portrait.

When the day finally came, what pleased me most about the service was that it represented something that had never happened before: For the first time in my life, all of my family was together. Seated in the Ocean View Synagogue were my black relatives—Granddaddy Drew, my Brown aunts and uncles, and my father—as well as my white relatives—Momma, Uncle Herbie, Bubba, Poppa Jack, Aunt Myrna, and my young cousins, Josh and Tracey. The men all wore *yarmulkes* (skullcaps) and white tallis prayer shawls—including my Granddaddy Drew who, until then, had hated white people and would not attend any white-sponsored event. Yet here he was, yarmulke and all. The women, seated by themselves, were beautifully dressed as well, and all of them were smiling.

This gathering of black and white faces made me so proud that when it was time to recite my part, I sang in Hebrew like a rabbi out of Israel. Next, I read the English speech that my mother had written. When I finished it all, and could see the pride in my friends' and family's eyes, I felt a rush of tremendous happiness. But why not? For the first time, everyone that I loved seemed peaceful, and in agreement on at least one thing: Despite everything that had happened, their Buddy Drew was impressive and growing up to be good.

The following day, a local newspaper quoted Bubba regarding the ceremony:

> . . . Unlike most other Jewish youngsters of his age, Buddy recited two pages of the Torah (the Jewish Bible) in Hebrew, considered quite a feat, added Mrs. Palestine.
>
> Like his hero [Muhammad Ali], Buddy is athletic. He has won two citations at school for his physical prowess, his grandmother indicated.

"He's also excellent as a student," she added. "He gets 90 and 95 percent in his grades, without studying. If he'd open a book yet, he'd get 110, he's so smart."

Afterward, we left the synagogue for the reception hall, but walking with Bubba along Brighton Fourth Street, we wondered aloud if my mother would get drunk. For weeks, I had been begging Momma, "Please, if you don't do anything, just don't drink at my bar mitzvah," because I knew that would ruin everything. To Momma's credit, she did make me proud that day. In spite of Bubba's protests, Momma wore a bright red silk Indian sari with gold trim. She looked as beautiful as only my mother could, almost like a queen. And she didn't drink or disrupt; throughout the reception, there was only love in her eyes for me.

Also during the walk, I realized that a remarkable thing was happening. From scores of residences along the route, old women at their windowsill pillows waved handkerchiefs, or threw kisses at Bubba and me, and many called out, "Buddy Drew!" "Beryl David!" It was as though everyone in Brighton knew that, today, the little black Jew had truly become a man, and that I had done it first-class.

At the reception itself, Bubba and I launched into our mission: Neither of my parents had paid for the reception in progress—even though Mother was now orchestrating this wonderful party—so Bubba and I had to come up with the money. But we had a plan. As the guests brought the traditional, money-filled envelopes by my table, my grandmother would provide hugs, then at length I would thank them while she slipped the envelopes into her ever-present shopping bag. When it was all over, I was shocked to discover that we had a bag full of envelopes. We had never *seen* so much *gelt*. After we counted it, there was actually enough money to pay all the expenses, with some left over to take, on Monday, to the Lincoln Savings Bank. What a team we were, my Bubba and me!

One of my most treasured moments was the picture-taking session. I took control of that. For the first shot, I positioned my father and Poppa Jack—black and white, with me in the middle—standing before the holy Torah. Next, I arranged the same shot, but with my black and white grandfathers on either side of me, and again before the Torah. Then my black and white aunts and uncles, standing with me before the Torah, followed by a similar shot of me with my black and white cousins. I wanted all the pictures to show that it was finally okay that my family looked different, because—like a well-brewed cup of coffee—I was special. I had a little cream, too.

Muhammad Ali had not come to the bar mitzvah because, once more, his advisors had persuaded him to fire my father from the Champ's entourage. Yet this time, Ali was unemployed too. In 1967, he had refused army induction during federal court proceedings in Houston, Texas, so the court convicted him of draft evasion. Later that year, the New Orleans appellate court also ruled against Ali, and he was stripped of his world heavyweight title. Finally, state after state refused to license Ali's fights.[2] So the Champ was halted at his peak as a fighter; and stymied along with him were all those men, like my father, who had devoted themselves to Ali.

In addition, the negative publicity surrounding these events—combined with my parents' inabilities to manage their bar business (in large part due to their own drug and alcohol dependencies)—resulted in the closing of Bundini's World. This hurled my parents back to square one. Deprived of income and saddled with business debts, they went deeper into the cycle of alcohol, drugs, and violence toward one another.

First, my mother moved in with us at Bubba's, but that didn't work. Then Momma got an apartment on her own in Brighton Beach. Meanwhile, Daddy just seemed to wander from place to place. He was the kind of man to whom people *gave* everything no matter what; so when he wasn't with another woman, he would stay over with friends, or would eventually come back to Momma.

But it was at this point that I discovered something horrible: When my parents were intoxicated, they were not in their right minds, so I could no longer get through to them. They acted as though they were in a different world, and completely different people from the parents I had known before moving to Bubba's. In a sense, they had become like Rosie the Witch, or Hymie, or the phone-booth fanatic. They were strangers, even to those of us who loved them.

This Dr. Jekyll/Mr. Hyde stuff hurt me more than anything else, and I didn't understand it. My parents were no longer partying. It had all become a bummer. Either my mother was drunk and dancing by herself, or she was frantically trying to figure out how to get more liquor. And my father, he would sit around in a dark mood on the couch, his eyes aglow and his nose running, while he talked about God, truth, and life.

Overall, it was gloom and slow death in my parents' lives. Yet this time I was shielded—if not from the hurt—at least from the repercussions. I was now under Bubba and Poppa Jack's care. Away from my parents' misery, I still had a family and security.

9

You know why some of us don't make it? Because some of us don't believe in ourselves. And if you don't think you're intelligent, you ain't gonna make it. Yet the truth is, you are smart enough, and I'm gonna show you why.

You go to class, and the teacher says, "Good afternoon, class. Today, we're gonna learn French."

Then you know what some of us do. You've seen them in the street, and they're like this: "Yo, yo, what's up, Ms. Johnson? Check it out. Does it look like I was born in Paris or somethin'? Hey, check it out. I don't be speakin' no French. I'm comin' correct, I'm in effect, baby. I ain't gonna parlay vous Français for nobody, home boy."

Really? Then how come these same guys can say something like this?

"Yo, home boy, what's up?"

"I met this def babe, that's what. We slid by the crib. We were kickin' it live on some cold def jams. But all of a sudden, she started buggin'."

"Yeah."

Talk about speaking some French! Ain't that a trip? But you know what the funny thing is? That street slang is the hardest in the world to learn, and if you know how to speak it, you better understand this: You have the intelligence to speak any other language that they teach in any school.

And you know why the language of the streets is so hard? Because you need updates. You can't even say the same thing you said five years ago! And you can't even ask your friends what the words mean. I've seen you. You walk around here, talkin' like, "Yeah, that's def, ain't it." Or, "Wow, that's rad." But you're really goin', "What the heck is rad?"

Yet you're motivated to be accepted by your friends, and to be cool, so you find out what rad *means, because you put that word in the context of a sentence—just like all your teachers ask you to do.*

So that's why you can speak street language so well, and why you can do the same with other languages: You have the ability, but you must believe in yourself. . . .

During my years at James Reynolds Junior High in Brooklyn, Bubba purchased a membership for me at the Brighton Beach Baths. It was a private club located on about ten acres next to the ocean, and membership there identified Jewish families as being solidly middle class, whether you actually had money or not.

That's where I met Eddie. He lived in the elite and wealthy Jewish neighborhood of Manhattan Beach, and his father owned several businesses in the garment district on the other side of the East River. Eddie and I liked each other immediately, because he was a renegade among these rich white kids, and didn't care that I was the only black Jew at the baths. And I liked him because we had something in common, and because he had everything that I had always thought I wanted.

Their home on Dover Street was a real mansion, built of stone, and so huge that I probably never saw all of its rooms. But the ones that I did see were straight out of the *Richie Rich* comics. These superbad furnishings were either antiques or the latest in style and technology. For example, they had color TVs and stereos when everybody else I knew had black-and-white sets and record players. Upstairs in the mansion, there were at least five bedrooms; and downstairs, in addition to a home's usual rooms, they also had a real library lined with books, and a pantry. I couldn't believe they had one room set aside just to store food! But this one contained goods by the caseload. Instead of going to the store, the way we did, to buy what you *had* to have in order to eat that week, Eddie's family bought for the entire season. And outside, the house had a full-size basketball court in the rear, plus a lawn out front so well-kept that it looked like a PGA golf green.

To me, they were the perfect family to complement these luxuries. Eddie's sister was beautiful, and his brother had been an All-American basketball player and scholar at Princeton. They even had a black maid named Arlene, who had served as a nanny when the children were younger. But by the time I met them, Arlene was the cool-headed matron of the house. She adored me, loved the fact that Eddie had a black friend, and regularly made pies and cookies and cakes whenever I came over for visits.

Because of all this, I would have given up everything that I had if Eddie's family had adopted me. They were my *Brady Bunch*. Compared to the way they lived The American Dream, my family life seemed like The American Nightmare.

At my bar mitzvah reception, Eddie had exchanged knowing glances while the photographer took the traditional picture of my father and me drinking from the same glass of scotch under the sign TODAY, I AM A MAN. To Eddie and me, that symbolized the fact that, once I became a man in the Jewish sense, I could start drinking. So in a few days, we did.

At the baths, each of us shared lockers with someone else, but Eddie's partner was an old rich man who kept their locker stocked with liquor. So gradually, Eddie and I stole booze from his locker, transferred it to mine, and then began drinking like the other kids. However, just as when my friends and I had drunk malt liquor in Central Park, Eddie and I regularly got sick on the scotch. Yet we persisted, because everyone else at the baths was drinking, and we figured that the Society of Drunks *had* to be right.

Soon, however, we desired a greater buzz, and a new drug. Eddie had the money. And a dealer promised that marijuana was *the* way to get high without getting sick. So we started scoring pot, hiding our stashes in the mansion's attic, and when the two of us could sneak there undetected, we would listen to Jimi Hendrix's albums and turn our brains over to grass. It was 1969. We thought that, together, we had beaten the world—

fighting The System and smoking weed in the safety of such a beautiful mansion—because nobody knew. Except, of course, the guy who sold the stuff to us.

Then one day we discovered that our stash was empty, and Eddie's dealer said he was out. So being the naive shmucks that we were, we went to the Boardwalk on 13th Street, called Bay-one, where all the druggies hung out, and tried to buy from strangers. "Hey, man, got some weed?" Eddie or I would say. "We want to score a bag." But these hippies looked at us like we were crazy.

Then finally, a strange-looking kid on a bicycle stopped, said "No" in a deep voice, then turned around and added, "But I got somethin' better."

"Like, what?" Eddie asked.

"I got acid."

Being young and dumb and game for anything, I responded, "Oh, that's great. Let's try some."

"Now I only have half," the kid cautioned.

"Man, we can't buy a half," Eddie said, resuming control of a transaction based on his money. "Don't you see we got two guys here? We'll need at least two apiece."

"Look," the kid said. "This is Orange Sunshine, and you don't need *four*. I guarantee you, this loaded half will blow your mind."

"Okay!"

Eddie gave him two dollars. Then the kid took his ring off, and underneath was the smallest object that I've ever seen. Suddenly, my mind flashed back to the stairwells in the project, and I thought, *We've been beat*. So I said, "No way, man. We ain't buyin' a *speck* of anything for two dollars."

"Trust me," he said calmly. "If you don't like it, I'll be sittin' here, and I'll give your money back."

We took the half, walked down the Boardwalk a bit, then faced the next problem. It was two halves of a half that we needed, and cutting this was like splitting an atom. So we went back to the kid, and he cut it for us. Eddie and I then took our individual specks, and headed back down the beach.

It was about five in the afternoon, dusk, and the longer we walked, nothing happened. "What's goin' on?" Eddie said. "This stuff is no good. We got beat." So we turned around to go find the kid, though I began to realize that the sky seemed to be turning a weird color. But we ran him down anyway and asked for our money back.

The trip was, when he answered, his teeth seemed to come out of his mouth. I realized that I was hallucinating, and when I looked at Eddie, I could see in his eyes that he was, too. Then I looked back at the kid, and his face transformed into that of a mutant humanoid. Immediately, Eddie and I spun around and started running in the opposite direction.

Back on the beach, we started watching the sea walls, and they looked like they were breathing. "Did you see that?" I asked, and Eddie described exactly what I was seeing. It was as if we had one mind together. Then the sounds of ocean waves crashing were somehow transformed into a serenade of symphonic music.

"Man, this is a trip," I said to Eddie.

"That's exactly what we're on."

As they sky grew darker, the beer cans on the beach began to look like one of those Wrigley's cartoon commercials of people lying side by side on the beach—except these white beer cans were teeth that snarled, and these toothy mouths began laughing at us. Seconds later, the beer cans turned into sharks, and the laughing teeth became devices of death.

Terrified, Eddie and I got very close to one another. I realized that we had packed our bags, left reality, and were tripping hard. We couldn't protect ourselves. So we jumped up and started running toward his house. Along the way, everybody we saw had long tongues hanging from their mouths, or eyes that bulged from their heads like bloody, pointing fingers. It was terrible. We couldn't stop it. The whole world seemed to be after us. And all I could think to do was pray—hoping against hope that we hadn't tripped so far out from reality that God could no longer bring me back. I knew that He was not of this world, so I feared that He could not hear me. . . .

That winter, Momma spotted a *New York Times Magazine* ad seeking exchange students to go to Israel. She discussed it with Bubba and me, and we agreed that I should apply—even though none of us knew where, if I was accepted, we'd get the money. My father was earning a meager salary as trainer of Jeff

Merritt, a new heavyweight prospect not widely known at the time[1]; and Momma's job at the Martha Jackson Art Gallery in Manhattan barely provided the additional income that she needed to get by. Nonetheless, officials of the American–Israel Program did grant me an interview at their Park Avenue office; and after that began our long, anxious wait until the AIP announced its decision.

Bubba, too, encouraged the move. I was fourteen, and had been living with her and Poppa Jack for over two years. Yet standing at the man-size height of five feet ten, I was no longer a boy. My grandmother still adored me, and kept saying how much she dreaded the separation, but recent events had proven that I was beyond her control. I had become a headstrong teenager, obsessed with the life that Eddie had, but that I couldn't share. Though my grandmother did not know the details, she could see that I was troubled. Bubba always knew. Yet she also believed that life on a kibbutz would steep me further into the Jewish faith, and would discipline me in ways that no one in our family could.

When the AIP announced that I would be its first black Jewish student and the recipient of a partial scholarship, I was elated. "Of course we're excited," the local newspaper quoted Momma as saying. "The whole family's excited." That same article described me as "a bright guy who is also hard to beat on the baseball diamond, the basketball court, or in the swimming pool." It also explained to New York readers that I would study during my freshman year at the Kfar Blum Regional School in Upper Galilee, on the site of a famous kibbutz.[2]

For a while, this event caused our entire family to pull together, just as we had done for my bar mitzvah. On the wall above Momma's desk, she kept a paper graph. On the bottom of it, she had printed BROOKLYN, and at the top, ISRAEL. Then each week, as she or Bubba or I saved money for the trip, Momma slowly moved the paper camel that she had cut from a cigarette package up a few more lines along the graph. Line by line, Buddy Drew was inching his way overseas.

And even Daddy got involved. From Otto Preminger, George Plimpton, and a couple of other famous men, my father got letters of introduction for me to use once I reached Jerusalem.

However, when the time came to send money for the costs

that my scholarship didn't cover, plus airline tickets, the paper camel still hadn't reached the top of the graph. So Bubba bought the round-trip El Al tickets, Momma got a loan from her boss for the rest, and once again, the women in my life sacrificed for me.

Upon my arrival at Kfar Blum, one of the first differences that I noticed was how they air-conditioned rooms on the kibbutz. We certainly had no such luxury while I was living in the Carver House projects; and in Brighton, only a few electric window units jutted from the apartment windows of wealthy families. The rest of us relied on the cool Atlantic breezes that crossed the Boardwalk to dispel the summer's heat.

But in some of Kfar Blum's dormitories, the Israelis devised homemade air conditioners. First, they stretched hay across the window. Then outside, and above the window, they positioned a hose that dripped water onto the hay. Back inside, they placed a fan in front of the hay, and its circulation would pull enough water-cooled air into the room to combat the Mediterranean heat.

During my ten months there, I lived in one of these dormitories along with other exchange students. I was also accepted into the home of a kibbutz family, Zvi and Mazel Rauch and their three children. This combination allowed me to experience Israeli life in depth. On the kibbutz itself, I worked in the *refet* (barn), and studied with other Jewish students in the outpost's school. The education was challenging, and because I was in another culture, the Israeli perspective helped me understand world issues from another point of view.

The Rauches also helped me personally. From them, and the friends they introduced me to, I discovered what it really meant to be Jewish. Their son Yossi and many of the other kids had skin that was as dark as mine, and hair just as curly. My being a black Jew was not unusual to them. As a result, I gained a sense of self-worth and being that I had never known, because these were the first Jews who genuinely accepted me as I am. And from them I learned a basic truth: *Prejudice actually comes from not liking yourself.*

Motivated by this self-awareness, I studied, and learned to speak and read Hebrew, including the idioms that make the language come to life. And that resolved something that had perplexed me since my days with Rabbi Lazar in Brighton. Even then, I had wondered: How meaningful is it for me to speak Hebrew, and pray to God, when I don't really know what I'm saying? The emphasis in America had been on how I pronounced the words, rather than what the passages meant.

But in Israel, I discovered, bar mitzvahs were different. Young boys on the kibbutz *acted* upon the words of God. They took their parents down to the River Jordan, cooked a dinner for them, and then, in conversation, each boy proved to his family that, with the mind and soul of a man, he could discuss matters of importance like life, truth, and God.

It was more of a family moment than a religious ritual. Most of the men didn't wear yarmulkes, and no rabbi conducted the service. But by the very act of cooking and by the meaning of what the boys discussed, they *showed* that they had truly become men. Only then, after this time by the river, would the families go to a synagogue for the traditional bar mitzvah service. To me, this made more sense than the American method of merely memorizing and reciting words of the Torah that few understood.

I also gained insights about war. Our kibbutz was literally a stone's throw from Israel's embattled borders with Lebanon and Syria. There, the hatred and prejudice between Arabs and Jews was obvious. Many nights, I watched from my window while the Arabs fired Soviet-made Katusha rockets and mortar shells into the fortifications that maintained Israel's hold on the region. War is the ultimate expression of racism, and these explosions etched into my brain how racial hatred only destroys, never uplifts, the human spirit.

Several afternoons, however, I was fascinated by the air maneuvers of Israeli jet fighter planes retaliating against the Arab attacks. At the time, I didn't know what these air combat maneuvers (ACMs) were. Yet their function was clear. Unlike the random rocket and mortar attacks that the Arabs used—which often destroyed homes and civilian lives while sometimes hitting military installations that the Arabs had targeted along the Gaza Strip—the Israeli F-4 Phantom jets were precise. They raced across the sky, zapped their targets, then whizzed back overhead again—all in a cool, no-nonsense manner that impressed me. What would it be like, I wondered, to be *bad* and to fly such a jet . . . ?

While I was out of the country, *Esquire* magazine came to Ali's defense. For the past two years, he had not been allowed to box while various appeals and legal hearings took place on the army-induction controversy. Then on the cover of *Esquire*'s November 1969 issue, twelve prominent Americans posed inside a boxing ring under the title: "We believe this: Muhammad Ali deserves the right to defend his title." In addition to the writers, artists, actors, film and sports personalities on the cover (including Richard Benjamin, Theodore Bikel, Truman Capote, Howard Cosell, Ernest Gruening, Michael Harrington, James Earl Jones, Roy Lichtenstein, Sidney Lumet, George Plimpton, Budd Schulberg, and José Torres), statements from ninety others appeared inside the edition. All demanded that the Champ get another authorized chance in the ring.[3] And that proved to be magical.

Ali got inspired again, and set out to regroup his old training staff. But by then, Dundee and my father were working with Merritt. This tall, rangy heavyweight had assumed the nickname "Candy Slim," and was coming off six straight knockouts as he trained above a drugstore in Miami, hoping for a title shot at Joe Frazier. Yet Ali was unimpressed, and decided to visit Dundee's Fifth Street Gym. There, overweight and absent from any workout in over a year, Ali challenged Merritt to a sparring match. At first, Dundee and my father protested. But the Champ sweetened the proposition. He gave money to my dad for Merritt, and said, "Tell him here's a thousand dollars if he shakes up Muhammad Ali."

Moments later, my daddy came back and whispered to the Champ that Merritt had agreed to give Ali a tough sparring match.

After the first round, Ali upped the ante to two thousand dollars. But before the next round ended, Merritt's financial backers called off the match; the timekeeper began banging the bell, and Candy Slim sank slowly into my daddy's arms. Alone in the ring, Ali shadowboxed for another round, then dressed and went to the airport.[4] He had made his point. Provided that his legal mess ever cleared up, the Champ wanted my father to know that he belonged back in Ali's corner.

Back in Israel, I turned fifteen in January, and was headed for problems of my own. I was a city boy who grew tired of cleaning barns every day. Kibbutz life, by itself, was not enough to stimulate me. So once I could use Hebrew well enough to function outside Kfar Blum, I began exploring the Galilean area during off-hours from my studies and chores. The young Israelis whom I met in these outpost villages were eager to learn details about America. I was equally excited about meeting strangers in a strange land, so we made friends quickly.

However, my principal (who was American, and the supervisor of the *Kita Americana* program under which I was studying) disliked what I was doing. He emphasized orthodox values and thought all exchange students should confine their friendships to the American class at Kfar Blum. But I always have to be different, and the fact was, the Israelis accepted me. I felt a fraternal bond with them. So I continued hanging out with the Israelis, instead of my American classmates. This irritated the principal, who was not accepted by the Israelis, and he began looking for ways to trip me up.

Being foolhardy, I paid no heed to his warnings. Then, during my tenth month there, just weeks from graduation, the principal expelled me. The charge was that I had broken the rule that forbade exchange students from having money that did not first go through the principal's office.

"The Rauches were strongly against what the principal had done, and solidly for you," Momma recalls. "They were aware that I had unknowingly contributed to the problem. Now and then, I had sent cash for spending money directly to you. But even when they told the principal this, he would not reconsider his decision, so the family never forgave him. We all thought the man just used you as an example to show all the exchange students that they couldn't get away with breaking the rules— not as much because of the money, as for other behavior."

Whatever the case, my study abroad abruptly ended. I was put on an airplane and sent home. In addition, I had to attend summer school that year, in order not to fall behind my class back in Brooklyn. So the whole experience left me disillusioned, angry, and hurting, but also a little wiser.

My first inclination, after returning to New York City in June 1970, was to move into Momma's Brighton Beach apartment. That way, I would not be reminded of my failure, because my expulsion had greatly disappointed Bubba. But there was a hitch. We had all expected that I would stay in Israel until September. Given that, and the fact that Daddy was rarely at Momma's apartment, she had taken in a boarder whose rental agreement ran through the summer. More to the point, however, I was growing up. I did not want the restrictions of living at Bubba's, but I also didn't want the looseness of life at Momma's house. So my only choice seemed to be going on the prowl again, searching for a new life, new experiences, and a family of my own.

Ironically, another event happened that same month. A federal court of appeals overturned Ali's suspension from boxing.[5] This allowed him to plan his first comeback—aiming to regain his heavyweight championship title from Frazier, who (only four months earlier) had become the undisputed heavyweight champion of the world.[6]

Daddy immediately left for Miami to make preparations for the training. But with him on the fast track once again, there was no room for me. So Daddy arranged with the Pugh family, who were his cousins, for me to live with them on Flatbush Avenue.

"I had a sense of guilt about that arrangement," my mother recalls. "I felt that I should be taking care of you. But I just couldn't. I was in bad shape, personally and financially. And by then, the life that I really hoped would happen, happened. Drew got his second chance in life. But none of it—the comeback, the money, and the success that followed—was to be for my benefit. I could just see my life going down the drain. After that, I just didn't give a damn anymore. The dreams that I had for myself, they were out the window. And all of my dreams for you, son—well, I had nothing to make them come true. They just turned into deeper hurts and guilt."

Yet, as she had done while I was in Israel, Momma continued sending me fifteen or twenty dollars each week for spending money. Brokenhearted and at the bottom, she still loved me as best she could. And me? I went to live with relatives that I barely knew. As it turned out, the Pughs would be very good to me. But that didn't stop me from feeling more alone than ever before.

10

Anytime someone tells you not to get high, don't listen to them. They're lyin' to you. You gotta get high.

If you wanna get high, I'll teach you how. Take your butt to med school. Become a doctor, and save somebody's life. You watch the gleam of life pass through their eyes. Then they hand you a check for sixty-five thousand dollars, and baby, you are toasted!

You wanna get high? Then become a lawyer. You save somebody from an injustice, and in this country, they'll say, "Thank you." You'll say, "You're welcome." They'll hand you a check for forty-two thousand dollars, you go buy a brand new Cadillac, and you are smoked!

You got to get high. Gettin' high is what life is all about. But if you use drugs, you're gonna die. Why do you think they call it dope, DOPE? . . .

Nothing is more painful than when teenagers bottom out in life, and at fifteen, I was at an all-time low. My need to feel accepted and my desire to belong had never been greater, yet I felt adrift—without a home or a family. In addition, I was having to attend summer school at Seward High in order to make up the work that I had not completed in Israel. I felt like a complete failure. And I made one of the worst mistakes of my life: I joined a Brooklyn gang.

We were called the Thunderbirds, and for initiation, I was required to steal a big, silver trunk ornament off a Ford Thunderbird and then attach it to my bike's sissy bar. But luxury cars like the T-bird were difficult to find in Brooklyn, and stealing an expensive ornament from one was even harder. In spite of these drawbacks, however, I went cruising to steal.

Yet I did not cruise alone. My street brother's voice—the conscience that every person has—persistently questioned me: *What if you're caught in the act, man? Don't you know the consequences could include being arrested, or at the very least, getting the crap kicked out of you by the car's owner?*

"I'm not afraid," I kept responding. I knew the streets of Flatbush. It was our gang's territory. I also believed that we had the right to fight for our flashy emblem, and because of these stupid convictions, I succeeded. Soon, I located a Thunderbird, ripped off its trunk ornament, affixed it to my bike, and earned my place in the gang. But that membership would be short-lived.

A few weeks later, two rival gangs were involved in a shooting, and the police turned the heat on Flatbush gangs. It was the highs of living dangerously that had attracted me to the Thunderbirds in the first place, but this heat from New York's finest was too much for me. I still needed to belong to something, but I didn't want to belong in the penitentiary or the graveyard. So I took my street brother's advice and abandoned the Thunderbirds.

While my personal plight grew worse, however, my father's status rose dramatically. Press reports in September 1970 dubbed him the mastermind behind "The Champ's Resurrection." Earlier, when it had become clear that Ali's three-and-a-half-year exile from boxing would not end with an immediate match against Joe Frazier—the newly recognized, undisputed heavyweight champion of the world—my father had engineered an exhibition for Ali at Morehouse College in Atlanta. *If you can't seize the title,* Daddy rightfully argued, *then win the people.* And that's exactly what Ali did. In a series of one-round matches against a succession of lesser-ranked heavyweights, the

Champ left the Morehouse crowd of about five thousand fans ecstatic.[1]

Years later, Ali would explain my father's contributions to this day of resurrection. But the Champ's words (recounting a postexhibition conversation that he overheard between his brother and my father) would also reveal how much my daddy was hurting, too. He would soon be forty-two years old, and so far, his life had been even more of a rollercoaster ride than mine. He did have my love as a son, and he was clearly regaining his reputation as a trainer. But Daddy had little else, until Ali reentered the boxing arena:

> ". . . And when the bell rings, the house roars so long the time-keeper has to ring the bell forty times before we can get The Champ back to his dressing room."
>
> "But that's not the best of it," Bundini goes on. "The best came in the dressing room. I hear The Champ talking to my old street buddies from New York, Teddy and Pal. He says, 'Angelo's got the connection and the complexion, but Bundini makes me fight.' That's all he said.
>
> "That was for me. It was the first time he ever give me my mojo back. I give it to him and he gives it back. I feel my body get younger. A man gets old quick when he don't get love. An unloved man is the endangered species. A man gets ulcers and brain damage when he ain't around love. But what he said smoothed out the wrinkles in my body. A man minus love is a wrinkled man, but a beloved man is smooth."[2]

The reason Ali's comeback meant so much to my father was that—more than anyone else in the entourage—Daddy had sacrificed himself during the exile. Even when he was not Ali's employee, my daddy remained as a friend and an encourager to the Champ. Others (except for my father and Gene Kilroy) went their separate ways for income during those years. But whenever Ali needed them, Daddy and Gene were never more than a phone call away.

So when the Morehouse exhibition ended, and Ali had proven himself fit to fight again, the comeback not only resurrected the Champ's career, but it brought Daddy back to life as well.

On October 26, Ali was set to fight Jerry Quarry in Atlanta. It would be the Champ's thirtieth career match, and Quarry, a white heavyweight contender, was the first of two that the Champ would have to defeat if he was to gain a championship bout with Frazier. Ali had not yet lost a match, though Quarry had been beaten more than once, but the press still touted the event as "The Battle of Atlanta," because it was Ali's comeback.

Yet I was excited about the fight for another reason. Daddy asked me to go with him, and I was thrilled. For the first time in years, I would be at my father's side while he did what made him famous. In addition, I would experience firsthand the jet-set life-style that he enjoyed away from Momma and me. But more than these things, Daddy's invitation proved that, even though he and I were apart, he had not forgotten his boy.

In retrospect, I now know that his cousins, the Pughs, had told Daddy about my involvement with the Brooklyn gang, and that Bubba had explained to him how difficult her life had become, dealing with me as a rambunctious adolescent. So Daddy *was* reaching out to me when he brought me to Atlanta. He *did* want something resembling a father-son relationship, in the hopes that such a boost might put me back on the right track.

But there was yet another reason. Just prior to the Ali-Quarry fight, gunmen shot through the dark of a Georgia night at my father and the Champ.[3] The two narrowly escaped death, and that threat had a sobering effect upon my father. He had struggled too long to lose it all, just days before finally seizing the glory. So for once in his life, my daddy became repentant. At least for a season. . . .

At Atlanta's Hyatt-Regency, I loved what I saw of the star-studded atmosphere. Twenty-three floors of that circular hotel seemed to be jammed with every black celebrity that I had ever wanted to meet. The Supremes. Coretta Scott King. Sydney Poitier and Bill Cosby. And of course, my "uncle" Sugar Ray and other legendary boxers. So like the poor boy in *The Prince and the Pauper*, I felt transformed overnight from a drifting teen into Bundini's heir apparent, and I savored every moment.

Subsequently, one writer would describe the Atlanta setting as *"Gone With the Wind* in reverse. Through one eye we could see Clark Gable and Vivien Leigh making their escape with horse and wagon as the battered Rebs fall back and the Old

South crumbles. Through the other eye we could see the afflu-
ent followers of Muhammad Ali arriving not in broken-down
mule trains but in Rolls-Royces decorated with psychedelic designs, and custom-made Cadillacs in all the colors of a Christmas tree, with TV aerials, telephones, and built-in bars."[4]

It was a happening, and almost more popular than the fight
itself were the parties—not the ones for everyday people with
ringside or grandstand tickets, but the private bashes—where
the in crowd, the beautiful people, the movie stars and enter-
tainers, the pimps and hustlers all got to mingle with Ali's re-
nowned entourage. But as Ali's "little brother" and Bundini's
son, I was regarded as a cut above these people in the know. I
was family, and that gave me celebrity status at the parties.

At one affair in the Hyatt's top-floor Presidential Suite, there
were more beautiful women in one place than I ever dreamed
possible, and most of them seemed to be dreaming of just one
chance with the Champ. But since that was physically
impossible—even for Ali—many of these women turned their
attentions to me. It was as though they thought that being with
me would somehow link them to the Greatest.

In any case, I loved the adulation. Just weeks before, I had
been wandering the streets of Brooklyn as a gang member.
Now I was a teenager being adored by adult women. I was sure
that I had finally arrived. So I was dancing up a storm with all
these babes when, just as I go into one of my James Brown
spins, I find myself face to face with Bundini Brown. All six feet
one inch of him. There are the equivalents of fire coming from
his eyes and steam from his ears and nostrils. He is the dragon
man I remember from my childhood. And though there are
hundreds of people in the suite, he is focused only upon me.

"Boy," he said in a low, stern voice. "Go to your room. Now."

My mistake was thinking that being at a grownup party had
actually aged me enough to discuss this direct command. So I
turned and got half of a response formulated in my mind. *Hey,
Pop, cool out. I'm just jammin'. . . .*

But as soon as my mouth opened, he exploded. "Boy, I'll beat
your ass," he yelled as he grabbed my arm. "Go to your room.
Now."

It was as if God Himself had spoken. The music fell silent,
and everyone stared at us—or more specifically, at me. But

what they saw was a kid who had been acting as if he were twenty-four suddenly shrinking in ego to years younger than my actual fifteen. All I wanted to do was shrivel small enough so that I could squirm, unnoticed, under the door and out of sight.

But by the time the Champ claimed his victory—chalking Quarry off as his twenty-fourth knockout victim—I had absorbed everything about the experience. And despite having been publicly humiliated, I promised myself that one day, I, too, would belong in this realm. *Inside my father's world.*

During the remaining months of 1970 I moved back in with Momma. She had leased a place on the corner of Brighton Twelfth Street at 1055 Brighton Beach Avenue, and her apartment was only about seven blocks from Bubba's.

Meanwhile, Ali trained intensely with my father in both Miami and at Ali's training camp in Deer Lake, Pennsylvania. The Champ was preparing for the December 7 bout with South American heavyweight Oscar Bonavena. That match—Ali's third ring entry in four months—would not only mark the Champ's return to Madison Square Garden and New York City, but winning it would also ensure a championship bout with Frazier.

But to me, this remarkable string of prize fights also meant that my father would finally come into some real money. Since I had always wanted a nice house where my friends would be proud to come over, I begged Daddy to give us that kind of home. He had not had one when he was a child, and so far, he had been unable to provide that kind of home for me. Yet with all this new money, surely he could . . . ?

To my surprise, Daddy agreed. He said that Ali was building a new house in Cherry Hill, New Jersey, so it was time that all the entourage settled down. And my father promised that, if Ali defeated Bonavena, thereby earning a title match against Frazier, then my father would fix up Momma's Brighton Beach apartment.

However, when I told Momma, she was skeptical. A host of Bundini promises had failed her over the years, and she knew something that I didn't: My daddy was living with someone new at the time—a woman named Audrey. In spite of all this, however, he showed up and told Momma himself, and in the weeks that followed, he did spend more time with us. To me, it all meant that my *Brady Bunch* dream was just two Ali knockouts away. . . .

In a sense, that was our winter of fragile contentment. But Gene Kilroy intervened. In addition to being a member of Ali's entourage, Gene had been a top executive with Metro-Goldwyn-Mayer. And at the time, he knew that the studio was looking for fresh new faces in feature films. Thus, after he called the right people, movie director Gordon Parks cast my father in *Shaft*. So a number of afternoons Daddy had me help him learn his lines and share in the excitement of that project. In addition, my parents were at least speaking to one another again, so the animosity of previous years no longer surfaced. Naively, I attributed this new bond to the glue called "Buddy Drew." I had not stopped trying to pull my parents back together, but I had reversed my tactics. I began saying good things about one parent to the other, and I continued to paint a television-pretty picture about how nice our family life could be.

Another factor in my life was that, earlier in the fall, I had enrolled in Brooklyn's Abraham Lincoln High School, where Scott "Scotty" Camer, Alfredo "Freddy" Garcia, and Ricky "Cubby" Katz became my good friends. Scotty and Freddy lived on my block, Cubby lived on Brighton First Street, and in a sense, the three became the brothers that I never had.

They immediately decided that my house was the place to be, the fun house, because they thought Momma was the coolest thing that ever walked. She was always joking and using the words and phrases that were current on the street. Sometimes, she even drank and got high with us. So they loved her, even though it was gut-wrenching to me.

What I saw was a mother out of control. Once again, my father was breaking her heart, but she used alcohol as her only medicine for the pain. So I set out to separate Momma from the booze in order to bring her and my father back together, and I stopped at nothing to accomplish this goal. I tried locking her inside the house by stealing the keys to our apartment's dead-bolt locks. That way, I presumed, she couldn't get out to buy more Johnnie Walker. But Momma was hooked solid, and once I caught her, she tied sheets together and tried to escape out the back window.

Ironically, my friends and I thought it was okay for Daddy and us to do these things, because we were men. Yet I held a double standard when it came to Momma. I was a male chauvinist who wanted my mother to be like Donna Reed. But Rhoda Palestine Brown—suffering from years of disappointments—was the farthest thing from Donna Reed that Brighton Beach had to offer.

Soon, however, Cubby, Scotty, Freddy, and I plunged headlong into our own substance abuse. Our routine began with them coming to the sidewalk beneath my window and yelling, "Buddy, Buddy." Then when I reached the window, they'd add, "Bother, Bother," which meant that they wanted to come up.

Most days, we listened to records by Jimi Hendrix, Johnny Winter, James Brown, or The Temptations. Hendrix, in particular, played the guitar as if it were a gorgeous woman, so the music set the pace for us to wrestle or do drugs. We lived for funk and rock 'n' roll. And because drugs and rockers went together in 1970, we started getting high whenever we could.

One day, for example, we bought some weed in order to get stoned before going to an Edgar Winter concert. At the time, the singer's brother, Johnny, had just completed a drug-rehabilitation program, and was straight. I had an inkling that this might be Johnny's "surprise" comeback performance. So my friends and I gathered in a ceremonial circle and rolled pot on one of his album covers. Then at the Fillmore concert, when Edgar introduced his brother and Johnny played our favorite song, "Be Careful of a Fool," we were so high that we thought our ritual of rolling joints had actually brought him back in concert again.

But Jimi Hendrix and Janis Joplin had not yet died from drug overdoses. So it was too soon for us to be frightened away from emulating our rock stars, and we lived out the myth.

On December 7, Ali knocked out Bonavena in a fifteenth-round victory at the Garden,[5] and our family's life shifted into top speed. For the first time in years, people telephoned Momma's house and asked for my father. Now and then, he took her with him to parties, and he began bringing friends over to visit with us. For once, we seemed like one big happy family.

But one of those friends turned out to be a big-time drug dealer—I'll call him "Candy Man." After a few visits in Brighton, he secretly invited me to his Manhattan apartment. He lived in an exclusive downtown building, and on my first visit, I was impressed by how clean and handsomely decorated his apartment was. What's more, the light-skinned man seemed charming and nice. He even had a beautiful white wife, and neither of them mentioned drugs to me. So nothing about him or his life reminded me of the street dealers I had known in Harlem or Brighton. I just had a good time with this couple, and the visits continued.

Then one afternoon, Candy Man took me to his bedroom where there was a big, silver-foiled package on the bed. He pulled back the wrapping to reveal the pile of snow. It was cocaine, and he said, "Don't you want some?"

Because I never wanted to feel naive, I said, "Sure." Then I snorted some, and soon my mind became very frozen and blank. The feeling was neither good nor bad—just different, somehow making me distanced from everything.

In the weeks that followed, I came back several times, and during each visit, Candy Man allowed me to snort more coke. But in these moments, he acted fatherly toward me. "Take it like this," he would say, or "Don't use too much, and you'll feel fine." That kind of stuff.

Yet when I confided in Scotty, Cubby, and Freddy about these visits, they chided me, "You two must be *gay*, Buddy. That's the only way anybody would give you *cocaine*."

That wasn't the case, and it hurt for them to accuse me of homosexuality. But I had no real answer for my friends because I didn't know the drug dealer's motives. He never made a pass at me. He never said anything wrong, or asked me for anything. He just let me do drugs for free.

Later, I realized that the Candy Man was using me to get to my father. Either the dealer wanted to turn me on to drugs, so that Daddy would then buy from him for me, or the dealer wanted my trust in order to gain access to the wealthy drug users in Daddy's inner circle of friends. At the time, however, I couldn't see through the dealer's generosity. All I understood was how good the cocaine seemed to be, and that may have been his real motive, after all.

In any event, I then tried to get Scotty, Freddy, and Cubby to share with me the cost of buying coke of our own. But they refused.

"Get outta here," Scotty said. "We don't have any money for that."

"Come on, fellas," I said.

"But it's so expensive," Freddy protested. "We can't afford that stuff."

"It's not that high," I argued. "Costs maybe fifty bucks."

"Man, we can't even put five dollars together for a bag of weed," Cubby said, and my boys just looked at me like I was crazy.

But gradually I talked them into it, and we devised a plan. We all went home, lied to our parents or relatives about why we needed money, or we snuck the cash from purses and other family hideaways until, with cash in hand, we headed for the street junkies who lived in filth under the Boardwalk. It didn't occur to us that we went to the dregs of society to spend fifty dollars for something to destroy our young bodies. Nor did we consider that, in lying to get the money, we were already being controlled by stuff that we hadn't even bought. We just headed for the coke.

The dealer took our money and handed me a tiny foil packet. Since Candy Man's packages had been so much larger, I *assumed* that the dealer was giving us a "taste." So when the four of us got to a safe place, I opened the tiny packet, held it to my nose, and snorted all the coke.

"What the hell are you doin'?" Scotty said, and they all stared in amazement. I explained that the sample wasn't as good as Candy Man's, but that we should go back for the rest.

"You idiot," Freddy exclaimed, "*that* was the fifty dollars' worth."

Not in my wildest imagination had I understood that Candy Man had *thousands* of dollars of cocaine on his bed. "There's no way," I kept saying to myself. "How could so little cost so much?"

Yet the only way that I could make this loss up to my friends was to replace the cocaine. So I schemed to go back to Candy

Man's and steal some from his package. I was certain that he'd never even miss it.

Back at his house, however, I found two packages on the bed. One was the usual large, silver-foil package—and this time, I was really amazed at how much he had—but the other was another foil package, half the size of the first.

I went right for the small foil, but the Candy Man cautioned, "Whoa, whoa. Be careful of that small package. It's *boy*."

Boy? I thought. *What's boy?* But I said nothing, because the whole thing in that drug culture was that, all the time, you had to act as if you knew what you were doing. So I proceeded to do some of the large foil, but every time he left the room, I also did a lot of the small package, too. Since to my mind *smaller* had to mean that it was better quality, I just knew that I would get higher from it.

But even more than the coke high itself, I was excited about getting something for nothing. Just like the day I ripped off that T-bird ornament, stealing something seemed a much bigger high than the pleasure of getting the object itself. I should add that my parents had taught me that stealing was the worst thing I could do. But by their actions, they had also shown me that ethics had no value in the drug culture. Thus, in stealing drugs, I didn't feel bad, because I knew that I wasn't stealing anything good.

So I took a dollar bill and used it to scoop out some stuff— particularly from the small package—to take to my friends. Then I stuffed the folded bill into my pocket, and slipped out of the apartment.

But on the train ride home, I got sick as a dog. I really thought I was going to die, though I did make it to the Brighton Beach stop. At home, I vomited profusely for hours and finally fell asleep.

My friends came over the next day, and Freddy said, "Well, did you see your faggot friend?"

"Guys, he ain't no faggot," I said. "Chill out and shut up"

"Well, what *did* you do?" Scotty asked, and I showed them the packet. That excited them.

"At least you came through for us," Freddy screamed, and we all sat down and did the dollar-bill worth. But within a half hour, everybody was vomiting in my toilet. Months later, I learned that *boy* meant heroin, and that we got sick because we snorted a near-lethal mixture of cocaine and heroin.

After that incident, therefore, I never saw or called or went back to visit the Candy Man. I had learned another lesson. Doing stuff that was bad was warning enough that adults who encourage kids to get high are no friends. They are manipulative pushers, and the stuff they offer is death. Why do you think they call it *dope*, DOPE?

11

*The funny thing is, they call drugs "a controlled substance." You know
why? Because the substance controls you.*

*How can you let a rock of crack cocaine—something no larger than
a watermelon seed—make you lie to your mother? How can you let some
alcohol, some cocaine, or some weed make you lie to yourself? You're the
only person who will wake up with yourself for the rest of your life!*

*If you want to get deep about it, we can. How are you gonna let some
cocaine, some marijuana, or some alcohol make you lie to God? You
better wake up! Why do you think they call it* dope, DOPE? *. . .*

My father liked money, but he believed in man more, so he
never signed contracts with Muhammad Ali. Instead, Daddy
settled, in financial terms, for whatever Ali thought that his
trainer should get, and in a strange way, Daddy believed that
their contract was signed by God. (Lesson learned: You don't
do business with God; you do business with man. Get a contract.) By the start of 1971, however, my father was getting
much more than money from his role with the Champ. Daddy
was gaining fame and personal power, and on several occa-
sions, I witnessed how he used these perks.

For example, in preparation for the title match with Joe Frazier that had been scheduled for March 8, I rode in a big beautiful Winnebago with Daddy and Ali, and we parked on the corner of 42nd and Broadway in Manhattan. It was a publicity stop, a few weeks in advance of the fight, so Ali got out to shake hands with the people in Times Square. But within minutes, traffic became gridlocked for fifteen blocks in either direction. Everybody wanted to see the Greatest.

What amazed me more, though, was that while Ali drew the crowds, my father kept pumping spirit in the Champ's ear. Of course there were the regular "Float like a butterfly, sting like a bee . . ." refrains, but the two of them also improvised on the spot.[1] That set cameras in action and evoked a rhythmlike applause from the onlookers. And once again, while the people responded, my father was leaning into the Champ's ear. His was the whisper of inspiration, and the insight of a street player who knew the ropes *outside* the ring.

But it was on the night of March 8 that I first understood what a great man my father really was. In some ways, it was Bundini's night, although there was a definite and powerful aura around Ali as well. The Champ had to prove that he was going to win. And this was not only his chance to regain the heavyweight title—which controversy, racism, and legal entanglements had taken away nearly four years earlier—but the commonly held belief on the streets was that "Ali was fightin' for his freedom." Granted, an appeals court had overturned his suspension from boxing the previous year, but Ali's basic charges of draft evasion were still pending before the U.S. Supreme Court.[2] Strangely enough, this night also became my opportunity to show one of the guys I used to run after that, now, I had the power. So I invited Jeff Hofstein, the ring leader of those Jewish kids who had shunned me, years before. And as Jeff and I accompanied Daddy to Ali's fight headquarters in the Statler Hotel, everyone seemed caught up in the frenzy. The odds were on Frazier, but anticipation and the people on the street were for Ali.

Once we entered the hotel lobby, a host of fans and reporters and boxing insiders acknowledged Daddy and me. Jeff had expected this for my father, but my Brooklyn buddy seemed amazed that many of these people knew me, too. I had the power. Then in the Champ's suite, Daddy gathered up Ali's gear and led us back outside toward Madison Square Garden where he, alone, would set up the locker room. That was part of the Bundini ritual, and he was primed for action.

At the Garden's side entrance, however, a lot of people were hustling tickets or waiting to see Ali, and police barricades held back the throng. But at the sight of my father, an officer motioned for the patrolmen to part the crowd so that we could enter. That blew Jeff away.

Just then, dozens of people started screaming the same thing: "Bundini, Bundini, get me in this fight, man. If anybody can do it, you can, Bundini. Get me in!"

Daddy stopped, looked out at the horde of begging faces behind the row of barricades and uniformed police, and he grinned. I knew that smile. It was straight from Harlem, because most of the screaming fans were brothers and sisters that he knew from those streets uptown. *They are here,* I realized, *not just for the Fight of the Century, as it was being called, but also because they believe in my father, the Black Prince of Harlem.*

"Let them in," he said firmly to the policeman nearest us.

"Hey, Bundini," the patrolman said in a low voice, "maybe one or two people, okay. But there must be forty or fifty people here. Come on!"

At that, the cop and my daddy squared off while the noise level rose. "Bundini, Bundini, I've been wanting to see the Champ all my life," several yelled in unison. "Get me in, man. *Please.*"

The cheers pumped my daddy up, so he set Ali's gear bag on the sidewalk and told the policeman, "If these people don't come in, I don't go in. And I got the Champ's gloves and his jock. So if Bundini don't go in, the world's biggest fight won't happen. Do you understand?"

Immediately, four policemen scurried inside the Garden and returned in haste with their captain. Meanwhile, the crowd was steadily pushing the barricades closer to the entrance, and their screams of "Bundini" and "Black Prince" seemed deafening.

The captain stared at the chaos, then at my father, and finally said, "Bundini, you *got* me." Then the officer snapped an order. "Let the man's friends go in."

Immediately, forty to fifty people pushed through and followed my father into the Garden. Trailing behind, I glanced at Jeff as if to say, "I told you so," but all the flies in New York City could have swarmed in his mouth, it was open so wide. My boy could hardly believe the persuasive powers of my father.

Inside Ali's locker room, I knew that this was no time for us to talk. "Daddy this" and "Daddy that" were taboo. The best that we could do was watch my father work, and he was the best at what he did. Meticulously, he checked every piece of gear and equipment in the room. I had never seen him so focused and careful. He was like a priest handling sacraments at an altar. Then moments later, I could almost feel the hush come over the building, and within seconds, Ali walked in.

Gone was the bragging, and the quick wit. Instead, Ali entered as a prepared, determined, but visibly shaken man. He didn't seem scared that he could not beat Frazier. No, Ali was scared because he had so much to prove. He was nervous and self-protecting. And the only person that Ali would let near him was my father. The Champ knew that my daddy would set hype aside, and tell the truth about the fight itself.

What happened next was another religious thing. The two of them went into the bathroom for privacy, and what I could hear was the low, steady voice of Bundini telling Ali *why* he needed to win. There was no talk of strategies or techniques, no mention of the purse or the Supreme Court case. Instead, my daddy talked to the Champ about the people—all the kids who believed in him, all the kids who didn't have enough to eat or drink, all the little people who make up America. "You're fighting for all of them," I heard my father say, "while ole Joe Frazier is just fighting for himself." And then they prayed.

Once Jeff and I entered the arena, I felt guilty about being so concerned that our family's best shot at riches hung in the balance that night. Like Daddy, I should have been concentrating only on the boxing—a match that *The New York Times* would subsequently describe as "a monumental epic fight." But we had been deprived for too long, and there was so much abundance all around me. For the first time in history, a championship match was being viewed by a truly worldwide audience. Elsewhere, about three hundred million people were watching it on closed-circuit television. And Madison Square Garden had broken all of its records by selling $1,350,000 worth of tickets to the people around me in the arena.[3]

Daddy can certainly keep his promise now, I kept saying to myself.

Just then, I saw him emerge, leading the Champ and his entourage toward the ring, and I was astounded to see what a changed man my daddy had become. His face was like the bow of a battleship, and his eyes were cannons, fixed in position and ready to fire. Right behind him, Ali followed, his gloved hands on both of my father's shoulders. The two men were silent, down-to-business, and serious, even though the crowd roared from the highest row in the Garden. It was as though Ali, my daddy, and Shorty had a closed-circuit connection of the heart. Words had become meaningless. It was time for only fists, minds, and souls.

But once Joe Frazier entered the arena, my daddy began pacing and staring, a ceaseless form of psyching pressure that never eased off of Frazier. At the same time, it was as if my father was drawing strength from the heavens above and pouring it into his man, Ali. My father often described this prefight moment as "being pregnant in public, pacing, praying, and anticipating, waiting for the baby to be born."

And when the bell rang, it was as if Frazier was actually fighting two men. Not just the remarkable and well-trained athlete wearing red velvet trunks and white shoes with bouncing red tassels, but also the loud man in the corner. The one whose stare-down could make a world-class heavyweight doubt his courage, or make a boy just turned sixteen believe in one more promise. . . .

During the first eleven rounds, Ali demonstrated his total dominance over Frazier, but Ali still lost. Throughout, the Champ taunted the sportscasters. He taunted the refs. He taunted the judges, and he taunted Frazier. Ali had predicted that he would knock his opponent out in the sixth round, so the Champ became obsessed with showing everybody how great he was. But in the eleventh round Frazier hurt Ali, and in the fifteenth round Frazier delivered a blow that knocked Ali to the mat. Unfortunately, the judges remembered that last image more than they did the Champ's earlier antics. Yet it was a trag- ically wonderful fight. Frazier spent several weeks recuperating in a hospital, while Ali's bruised, beaten, and bloody body re- quired no more than an examination, X rays, and bandages. Be- fore midnight, he returned to spend the rest of that night in his suite at the New Yorker.[4]

Despite the defeat—Ali's first, after thirty-one straight victor- ies—my father received over $70,000 in earnings from the $5 million purse that Ali and Frazier divided. Two decades ago, that was a lot of money, and true to his promise, Daddy began trans- forming our Brighton Beach lives. He sent me on the spring break excursion to Miami and the Bahamas that I've already de- scribed. For himself, he bought a Fleetwood Brougham Cadillac that he named "Black Beauty." It was black with gray interior and had psychedelic lighting in the rear passenger section. Then, as if signing a peace treaty with Momma, he sent workmen to 1055 Brighton Beach Avenue and began renovating our house.

In a matter of weeks, those Brooklyn digs were transformed into the equivalent of a swanky Manhattan townhouse. New, plush carpet ran throughout the house, and black-and-white ornamental tile adorned the foyer, not unlike the type I had admired in the lobby of Bubba's building. Daddy also had all the walls and woodwork repainted, and he had the kitchen redone so that it included a bar, complete with western-style saloon doors and a large "Float like a butterfly" logo painted on the wall.

For new furnishings, he and Momma selected African sculp- tures for various parts of the house, including a life-size one of a man and woman kissing. There was also a color television, new couches and chairs, and an enormous platform waterbed for their bedroom. My bedroom, however, they left to my de- sign, so I had the workmen paint it red with black borders, and I chose red carpeting. It looked just like a Jimi Hendrix album cover.

And when all the work was done, our remodeled place looked like a dream house—the one I had yearned for—and except for the bars that my daddy had the men install across all the windows and doorways, I could find nothing to object to. The Browns of Brighton Beach had finally arrived.

*   *   *

What I didn't know was that Daddy had also asked Momma for them to get remarried.

"But I said no," she recalls. "I just didn't want to put myself back in that same position. I simply wanted to let things be the way they were, and see if they worked out. I knew that he wanted things rights—a home and three of us together again—at least for your sake, son. But I was forty years old, and you were nearly grown. So simply 'doing the right thing' was not reason enough to get remarried."

Looking back, however, I also think that Momma knew what was coming. . . .

April through June were remarkable months in our family's time together. They seemed almost too good to be true. It was wonderful to wake up each morning and know that my parents were in their bedroom and that I was in mine. I loved the odors of fresh paint and new materials that lingered throughout the house, and I took great pride in bringing my friends to the fancy place that my father had created. It all seemed very normal, as if my previous sixteen years of agony had never happened.

But these joys disappeared just as quickly. In June, my father moved a woman named Sherry into our home. She was the first black woman I had ever seen him with, and one of the few people my father never got total control of. Sherry was tall, light-skinned, full-busted, in her mid-thirties, and she had two children.

I liked her, but the night that he carried her luggage into Momma's new home, I realized that all of my family dreams were crushed. Forever. And sure enough, when Momma discovered Sherry the next morning, my mother packed up and moved back to Bubba's.

That left me with Daddy and Sherry and all our new things. But as brokenhearted as I was over Momma's departure, I had no intention of moving out. I had fought an entire childhood for exactly what we now had. So to me, my situation was the equivalent of Custer's Last Stand. I refused to give up what we had just gained, so I resolved to be the last person to leave 1055 Brighton Beach.

*   *   *

Several days later, the showdown came. Momma returned to pack up more things, and an argument ensued between my parents. It was just like their old fights, in that they started screaming and hitting one another until, finally, my mother ran outside for self-protection. But I could take no more.

I lunged across the room, grabbed my father in a crushing bear hug, and threw him to the floor. In the process, bar chairs and glasses and a sculpture crashed around us, but I didn't care. I pinned him to the floor by placing my knees on his chest, and then I shoved my fist in his face. "If you ever touch my momma again," I screamed, "I will kill you."

Even though I could barely bring myself to hit my father, I was determined to knock him around. It was a resolve that went back years earlier, to the night in the projects when I cried in my room while he beat Momma. But to my surprise, I didn't have to hit him. Not once. When he realized that I had already overpowered him, and was serious in my threat, my father surrendered.

You see, when my father was right, he had animallike strength and magnetism. But when he was wrong, he was powerless. And when he felt powerless that day, he surrendered. That was my father's way. He was always honest about right and wrong, and when he was wrong, he always backed off.

He also knew that I could do it, and that I was telling the truth. And the worst part of it all was that Daddy knew he was wrong. In fact, he acted as though he was glad that I had finally stuck up for my mother—as if he remembered, in that same moment, the many times during his childhood when Granddaddy Drew had beaten Elizabeth. But my daddy had been too young and too small back then to do what I was doing now.

Within the hour, he and Sherry moved out. Later that day, Momma was restored to the home she deserved, and my defiance proved that, at last, I had truly become a man. I was the only one who didn't have to move. I won. But at a price. Daddy took most of the furniture. Momma and I got a boarder to help us with expenses, and that encounter ended my parents' on-again, off-again, twenty-year relationship. And I would never again dream of Momma, Daddy, and me becoming *The Brady Bunch*. That was history.

*   *   *

Later that month, Ali won his political freedom. The U.S. Supreme Court ruled unanimously that his conviction was invalid, and the Champ was subsequently granted the status of conscientious objector to the military draft on the grounds of his religious beliefs.[5] But for once, I was disinterested in Ali and Bundini. My heart was still a boy's, and it was shattered. So I planned an escape.

During previous summers I had worked at the Brighton Beach Baths, but this time, Cubby and I joined a band called "Sargent." We had been into rock 'n' roll for a while, and among my Jewish friends, the best summer jobs were in the Catskills, where teenagers could do dishes or wait on tables at one of the resort hotels. But since most bands of that era in the Catskills were strictly rock 'n' roll, we became a rock band with soul. That was an unusual mix for the hotel circuit, so we became an overnight sensation in the resort's "teen rooms."

Since I was the band's lead singer, I had no problem finding a girlfriend, and within a few days I chose Meryl. She was a down-to-earth white girl, and very liberal. Her long hair looked like Joni Mitchell's and her devotion to me was the balm that I needed to heal.

The whole mountain setting in the Catskills was therapeutic, too. It reminded me of the good times that I had enjoyed as a child in summer camps, and I turned on. I bought Nehru jackets and bell-bottomed pants. I let my hair grow into a thick, impressive Afro. And even though drugs were very prevalent in these resort settings, I preferred booze. My father did drugs, and I shunned anything that reminded me of him.

So one night I was drinking some Thunderbird wine while Cubby and Freddy did some weed. We were in my 1965 white Grand Prix, and after our band's gig, we drove to a dance at a nearby hotel. Since Meryl had gone home for the weekend, and Alfredo had come up from Brooklyn, we three guys began cruising the dance for women.

Alfredo, who was Cuban, immediately linked up with an attractive white girl, whom we subsequently found out was the county sheriff's only daughter. But what we didn't know, Freddy wasn't belaboring. He liked this gal. Meanwhile, I kept drinking too much, so none of the babes showed much interest in me. And Cubby was growing concerned with my behavior.

Eventually, I got sick and headed outside to vomit. Cubby, my main man, escorted me to the exit, but Freddy stayed. From the doorway, I could see through double vision that he was making heavy moves on his girl, even though some of the white boys at the dance were becoming increasingly upset. I asked Cubby to persuade Alfredo to ease off, but Freddy refused. "She's digging on me," he told Cubby, so the two of us wandered into the parking lot.

Later, we learned that while we were outside, one of the white boys telephoned the sheriff and said that a black and a Puerto Rican were disturbing the peace. But Cubby and I, oblivious to what was coming down, were relaxing in my car when several patrol cars arrived, sirens blaring and their spotlights shining into the parking lot. So when the sheriff approached my car, I was shocked.

"Stay where you are, and stop whatever you're doing," the official yelled.

I didn't know any better, so I stepped out of my car. But immediately, I heard the peculiar sound of guns being pulled from holsters, and I froze.

"We're not kidding, boy," a voice yelled. "We'll blow you away. So stop where you are. Stop right now."

Suddenly, my intoxication seemed to vanish and I was totally straight. I knew we were being harassed, but I didn't know why, so I asked, "What's going on?"

Without answering, the sheriff's deputies began searching me and Cubby, and they were rougher than they had to be. Then Alfredo walked outside and approached the scene. "What's happenin'?" he asked, in a nonchalant voice.

The sheriff turned his gun on Freddy and said, "Stop where you are. Do you know these guys?"

Our street pal looked at us with the most amazing Hollywood eyes, and his transformation from a Brooklyn Cuban to an upstate white boy was incredible. It even convinced us. "No, sir," he said. "I have no idea who these guys are. I just came out because I lost my hat." Then, confidently, Alfredo turned around and walked away.

Well, the authorities found two marijuana joints in Cubby's

pocket and a hash pipe in the glove compartment of my car. So the two of us were arrested and taken to a county jail. Inside, I thought the place was amazing because it was so small that they didn't even have a cell available for us. But being a kid and still intoxicated, I felt like James Cagney behind bars and wanted to play "the real jail thing," so I resented the fact that we had to sleep in the hallway outside the regular cells.

Cubby was scared to death, even though I kept saying that we weren't in much trouble and that, hopefully, we would get out in the morning. "After all, man," I argued, "we didn't kill anybody."

The next morning, we were served nasty coffee and cereal. The corn flakes and milk were in a metal bowl, and the flakes were so soggy that they tasted like mush. The coffee was too bitter to drink, so we just left all of it. Minutes later, however, I got an idea. I poured my coffee into the cereal bowl and started banging on the bars with the metal cup. Then, just as I had seen jailbirds do in movies, I yelled, "We want out of here. We're going to break this joint."

That tripped Cubby out. "You can't do that," he screamed. "Are you crazy?"

Yet I persisted, knowing that my voice was loud enough to penetrate the steel door leading to the officers' area. But nobody came. When we realized that they were ignoring us, we decided to become socially cool prisoners, and I began asking the other guys, "Hey, what are you in here for?"

One guy said a traffic violation, which disappointed us. Then a tall guy, who was barefooted and mopping the floor, said in a funny-sounding voice, "I like little girls."

That even scared me, so Cubby and I went back to our corner of the hallway, and I cooled out. Later that same morning, Cubby's father arrived. He was a big man, six feet three and imposing. He worked as an art auctioneer, and was the straightest adult I knew. So when we saw the stern expression on his face and realized that he had driven all the way from Brooklyn to the Catskills, we fell silent. He got us out of jail, drove us back to Brooklyn, lectured to us all the way, and then waited in my house while I told Momma what happened. I could see in her eyes that this was one blow she didn't need.

*   *   *

Two weeks later, we returned to the Catskills for the trial, and the judge let us off because Cubby and I were minors and these were our first offenses. But the charges remained in our juvenile records, and suddenly, the realities of The System hit home. Even though my parents had always operated outside The System, I had wanted to become a part of it. To be somebody. Yet this criminal record, I understood, could dash such hopes before they ever began.

That's when I realized that drugs and alcohol had not been a part of my life *inside* high school. They were things that I did in my *void* time. And everybody needs something to do when there's nothing that you *have* to do. But drugs and alcohol had gradually taken control of most of my spare time. They had answered the nagging voice inside me and my friends that said, "Let's do something, and let's do something intriguing." But when the realities of jail redefined the word *intriguing* for me, something had to give.

Fortunately, what really saved my life, and started me back on the right track, was sports. My senior year at Abraham Lincoln, I was bigger and taller and stronger than most guys, and thank God, I had some skill in playing basketball. What's more, I had some friends who were also athletes, like Gary "Princey" Prince and Danny "Rap" Rappaport. (Princey, by the way, was the epitome of hard work. He worked harder than anybody I knew. Though he wasn't as talented as I was on the basketball court, his tenacity overcame that. He is now a famous doctor in New York. But nobody ever gave him anything.)

Our adventures in Florida and the Bahamas had bonded us together. So Rap, who played football, started encouraging me to study, and Princey was on the school basketball team, and they weren't into drugs at all. Their high was basketball and football, and by example, they encouraged me to share that trip. Soon, learning to jump and shoot better became my thrills. And after I was able to jump more effectively, the next big high was that I could dunk. So even though I wasn't a star player, I did start smokin' with moves on the basketball court, and that began to satisfy my earlier needs to get high with drugs and alcohol.

At most games, my buddies were usually disappointed because Coach Chuck Tayer would not start me, even though I had told them that he would. But Cubby, Danny, and Freddy still came to every game and cheered for me, even when I did nothing more than pass the coach's clipboard down the bench. But finally, my big moment came. Coach Tayer sent me in to pair up with a tall black kid on the opposing team, Lafayette. That kid was Sam Jones.

After all those months of practicing hard and languishing on the bench, I was primed. So the first time I got the ball, I went to the left corner for a jump shot. Behind me in the stands were my buddies, yelling and cheering, and when I took my shot, Sam Jones blocked it. But he didn't knock it out of bounds. Instead, it came flying right back into my hands.

I was shocked, but I knew what to do. I had to prove to everybody that Sam *shouldn't* have blocked my shot, so I jumped up and shot again. It was supposed to be a long, arched, sweet jump shot, but again, Sam blocked it.

Stunned but determined, I caught the ball a second time. Now it was me against him, and I didn't care if I ever made another shot. I just had to put the ball up. So I shot a third time, but Sam blocked the ball so hard that he threw it out the gym window. Then, adding to my embarrassment of having had three of my shots blocked in a row, my friends fell on the floor in such hysterical laughter that I thought we would need medical attention for them.

After the game, however, as Danny, Cubby, Freddy, and Princey gathered around me, the ridicule was gone. The five of us were high as a kite, and not a one of us had a speck of drugs or alcohol within us. And that's when it hit me: *You've done it, man. You've accomplished what neither your mother nor your father could do. You've found a natural high that satisfies.*

PART THREE: Plus Hard Work

12

Some of you might say, "I'd like to go to college, but I can't afford it."

Don't you dare lie to me, and don't you dare lie to yourself! If you can't afford to go to college, you better start bustin' your butt in high school and getting a 3.8, 3.9, or 4.0 grade-point average, and your teachers can get you into any college in this country for free. It's called a scholarship.

But if you can't get those kinds of grades, then you go to work in an organization like McDonald's and send your own butt to college. Or join the army, air force, coast guard, navy, or marines, and they'll send you to college.

I don't care what you do. You get a loan. You get a grant. You work nights. You work days. But take your butt to college. See, it's not that you can't afford to go to college. The fact is: You can't afford not to go to college.

Of course, some people are just so cool that they won't listen to me. But that's okay, 'cause that's what makes the world go around. I got a big, long, black Cadillac at home. And when I drive up to that drive-thru window, and I hit my button for the electric window—booop—and I stick my hand out, I'm gonna need somebody to hand me a large order of fries.

So you see, you have two choices. You can slide now, and bust your butt for $3.35 an hour—with the decimal point after the first three—for the rest of your life; or you can bust your butt now, studying and going to college, and maybe one day work for $335 an hour—with the decimal point after the five—and slide for the rest of your life. It's up to you.

That's the bottom line. If you don't plan on going to college, and staying in college until you get a four-year degree—This is the 1990s!—then you ain't gonna make it. You're gonna be a bum.

Accept it, now. . . .

No matter what our family faced over the years, I was always expected to go to college. I didn't really have a choice. My father repeatedly said, "I'm giving you two choices in life, son: college or death," and since I was no fool, I picked college. It was the best way out of home-life troubles and New York City, and I wanted to run away from both. But unlike other teenagers, I planned to run away to college.

Yet I wasn't good enough in academics or athletics to get a scholarship, so I decided: If college recruiters aren't seeking me out, I'll go looking for them. Then during the winter months of 1971–72, I wrote letters to a host of college coaches. I told them about my abilities and my accomplishments. I told them about my C average in grades, but I made certain to explain how motivated I'd become. I promoted Buddy Drew the way my daddy promoted Ali, and I got some offers. Several schools extended partial scholarships or grants, and in New York, both Yeshiva University and Hunter College wanted me for a full ride. But my number-one criterion was to go as far from the Big Apple as I could.

Then one day, my high school coach received a letter from Las Cruces, New Mexico. "We would be very happy to have [Drew] come out for basketball next year," the letter stated. "We usually try to help any of the players that can contribute to our team. So have him contact me when he comes down to attend school." And it was signed by Louis "Lou" R. Henson, who was then the director of athletics and head basketball coach at New Mexico State University.[1]

To me, that letter represented my passport out of misery, and a roadmap to success. I was so excited that I carried it around everywhere and showed it to everybody. Amid all the

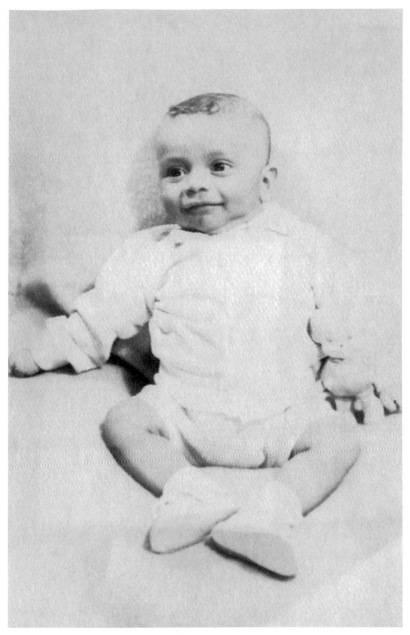

Conceived above *Sugar Ray's*. This baby picture—taken within days of my birth, January 20, 1955, at Sydenham Hospital, Harlem, New York—shows how I looked when my maternal grandmother, Mildred "Bubba" Palestine, said sarcastically, "He's not so bad. A little baby powder on his face, and my first grandson'll be all fixed up!"

Surrounded by my "family" men. During my first birthday party, hovering around me in the high chair are (*from left to right*): my Harlem "uncles," Wali "Youngblood" Muhammad and Oliver Shelton; my father, Drew "Bundini" Brown, Jr.; and my maternal uncle, Herbert "Herbie" Palestine.

An afternoon on Brighton Beach. Under the protection of a beach umbrella, Bubba watches while my grandfather, Zeda "Poppa Jack" Palestine, and I play in the sand.

An evening at the Apollo. My mother, Rhoda Palestine Brown, and I enjoy an evening in Harlem, New York, with my father. We're standing in front of the famous Apollo Theater on 125th Street near Amsterdam Avenue.

The Champ comes to school. *Left to right*: Bubba, Muhammad Ali, and I pose in front of the other sixth-grade students, after the Champ made an impromptu appearance in my honor at P.S. 171.

My *Brady Bunch*. Posing between my parents, I was considered "a man" at thirteen, during my bar mitzvah, February 17, 1968, at Ocean View Synagogue in Brooklyn, New York.

(Courtesy of Contemporary Images by Sylvette, Huntington, New York)

Bridging the family gap. My paternal grandfather, Drew Brown (*left*), was born in segregated Florida, and my maternal grandfather, Poppa Jack (*right*), was born near Kiev in Russia. Standing on either side of me at my bar mitzvah, this is the first time that I remember them being together as members of my family. They were born slaves; I was born free.

My bar mitzvah sponsors. Had it not been for Poppa Jack and Bubba, there would have been no bar mitzvah for me. They sent me to Hebrew School and provided for me when my parents could not. So posing with them here, I could almost feel their pride.

(Courtesy of Contemporary Images by Sylvette, Huntington, New York)

"Buddy Drew" visits Jerusalem. I am fourteen (*second from left*) in 1970 and emotionally affected, after slipping a piece of paper with my prayer written on it into the Wailing Wall in the ancient section of Jerusalem. This picture was taken during the year that I studied at Kfar Blum, an Israeli kibbutz.

Pretending to conquer *Jaws*. A dead shark, beached in the Bahamas in 1971, falls prey to a sixteen-year-old "Buddy Drew," as I enjoy spring break from Abraham Lincoln High School in Brooklyn, New York.

Jimi Hendrix's best Brooklyn fans. My friends Scott "Scotty" Camer (*center*), and Alfredo "Freddie" Garcia (*right*), rap at curbside with me during our senior year in high school.

Graduating, Sixties style. A well-cultivated Afro serves as my senior cap in this 1972 graduation portrait from Abraham Lincoln High School.

A slam-dunking Lion. After an academically disastrous year at New Mexico State University, I started my college career over at Kingsborough Community College in Brooklyn, New York. And by the second semester of the 1973–74 school year— as I demonstrate here while dunking the ball—I became a star basketball player for the Kingsborough Lions.

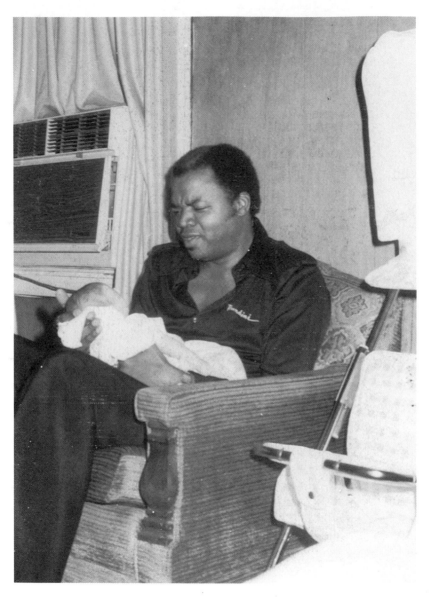

Bundini's first grandchild. My father seems particularly proud as he holds my daughter, Taryn Christine Brown, who was born in August 1977, during the summer following my graduation from Southern University in New Orleans.

The host of Bundini's. Dressed in a tuxedo—which was regular work attire at my New Orleans after-hours club named after my father—I am celebrating the enterprise's success during the winter of 1980.

The Greatest in the Big Easy. Muhammad Ali (a year before the world heavyweight champion's 1981 retirement from boxing) visits with me at Bundini's during the club's heyday.

Grinning to bear it. A fellow naval officer candidate, Paul Anderson, enjoys one of the rare relaxing moments with me during the summer of 1981 at Aviation Officers Candidate School in Pensacola, Florida.

A gentleman for a lady. Laurie Guimont Brown, my wife, is the best-looking woman at the Military Ball, held in July 1981, midway through my AOCS training in Pensacola. Dressed in naval "whites," I am clearly succeeding as the gentleman en route to becoming a navy officer. (Courtesy of the U.S. Navy)

An officer's first salute. Gunnery Sergeant Stephen W. Clark, USMC, gives me his finest salute, following my commissioning as an ensign in the United States Navy. He was the "gunny" sergeant who supervised our class through AOCS training in Pensacola. (Courtesy of the U.S. Navy)

"Dark Gable" in readiness. I am in full flight gear (with the helmet cropped out of this picture) as a naval jet attack pilot, stationed at the time on the U.S.S. *Nimitz*.

(Courtesy of the U.S. Navy)

The Browns of America. Dressed in my naval "whites," I stand with my wife, Laurie, and our children, Drew Jacques Brown IV and Taryn Christine Brown, for a family portrait in 1983.

euphoria, however, nobody mentioned the fact that I didn't *actually* have a scholarship or grant offer from NMSU, or that I didn't have the money to go to college. Oh, *How do you expect to pay for this, Drew?* did cross my mind. But I couldn't deal with such an unhappy thought. I'd had enough of those in earlier months, so I just let it pass.

And since Daddy had said "College, college, college" so often over the years, I figured that, somehow, he would come through for me. I didn't specifically expect *him* to pay for it all, and I knew that Momma didn't have that kind of money, but I figured, "Hey, give it a shot." So I told Daddy about the chance to be an NMSU walk-on, and I explained how much money it would take.

To my delight, he was elated that *his* son had gotten accepted at a university! He liked the sound of that. "Don't worry about it," he promised. "I'll get the money for you to go to college." Well, that did more for me than actually securing the money itself. My fears vanished, because I just knew that everything would be okay.

Yet experience did warn me to devise a backup plan, so I also talked to Momma about the money. She expressed no faith in Daddy's ever paying for my college costs, but she also promised to start putting pennies away. "I definitely want you to go to an out-of-town college," she said. "You deserve it, and your father can afford it." So she began pressuring him for the money, and he told her that he would get it from Ali.

But when the NMSU bills began arriving, I still had no money. And when I mentioned the problem to my father, he simply repeated his *don't worry* lines. Years later, I would learn that Ali had given the money to my father, but Daddy had drunk and gambled the cash away. At the time, however, all I knew was that promises failed to produce money.

Finally, Momma and Bubba paid the airfare and came up with some spending money for me to use until Daddy could send the rest. So there I was, the night before my departure for college. I had an airplane ticket, a little cash, my luggage, and Coach Henson's letter. In reality, I should have been terrified, but I was ecstatic. It wasn't so much that I *wanted* to go to college as that I couldn't wait to start my own life, and I knew college was the key.

Also, I was the only one of my friends—that is, among the group that included Scotty, Cubby, and Freddy—who had this route out. And it was Cubby who emphasized the point. That hot summer night, he and I went cruising for some fun, but we ended up sitting in front of the Lincoln Savings Bank on Brighton Beach Avenue. For a while, we joked and talked about the girls who walked by. Then quite unexpectedly, he said, "I'm proud of you, Drew. This is great, you going to college and all."

I teased Cubby about the uncharacteristic earnestness in his tone of voice, but then I realized that he was serious. That got to me. "You mean it?" I asked.

"Sure," he said. "It's just like I was going, too. 'Cause you're the guy from Brighton who's going to make it, and while you make it, man, we're gonna be right there with you, makin' it, too."

Because I arrived at college with no money, I had to spend the first weeks on campus using my street smarts to delay demands for payment from the business office. And those people were persistent. They could have given lessons to loan sharks, because they called every day.

"The money is on its way," I kept saying, even though I fully expected them to call my bluff at any time. But they didn't. Instead, they allowed me to register, to move into a dorm, and subsequently, to start classes before the first nickel arrived toward my bill. And eventually, my father did get the money to the school. He had to go to Ali a second time, admit that he had squandered the first funds. Gene Kilroy intervened once again and told the Champ that a son shouldn't suffer because of what his father does. To Ali's credit, he paid twice for my freshman year at NMSU.

I had never been to a major university campus before I arrived in Las Cruces, New Mexico. It's about forty-five minutes from the U.S.–Mexican border where El Paso and Juárez face one another across the Rio Grande, and at the time, NMSU was the largest campus in America. It had big, beautiful facilities, and an enormous basketball coliseum had just been built.

Our campus nickname was the "Aggies," because the university featured a major agricultural program, and that impressed me. I hated the name and had no interest in farming, but the irrigation process made NMSU look like an oasis in the middle of the otherwise arid climate. Grass on campus extended right out to a line, beyond which cacti and sand covered the land to the horizon.

But because the campus was so large, getting from one place to another often took a good ten to fifteen minutes, and there were no subways. If these people could figure out how to transport water from the Rio Grande onto campus, I wondered, why didn't somebody give some thought to human transportation as well?

What I did like were the dormitories. These two-storied buildings were like motels, with two students per room and pairs of rooms sharing a common bath. So it was as if we were on vacation and at summer camp, all rolled into one. Most of us black students taped up our windows with silver foil so we could use "black lights" to make the fluorescent colors on our posters glow, night and day. But this practice also shielded our rooms from the intense sun and dry heat of the Southwest.

On the other hand, nothing could protect us from the area's periodic sandstorms, and this phenomenon astounded me. In New York, I had thought that getting caught up in wind funnels of trash was bad, but whirling sand makes you feel helpless. Sandstorms are like torrential rainfalls minus the water. And when millions of these miniature granules surround you at once, they irritate your eyes, often causing you to become temporarily blinded. Somehow that reminded me that I was on my own. For the first time, mornings came and Bubba was not there to shove One-A-Day vitamins and a glass of OJ in my face, or to call Momma's and make certain that I was awake. I now had to do it all by myself. Yet everything seemed like a whirlwind that proved even more blinding than the sandstorms.

I had come to campus as early as NMSU would let me. So although I had a walk-on letter for basketball, I reported to football practice. Preseason activity was just beginning, and I could see that the university's football players had a certain aura about them. First of all, most of the team was black, and their "hell week" was the envy of other campus groups. In addition, I liked the way the players looked. In uniform, they were modern gladiators, with black stuff painted under their eyes, and cleats that crunched when they walked on the concrete. So I said, "Why not? Football's my style," and I became a football walk-on, even though I had never played the game on any organized level.

But I started working out and bulked up from 205 pounds to about 220 pounds in just over a month. I was big, I was strong, I was fast—and except for the fact that I knew nothing about football, I was ready. When the day came, however, that the coach asked what position I played, I said, "Tight end or linebacker." Those were the two coolest positions that I could think of, and I would have said quarterback, except that I couldn't throw the ball.

He placed me as a linebacker, and during the first practices, I loved hitting. The only problem with being a linebacker was that I couldn't stand my ground. When the ball was snapped, I always backstepped in order to find out what was going on before I went for a hit.

At every huddle, though, the defensive captain would say, "No, no, Drew. Stay in your spot, and then go forward. Don't give an inch, and for godsakes, quit chicken-footing backward." But it never worked. My movements were habitual, and by the next snap, I would scrap backward again, so the guys started calling me "Chicken Feet" Brown, and the coach moved me from linebacker to tight end.

I was good in this new position and held my own against older guys on the team until our first offensive scrimmage. It wasn't an actual game, but we ran through a series of plays—the team's prospective offensive crew against its crack and proven defensive players. I felt psyched, and during one of the first plays, the quarterback tagged me in the huddle to receive a pass. The play was a slant six right over the middle. At the snap I hit my man, then watched for the pass and caught the ball— although simultaneously, two seniors crunched me. They hit me so hard that both of them bounced off. But I felt no pain, so I ran ahead for the touchdown, and when I crossed the goal line, I tossed down the ball and yelled, "This is my game, and I'm the man!"

Back in the huddle, I was high as a kite. The quarterback said, "Same thing," and I responded, "All day long."

Again the ball was snapped. Again I hit my man and turned for the pass. But this time the quarterback threw it high, so I had to jump and catch it. My body was outstretched and two feet off the ground when a defensive linebacker's helmet caught me dead in the stomach. It was a solid hit. It felt like his best shot, and I plummeted.

All the guys gathered around me, but all I could do was pray, "God, just give me my breath back." Meanwhile, my mind was racing with the thought: *This is it, man. Forget football.* Then a week later, I got the tendons in my hand torn during a game, and that convinced me to hang up my cleats. I had my injury. I had the experience. So as far as I was concerned, I won. Momma didn't raise no fool.

Good athletes got away with not going to class, so even though I wasn't that good an athlete, I still hung out with the jocks and did what they did. I skipped. But this decision was reinforced by what happened when I went to my first lecture class. I was surprised to find an auditorium-sized classroom in which hundreds of students were enrolled. I looked at my friend and commented, "If the professor takes attendance, we'll never learn anything. It's got to take the whole hour just to call out the names."

"Chicken Feet, they don't take attendance here," he said.

Remembering how schools were run in Brooklyn, I was shocked. "Then how will the professor know that I'm here?" I asked.

"He doesn't know, and doesn't care," my friend said. "You're just a number. They don't take attendance." That did it. *Boop*— I sneaked out the door and didn't go back to the class for the rest of the semester.

At the time, blacks were a small minority within the NMSU student body, and since most of us were athletes, we all hung out together. It was a lot like being back in Harlem, except that all of these brothers were educated. They were on their way to being something, and sports was their ticket. The early seventies were also the heart of the Black Revolution in America, and the beliefs of that movement were prominent among our NMSU crowd. They gave us a cause to believe in. But the revolution gave me something more. Just as living in Israel during the late sixties had given me a sense of worth as a Jew, living among NMSU's black athletes gave me a renewed sense of my blackness. So I jumped on the Black Is Beautiful bandwagon.

In part, my father had primed me for this black awareness when he emphasized the same theme during Ali's publicity campaign against Frazier. One of the Champ's statements, in particular, remained with me. "When I climb into the ring, I'm thinking about God, and I'm thinking about all those people in every ghetto in every city in the United States of America," Ali had said. "I'm out to whip all the hypocrites of the power structure. I'm fighting for my freedom and carrying the hopes of my thirty million black people who also suffer here."[2]

When I first heard this, I thought it was hype. Tough, truthful stuff, yes, but just words. Then at NMSU, I participated in campus demonstrations, and I witnessed one riot. I entered the struggle. I joined the fight. And as my actions began to show me, words like Ali's can become battle cries when the cause is real.

However, NMSU put its own spin on the Black is Beautiful movement. We not only took pride in being black, but for the first time in my life, I heard black guys say, "We're *better* than they are," meaning that black was not just equal to white, but superior. In fact, our first line of defense became "They all want to hang with us, but they can't."

"You know what it is, man," explained Smokey, who was one of my best black friends. "White dudes are always lookin' for us, partyin' where we party and hangin' out in the spots that we make cool. But the real thing is that white girls love *us*. And that drives white boys crazy. So it's still them against us—except now, *them* is the weak ones."

Male strength, then, became part of our black awareness. For the first time, women were looking at us as men, and since there were very few black sisters on campus, it was the white girls' glances that affected us. Our Afros became a Samson and Delilah thing. The longer and prettier and puffier and shinier a guy's Afro was, the more strength he was perceived to have. So we black guys cultivated our hair as carefully as the white ag majors worked their campus crops. Long was strong, and we were defiant about it. When, for example, a sister's hair wouldn't grow long, we called her a "TWA girl," meaning that she had a "Teeny Weeny Afro."

And we became intensely loyal to black rock groups like Parliament-Funkadelic. It was the first group of brothers who played hard rock with the funk that I loved. Their album *Maggot Brain* was a funky rebirth of Jimi Hendrix. It was The Temptations on acid, and we all listened to Funkadelic. We plastered their psychedelic posters on our walls. They brought the revolution home to us. But in those posters, another phenomenon was obvious. Though we enjoyed attracting white girls elsewhere on campus, in our rooms, all the brothers' posters and pictures were of the sisters. Black women were done in caricature, beautiful women with large Afros and gorgeous breasts— but all of these posters were accented in fluorescent colors of yellow, pink, orange, purple, and black. When our black lights came on, white was not a color on display.

Later that fall, Coach Lou Henson saw to it that I made his opening practices with the Aggies basketball team, and I was overwhelmed at how good these ballplayers were. At the time, the Aggies were nationally ranked contenders. From 1950 until 1970, they had logged nine appearances in the NCAA playoffs, and their collegiate-year records between 1968 and 1970 were 23-6, 24-5, and 28-3. So it didn't take me long to realize that I was a walk-on for a first-class squad.

Yet at six feet five I was not this team's big guy, and that took some adjusting. Always before, I had been the tallest player on any basketball team in Harlem or Brooklyn. But my height was just average for NMSU's roster. For example, "Truman," a junior and an excellent player, was six-nine. "Bostic," another upperclassman, was six-eight. And the guy who was seven-two we called "Tree," for obvious reasons. These guys were so tall that they could slam on me, and I'd never been around that kind of power before.

Still another teammate, "Super" John Williamson, went on to play pro ball. At that time, though, he was only six-three, but he had an enormous body. He habitually walked around with a toothpick in his mouth and rarely spoke, on court or off, but he was an unbelievable basketball player.

One day, a white kid was trying out for the team, and Coach Henson assigned him to guard Super John. Well, the white kid wasn't on the court more than a few seconds when Super John elbowed the kid right in the mouth. Blood went everywhere, and it was like, "I'm the star here. You're the punk. Now get away from me, or your eye will be next." Back in New York, we played basketball intensely, but Super John astounded even me. I had never seen anybody blatantly cheat and get away with it.

Yet he taught me something that I used for the rest of my basketball career. Remember, he never spoke. But anytime he shook a guy who was guarding him, Super John would slide past his opponent with a move, and then whisper as he passed, "Excuse me." It was a cool but calculated play, like rubbing salt in the wound, because Super John didn't say it in a bragging tone. He said it so softly and politely that it stung. Worse, he didn't embarrass you loud enough for others to hear; he kept it between you and him, and that made the result more intense.

Looking back, these were the first black guys who were older than I—and whom I admired—who actually weren't junkies, or into drugs, or in some other way operating outside The System. Instead, NMSU's black basketball players were powerful contributors to The System itself. That season, we played in basketball's National Invitational Tournament, and Super John Williamson ranked ninth among the nation's leading college scorers. He averaged 27.2 points per game, for a season total of 490 points.[3] Yet these basketball stars and my roommate named "Rocky" accepted me as just another guy. It was a great sensation, and one that I had not felt since my time in Israel.

After two semesters of skipping classes and hanging out with the jocks, however, my grade-point average was a 1.6. That was a *D* overall, but I still received an academic deficiency notice from the registrar. So I went to the office, as the notice instructed, even though I wasn't worried. "Next year, I'll do much better," I told the man. "I now know how to bring this GPA up."

The registrar seemed unimpressed. So I apologized, told him that I felt bad about the whole thing, and once again, I promised to do better.

That's when he cut me off, and his words were like a brick

wall: "You won't be able to come back next year. That's the rule, any time a student's GPA drops below a certain level."

Only then did I realize what was happening. In a year's time, I had developed a bigger Afro, a broader chest and shoulders, new skills as an athlete, and a great bunch of friends. In addition, I was good-looking, and girls were after me. But until that precise moment, I had not realized how little I had actually matured. I hadn't gone to class because of a peculiar rationale: *College is heaven. I don't want to be anywhere else. But if I go to class, then I'll graduate and have to leave. So I'll just never go to class, and never graduate. That way, I won't ever have to leave heaven.*

That's how naive I was. Yet faced with the actual consequences of my actions, I felt not only dumb, but cheated. I was having to give up the greatest party of my life—all because I hadn't made it my business to find out that if I didn't make the grades, I couldn't come back.

And I did have to leave. The Buddy Drew who had been given a proud Brooklyn send-off in the fall of 1972 was returning home in defeat. But that summer of '73, one thing was very clear to me. Somehow, I would be at a university, by hook or by crook, because Buddy Drew was going back to college.

13

But you know what the really big one is? If you dare have the nerve and audacity to disrespect the teachers, secretaries, coaches, counselors, principals, or even the people who sweep the floors in your schools, I'll promise you one thing: You will be a failure in life. *Why? Because good teachers are God's gift to this country, and anytime you disrespect a gift from God, it's a sin and you're gonna pay for that sin.*

These teachers are a gift because they're some of the last people you'll ever meet who work and don't get paid enough money for it. They do it for another reason: They're all junkies. That's right. The best teachers in this country are junkies, and do you know what they get high on? They don't use drugs. They get high on you.

When one of you in here who thinks he or she is so bad finally wakes up and finds out what time it is—not on your watch, but on your life—and you finally say, "Maybe I can be somebody," then you change. You finish high school, you go to college, and then you become a doctor, an electrician, a lawyer, a teacher, an engineer, or the head of some corporation. . . .

Well, when you do that, you'll never forget the teacher who helped you believe you could be somebody. And someday, when you come back—and just say, "Thank you"—that's when you pay them back.

Every time one of these teachers sees a former student come back and walk down the halls to prove that he or she has made it. Every time one of you tells a teacher, "Thank you for what you have done for me." Every time these teachers see that education does make a difference in one of your lives, that's when they really trip out. You are their greatest highs. You are what they're addicted to. . . .

Like a puppy dragging his tail between his legs, I returned to Momma's house in Brooklyn. It was easy to get my old job again at the Brighton Baths, but nothing else during the summer of 1973 was the same as before. I was too devastated at being unable to return that fall to NMSU; and I wondered how I could be happy again.

But I was too proud to tell my family or friends that I had flunked out. Only Momma and I knew, and as usual, she was sympathetic but determined that I go back to school. With the others, I simply used the lie that Momma's problems necessitated my coming back to help. And if they asked, I said that I would transfer to a Brooklyn college in the fall. After all, I was back in New York City where streetwise habits are second nature, so the con was easy.

My most blatant lie, however, I saved to get what I really wanted. And I justified the plan based on the fact that the NMSU grades were *my* failure and that they jeopardized *my* future. So I took my high school transcript to Kingsborough Community College, and with a convenient lapse of memory about the year at NMSU, I told KCC's admissions office that after having taken the previous year "to find myself," I had finally decided to start college. I must have appeared convincing and motivated to study, because they bought it, and that autumn I started classes as a KCC freshman with a clean academic slate.

Instead of riding a 50-cc motorscooter along the green and expansive New Mexico campus, though, I now took the number 21 bus along the drab streets of Brooklyn. KCC had a nice campus, but it was fenced in and enclosed—creating just another collection of buildings in the conglomeration that is Brooklyn. So, in contrast to the snow-capped Organ Mountains and the vibrant blue sky that created Las Cruces's broad horizon, litter and garbage now swirled in the murky city air that formed my horizons at KCC.

For all practical purposes I was back in a high school setting. Gone were NMSU's classes of 350 students that I had hoped to conquer. At KCC, I sat in small classes of twenty-five and thirty people. I was paying the dues of last year's college folly. Yet some of this proved to be for the best. Not having NMSU's advantages to lure me into self-deception, I *had* to do better work in KCC's smaller and less distracting classrooms. It meant very little that I was now king of the hill, because I knew that Kingsborough was small in comparison to what I had lost. So I *had* to take pride in my work. I was on a mission, dedicated to getting back to a university out of Brooklyn where the real fun is.

To accomplish this, I first had to succeed in KCC's classrooms, and this task became easier because, in some cases, I simply repeated courses that I had taken at NMSU. But in going over familiar material, I could not also repeat my poor study habits. I had to attack KCC's classrooms with a different strategy, and that's when I began developing my "Getting the *A* Theory."

The first rule is that *students must go to class every single day.* That seems obvious enough, but skipping had been my first mistake at NMSU, so I never missed a class at Kingsborough.

The second rule is that *students must ask for the A.* College is no different from life itself. In both, you get what you ask for. So I started every new class at KCC by going to the professor and saying, "My name is Drew Timothy Brown III, but you can call me 'Buddy.' Now, I want to start this semester off right by assuring you that I need an *A* in this class. And to get that, I'll do whatever you say. So please tell me what you expect from *A* students in your classes?"

The third rule is that *students should sit in the front of each class and pay attention (or at least act as though you are!).* Even though I was living back at home, I had not forgotten what it was like in New Mexico to live on my own. Getting up every morning had been difficult. So seeing KCC's underpaid professors arrive each day and show up for classes made me realize that they weren't doing this just for the money. The real reason they came to class was that they *respected* us as students. Thus, returning that respect was the least we could do. And if I respected the process of learning as much as the professors did, then I was certain that Buddy Drew would make the grades.

My year at NMSU had been a difficult period for my father and Ali. From the summer of 1971 through late 1972, Joe Frazier's manager, Yancey "Yank" Durham, had repeatedly postponed a return bout between Frazier and Ali by haggling over terms with the promoter, Jack Kent Cooke of Los Angeles, who held the contract for that event. While Durham held out for Frazier's benefit, however, Ali was forced either to wait on Frazier or to fight other contenders. The Champ chose to fight, and in February 1973, he won a twelve-round decision in Vegas over England's Joe Bugner. But on March 31, Ali was dealt the second-ever loss of his professional career by Ken Norton, a twenty-eight-year old boxer who was virtually unknown at the time.[1]

Beyond the beating that the speedier Norton levied upon Ali that night in San Diego though, Norton also broke the Champ's jaw. Yet Ali continued to fight, round after round. It was an inconceivable risk for him to take, and years later, the Champ described how my father helped him through that ordeal. Coming back to his corner, Ali's memoir explains, he asked Bundini and Angelo how to determine if a boxer's jaw is broken. My father made a sharp sound with his tongue and moved his own jaw to demonstrate the signs. But when the Champ followed suit, they all heard the crack as he spit blood into the bucket.

Immediately, Daddy told Angelo that the bout had to be stopped. However, there were more than a dozen rounds left, and Ali was still convinced that he could fight. *If* his jaw lasted. So the pair reluctantly agreed to let the Champ continue. But when it came time for Ali to head back into the rumble, Daddy whispered to him, "Shorty is in the living room, watching. Shorty is sitting down, crossing his legs and watching you. Just remember that. . . ." Then throughout the remaining rounds, my father kept screaming this refrain while the Champ miraculously kept their secret about his jaw, fought off Norton, and survived to walk away.[2]

But if Shorty had merely been in the living room that night, Ali might not have survived. To be sure, Shorty also entered the ring with the Champ, and huddled in the corner with my father. Psychological warfare by itself could not have accomplished what happened that night. It took spiritual, magiclike intervention to shield Ali, and that was what Shorty did.

He had to. The Champ's emotional resources were dangerously low. Months before, he had become depressed and out of shape. Many considered him, at the age of thirty-one, to be "just another over-the-hill fighter with the years hanging heavy around the middle of his once magnificent physique."[3] Ali resented this, but his weariness came through in an inscription that he wrote, earlier in January, on a photo of him and my father: "The man who has no imagination stands on earth. He has not wings. He cannot fly." It was as though the fighter that once floated like a butterfly had somehow become grounded, and he knew it.

So did my father. He knew something was wrong with Ali. Daddy could feel it. What's more, for the first time in their years together, my father could not find the right buttons to press in order to motivate the Champ. So after the first Ali-Norton fight, while the Champ flailed his body back into shape at the Deer Lake camp, Daddy backed off. He spent time with Ali when the Champ wanted. Otherwise, my father resumed working in Harlem with Jeff "Candy Slim" Merritt, the young heavyweight contender who, some years earlier, had persuaded my father to be his trainer.

By the time I returned to New York from New Mexico, therefore, the best way for me to see my father was to show up for Merritt's workouts. I also took a real interest in Jeff's abilities and his natural kindness. Then, because of my input and because Jeff and I became close friends, he and Daddy named me as assistant trainer.

This was the boost that I needed. Working alongside my father in boxing helped both of us heal some wounds from previous years. And combined with my renewed discipline in academics at KCC, the two responsibilities provided the focus that I had lacked at NMSU.

In September, I got my first shot as a ringside trainer. Jeff was scheduled to fight at Madison Square Garden in an undercard match against Ernie Terrell. But Daddy had to be in California on those dates because Ali had a return bout with

Norton at the Forum in Inglewood, California.[4] So it was agreed that I would work Jeff's fight in Manhattan.

It was to be an all-out publicity night, because Candy Slim had a very streety image, and I wanted his Garden appearance to counteract that. We landed several prefight interviews for him with high-profile sportswriters, and I even had a celebrity date for the event, Gail Fisher, who was costarring that season in the hit TV series *Mannix*. We left nothing to chance. And neither did Merritt. That night, he knocked out Terrell in the first round, and we immediately left for a series of parties in Harlem. We wanted the word on the street to be that Candy Slim had class and was the new kid on the block.

The Harlem celebrations were great, and most people seemed impressed with Jeff's win. But late in the evening, we ended up at a private affair, and within minutes, the victor was nowhere to be found. I started checking the apartment, room by room, until I located Jeff in the bathroom. There, sitting on the floor, his arm outstretched over the toilet, Jeff was shooting up heroin.

I was no longer naive about drugs, but I tripped out. I couldn't believe the power of dope. Why else would a young man with a chance of becoming the next heavyweight champion of the world be shooting up heroin? And in some ways, that moment hurt me more than it was killing Jeff. He was hooked, but he was my friend; yet I also had a responsibility to my father. So when he returned from Ali's narrowly won revenge victory over Norton in L.A., I told Daddy what had happened, and the next day we resigned from Jeff's staff.

Meanwhile, basketball season had begun at KCC, and by then, the college's officials had discovered that I was actually a transfer student. So following NCAA rules, they declared me ineligible for first-semester play. As a result, I had no time to devote to Merritt. Instead, I had to focus on college and make the grades or I wouldn't see any second-semester action, either.

KCC's basketball team was known as the "Lions," but we should have been called the "Cubs," because we were the first squad in the college's history to compete on an intercollegiate basis. And it was a rough season.

Instead of a traditional gymnasium, we practiced and played

home games in a small airdome called "The Bubble." It was not an inspiring place, and our first-semester record lived up to that fact. We lost more than half of our games. But because I had a year's experience at NMSU, and because I was older and stronger than most of his players, Coach William Lopez gambled on me. Once I qualified for the second half of the season, he made me the team's starting "star" forward.

Looking back, I know that Coach Lopez was the first coach who truly believed in me as an athlete. And as a year-end news story confirmed, I did not disappoint him:

> For Drew Brown this is just the beginning of something big. This 19-year-old sophomore out of New Mexico State is out to make a name for himself. . . .
> When January came around, Drew became eligible. . . . With his 6'5" muscular body, [he] paced the Kingsborough Basketball Lions to a convincing 12-11 season after a horrendous first half of torrid basketball. Among Drew's best games [was] a 35-point performance against a Queens team, which also included 13 rebounds and five blocked shots.
> The KCC Lions needed rebounding and Drew supplied it. This turned the team around. According to Brown, the team played differently with him on the court. . . . According to his coach, Bill Lopez, Drew has much potential. [Though Drew] needs help with his defense, [the coach] has no complaints about Drew's offensive capability.
> Outside of basketball, Drew is a very outgoing person. He surprises everyone with his vast knowledge about the world. . . . Drew is studying liberal arts and hopes to be a public-relations man in the future. He is very concerned about the world's situation and is deeply involved within himself to root out the wrong in today's society. . . .
> Between his basketball skills and his knowledge, Drew is destined to become a great man.[5]

Meanwhile, I succeeded in the classroom, too. By strictly complying with my Getting the A Theory, I finished that year at Kingsborough with a 3.2 grade-point average. And with Coach Lopez's support, I received offers to play basketball at Brooklyn College and Yeshiva University in New York City, as well as offers from colleges in South Carolina and Louisiana.

The last one came from Southern University in New Orleans, and theirs was for a full athletic scholarship. Joe N. Hornbeak,

Jr., who was SUNO's head basketball coach at the time, wrote, "[W]e are in the process of lining up possible recruits for next year's team and would like to include you in that number. Enclosed is a copy of our Letter of Intent and a grant-in-aid form. These need to be signed and returned as soon as possible. . . ."[6]

Even though it was a matter-of-fact offer, Momma was ecstatic and glowing with pride, so I grabbed at the chance. To me, Coach Hornbeak's letter promised a university setting like the NMSU one that I had lost, so I stopped looking. I could imagine nothing better than hailing from a university in the Big Easy. What's more, the SUNO scholarship meant that my education could survive whatever happened in my father's career.

Because I was a full-scholarship athlete, instead of a walk-on, I expected reporters, banners, fans, a limousine, and maybe even a marching band to greet me at the airport in New Orleans. But there was nobody on hand, not even a fellow student to pick me up, and that should have been a signal. Finally, I walked out of the terminal to get a taxi, only to have the humidity plus the heat drive me back inside. Heat in New York City and New Mexico can be miserable, but this Gulf Coast humidity was like steam from a boiler. My first thought was to purchase a return ticket and head back north.

Thirty minutes later, however, Coach Hornbeak arrived. He was a young black guy with a big Afro, and he seemed proud to have a basketball player from New York City join his team. His T-shirt had BLACK KNIGHTS printed across it, and I liked the sound of the team's nickname, so I loaded my luggage into his car. *How bad could it be?*

SUNO turned out to be a small southern black college. Its campus had half a dozen buildings neatly arranged amid lush green grass and trees. And though the campus was bigger than KCC, it didn't even approximate NMSU in size. The only *newness* was in the name, New Orleans. Everything else in sight was definitely the Old South—including our jock residence, which wasn't even on campus. For that, we had to cross the railroad tracks. And I do mean go on the other side of the tracks.

"The House," as we called it, was on Peoples Avenue in an area known as Seabreeze, and it served as home to ten big black athletes. Carrying my luggage inside, I saw that all the mattresses were on the floor, and by the odors and disarray in the kitchen, I realized that all ten of us were left to our own devices. But I didn't complain. As bad as the facilities were, this was now my school. I had earned a scholarship here, and I intended to make the most of it.

Later, I would learn that SUNO had been developed during the "separate but equal" era. Across town was its "white" counterpart, the University of New Orleans. It boasted an enormous campus with top-notch facilities, even though both campuses were built about the same time. Yet the only equation between the two campuses that I could discern was that for every ten UNO buildings, SUNO had gotten one.

SUNO's most striking aspect was that all of its administrators, professors, and staff were black. All of its nerds and bourgeois were black. In fact, everybody on campus was black, and it immediately hit me that the Black Revolution didn't exist here. There was nobody to protest against. Everybody was the same. And that did something to my head. Namely, it yanked out the rug from under my lifetime of excuses.

Always before, I could say that I failed because the teacher was white, or because the coach was white, or because the girl that I liked was white, and that their racism kept me from succeeding. That line, however, didn't work at SUNO. There was no "color" excuse on this campus. All that mattered here was what you did, who you were as a person, and what you could accomplish. Even in Harlem, the power and money of downtown whites had dictated how we lived uptown.

But not at SUNO. It was an all-black world unto itself where, devoid of color excuses, it was as if nobody were black. And since everybody was the same, then for once in our lives, we were just people again. *Just people.* I liked the feeling of that. *Just people.* It also made me wonder once more if black and white really mattered at all. . . .

Despite SUNO's poor exterior, inside these buildings I would encounter the best and most caring educators possible. And foremost among these, in my experience, was Dr. Norman Wilson. An old-style southern black, he had thick eyeglasses and routinely wore his salt-and-pepper hair in that short, cropped fashion that looks classic and academic. He always kept a plastic pencil holder in his shirt pocket, and each day he filled it with half a dozen well-sharpened pencils. Nothing important ever escaped him.

He was also the most polite man that I ever met—so polite, in fact, that he disarmed my streetwise New Yorker tactics. I did not dare to con Dr. Wilson, and because of that, I could do nothing but study and learn. Unwittingly, he even came between my father and me on one occasion.

During much of 1974, Daddy and Ali had been concentrating on what, until then, was the most valuable fight purse in boxing history. It was touted as "The Rumble in the Jungle," and President Mobutu of Zaire had guaranteed five million dollars each to both the Champ and his opponent, George Foreman.[7]

That event would also be Don King's first big break in major fight promotion. Prior to "The Rumble," he had been a young, hardworking black promoter. But my father convinced Ali to let King put together the Zaire extravaganza. Daddy told Ali that signing with King was the right thing to do. "Words are cheap," my father said, "so now is the time to put your money where your mouth is." And when Ali agreed, Daddy witnessed the Champ and King signing their contract in a bathroom; that contract launched Don King's boxing empire. To his credit, King never forgot how Daddy had helped him. But then, my father never let him forget it, either.

So when Daddy telephoned The House and asked if I wanted to go along for the African trip, I was thrilled.

"Fine," he said. "Give me the number of your teacher. I'll call and find out if you can go."

"Daddy, I'm in college," I said. "We don't have 'teachers.' We have 'professors.' And this is not elementary school. We don't need our parents' permission to skip—"

"—Boy," he interrupted. "I want your teacher's phone number."

Since I had an *A* in Dr. Wilson's class, and I thought his politeness would disarm my father, I gave him the professor's office number.

Later, I learned that Daddy did telephone Dr. Wilson and asked if I "had school" during the week of the African trip. My professor explained that he told my father, yes, I did have class, but Dr. Wilson could give assignments in advance so that I could study while traveling, and he said the trip could be educational for me.

But my father interrupted the polite professor. "I didn't ask you all that," Daddy said. "I just want to know if Drew has school that week."

"Yes, sir, he does," Dr. Wilson responded.

"Then thank you very much," my daddy concluded, and said good-bye.

Moments later, The House phone rang, and as soon as I picked it up, Daddy said, "Boy, you can't go to Africa. You got school that week." So I didn't go. On October 30, 1974, Ali regained the World Heavyweight Championship during what turned out to be an historic match in an African stadium. But I didn't get to witness it. The eighth-round knockout also marked Ali's second capture of a world title, and until then, that feat had been accomplished by only one other boxer, Floyd Patterson.[8] But I missed it all.

In the process, however, Daddy and Dr. Wilson demonstrated how important rule number one of my Getting the *A* Theory really is. No matter what, a student should not miss class.

And I didn't. During my first year at SUNO, I added real concentration to that theory. I played basketball and I went to class. I played basketball and I went to class. That was it. And my spartan habits were in sync with SUNO's athletic program which, like everything else, operated on a nickel budget.

Our arena looked like a broken-down high school gym, and the equipment was minimal at best. At NMSU, we athletes had drawn upon a virtually unlimited supply of sneakers and supplies. Yet SUNO issued us—per season—one pair of white Converse for practice and another for games, plus a grand total of four pairs of socks. Just as skimpy was our basketball team's record for the year. We traveled to other southern black colleges for games, but we lost most of them. Needless to say, we didn't get into a playoff, either, though I was having the time of my life.

I learned to enjoy being a Black Knight because, at SUNO, I

felt wanted and needed. Guys such as "Big John," "Cornell," "Speedy," "Tex," and "Footsie" became like family to me. We lived together, ate together, and played the same sport. This was particularly the case with another guy named Craig Allen. He was from Detroit and had that northern coolness about him that made the two of us instant buddies. We really hung tight all through the remainder of our college years.

In essence, then, SUNO formed athletic teams the old-fashioned way—meaning that everybody helped one another—and that attitude made my basketball playing improve consistently. Yet I did not become the college's basketball star that year. At SUNO, the *team* was our star. So in addition to the disadvantages, SUNO athletics also lacked one major hindrance that frustrates players at most major college programs today: We were not dominated by a win-at-any-cost mentality. In the best sense, we were *student athletes.*

I was equally intrigued at SUNO to see how the mindset of southern blacks differed from that of blacks in New York, or even of blacks in New Mexico who were predominantly from California or other western states. To me, New Orleans blacks who were mostly from Louisiana and Texas seemed a breed apart. Even their motto was the reverse of New York's. "If you *can't* make it in the Big Easy," they explained, "you can't make it anywhere." And as soon as I heard that, I promised myself that I would become a Big Easy star.

Why not? On the surface, the competition didn't seem that tough. For example, at the first rock concert that I attended, I saw seven black guys standing in the auditorium's lobby. They ranged in height from five feet to six-five, and they had assembled themselves in order from the shortest to the tallest. All seven had on the same type of polyester jumpsuit, yet each outfit was a different shade of purple, ranging from pale to dark. Each brother held a cane, and they all wore sunglasses, oversized "gangster" hats, and white gloves. It was clear that these guys thought they were the coolest brothers that ever walked—except that not one of them spoke to a single girl, and the dudes really looked like characters from *The Jackson Five* cartoon show.

It wasn't, I discovered, that southerners are "slow." The New

Orleans crowd just didn't see any value in trying to be fast. But along with that mindset, they showed me a redeeming quality, too: They trusted people.

At the end of my first academic year, for example, I tied with "Big John" Williams for SUNO's Scholastic Athlete of the Year award. He was a six-eight player from Louisiana, and back at the start of the year, he taught me a solid lesson about trust. We had known one another less than twenty-four hours when several of us decided to go to Bourbon Street. I went along, even though I had no money, and when we got there, I asked to borrow some from Big John. Now I was thinking five, maybe ten dollars at most. But without hesitation he hands me a fifty.

I was astounded. Nobody in New York would do that for an *old* friend, much less a new acquaintance. Yet it was clear that these southerners enjoyed helping other people, and gradually, that affected me. It smoothed out some of the rough edges that the worst of Harlem, Spanish Harlem, Brighton Beach, Israel, and Las Cruces had etched into my personality.

By the end of my first year at SUNO, I really started enjoying life. I juggled six or seven girlfriends at a time—the prettiest women on campus. I even dated seniors, which was unheard of back then. But I was a smooth-talking New Yorker. They listened to what I had to say, and they wanted to hear more. I was also asked to join the Alpha Phi Omega fraternity.

As in the movie *School Daze*, the APOs subjected me to every aspect of hazing that was common to fraternity life back then. They really beat my butt. But I knew that a lot of guys were merely expressing jealousy, because I came from New York, because I was cool and fast-talking, and because attentions from the sisters gave me power on campus. So I took the hazing, and took it in stride. After all, unlike the experiences in Israel or New Mexico, I was not being asked to leave SUNO. Instead, I was being initiated into belonging.

On September 30, 1975, during my junior year at SUNO, the Champ got a third bout with Joe Frazier—but by then, their status had reversed. Ali was once again the championship title-holder, and in the "Thrilla in Manila" match, he defeated his challenger after the fourteenth round when Frazier's trainer stopped the fight.[9] For my father, this TKO was a sweet victory, finally putting to rest Frazier's shadow over Ali's successes and culminating the most productive twelve months in the Bundini-Ali relationship. For the Champ, this win brought between $4 million and $7 million into his bank account.[10]

Meanwhile, my attitude had never been better. I was doing well in both academics and basketball, and I had an apartment at 1707 Esplanade Avenue. Fraternity life and dating had restored my self-confidence. But I did have one problem. A car that I had bought for a hundred dollars kept breaking down.

So after Daddy returned from the Philippines, I telephoned him. "Pop, since I'm here on scholarship, you don't have to pay for my college," I began my pitch. "And I'm getting along fine in school. So can you send some money for me to buy a car?"

He said yes, but I thought, *What?* because I couldn't believe that he agreed so quickly. "You *are* doing those things, and I'm proud of you," he added. "So I'll send money for a car." During the next few days, I was so psyched up that I went to nearly every auto dealership and showroom in New Orleans. I figured Daddy would be sending between six and ten thousand dollars, which would buy a nice car, so I picked out several sporty options. But the days wore on, the check didn't come, and I had bad vibes that this was a repeat of the NMSU disappointments.

So I telephoned him again, he said the check was in the mail, and four days later the check arrived. But I was so excited about getting it that I didn't open the envelope until I reached the car dealership. And when I did, and saw that the certified check was for $150, I almost fell out.

My first thought was that Daddy was such a trusting man with bankers that, somehow, they must have cheated him and sent me an amount less than he had released. He must have intended the certified check to be for $15,000, but they put the decimal point in the wrong place. So I ran to the telephone, reached him and said, "Daddy, Daddy, guess what? Your check came in, but they messed over you, man. It's only for one hundred and fifty dollars."

"No," he said. "I sent you a hundred and fifty."

I couldn't believe my ears. "Whoa, whoa, whoa," I said. "This is not Nineteen Forty, Daddy. I can't even buy tires for that."

"Oh, yeah," he responded, "you can find a good used car,"

and then he began telling a story about one of the Rockefellers. "You see, he sent his kid off to this Ivy League school, and he gave the boy a new luxury sports sedan to drive. . . ."

I had no idea what this story had to do with my father embarrassing me. I had already told my friends that the check had arrived, and that we would be going to get a car. But here I was, looking at $150 and listening to a story about some billionaire.

"But after a few weeks," Daddy's voice droned on, "the boy's roommate's father called up Rockefeller and said, 'Ole pal, I'm pulling my son out.' This stunned Rockefeller, and he asked why. 'It's simple. My son can't compete with yours driving a car that costs more than four years of tuition. So I'm pulling my boy out.' When it came to money, Rockefeller understood, and he knew that his friend was right. So he took back the luxury car and sent the boy enough money to buy an average used car. . . ."

By that point, I was fuming. My daddy is thinking that *he* is Rockefeller and that, somehow, a $150 check is doing me a favor? So when he finished, I said, "Daddy, I understand. You made your point very well. But in today's prices, I cannot buy a car with this money."

But my father simply said, "You can do it, boy." Two days later, however, I received another certified check from him. It was for $1,500. He had been right, and I had been right: That's what the higher check represented. So I took that money and bought a used white 1974 Karman-Ghia. It was still the coolest car on campus. It lasted me the rest of my college career. And like working as a trainer with my father, this gift healed more of the wounds that had distanced us for so many years. We had learned to talk again, and to compromise.

14

The other day, I drove up to a stop sign. There was a father, a mother, and two kids in the car next to me. I thought it was raining in their car, because they all had on shower caps! I almost tripped out.

If blacks ever want respect as a people, we better start walkin' around these streets like we deserve respect and expect it. But shower caps are bad, because people don't know why we wear them, and people don't respect what they don't understand.

At least when you see a woman on the street with curlers in her hair, you know she's triflin', but you do know that she's tryin' to curl her hair. But people don't know why we wear shower caps.

So I have to explain the psychology of the shower cap. For anybody who doesn't know why, we wear shower caps to preserve the moisture in the Jheri Curl. But you know why most people don't understand that? Because they see brothers and sisters dressed up with tuxedos and evening gowns on, out in the street, but they still got the shower caps on. It's like, "When do they take the caps off? Do the caps have a religious meaning? Is there a tribe called The Shower Cap People?"

To tell you the truth, I don't know when some guys take the caps off, either. Only thing I can think, it must be on Saturday evenings about eleven-thirty or a quarter 'til twelve. The candles must be lit, and

*the moon glowing, with a slight breeze in the romantic autumn air.
And the guy's got his girl in his arms, and they're listenin' to Anita
Baker on the stereo.*

*And that must be when he looks down into his girl's eyes, and he says,
"Baby, baby, baby." Then he carefully lifts the shower cap off and says,
"The curl!"*

During the fall of 1976—my senior year at SUNO—the basketball team elected me as its captain, and that season looked
promising. As upperclassmen, we had the experience to be
competitive with opponents on our schedule, and we also had a
new coach, Cirilo Manego. So I was determined that we would
succeed. We needed a strong winning record.

I particularly needed one, because I wanted to follow up
graduation from SUNO by playing pro ball in the NBA, and I
knew that pro scouts looked first for prospects from teams with
impressive records. At the time, the best team in the city was
across town at the University of New Orleans. So several of us
teammates went to a UNO game one night to check out the
competition.

We hadn't been in the gym very long, however, when all the
way on the other side of the court I saw a woman. I looked at
her, and looked at her. It was like a dream. Meanwhile, the
crowd kept standing and cheering, but I was so focused that I
didn't hear a sound. Finally, I turned to my friends and said,
"You see that girl over there?"

While they argued over which girl I was talking about, I kept
staring at her. I was in a trance, and she was gorgeous. Tall,
dark-haired, and classy, she had a presence about her that fascinated me. She was unlike any woman that I had ever seen. On
our scale of women—from a "quarter babe" to a "total babe"—
she was what I called a "super babe." So I turned to my friends
and said, "That girl, right over there. She's going to be my
wife." But my boys thought I was crazy.

Later in the game I found out her name, where she worked
and lived, and if she had a boyfriend. It was love at first sight. But
the real test was to find out if she would feel the same way—once
Miss Laurie Guimont had the chance to get a load of me.

For the next several days, I dropped in D. H. Holmes Department Store where she worked, yet I never approached her.

I simply walked past while she worked the register in the women's clothing department. I *couldn't* speak. My mouth kept going dry. So each time I passed, I only looked, very casual like, and I loved what I saw. Laurie was a fair-skinned Creole who had an aura of goodness about her, and that convinced me that she could be the start of my real, live *Brady Bunch*.

Of course, I still had to meet her, and I was trying to figure out a cool reason to call when a terrific storm hit the Gulf Coast. I was alone in my apartment, so I telephoned Laurie. She admitted to having seen me repeatedly passing her at D. H. Holmes. I gave her a hard-luck story about me being a city boy from New York who knew nothing about hurricanes, and I asked for some pointers about what I should do. We ended up talking for eight straight hours—through the entire storm. And near dawn, I asked if she would be my girl. But in fact, God had told me that she would be my wife.

What we learned about one another, that night and in the days that followed, sealed fast the love between us. We were opposites, and that made the attraction stronger. She wasn't Jewish, but Roman Catholic. She seemed naive, but I was experienced. And she wasn't an only child. Instead, she was the eldest of seven surviving children born to Lynne Smith Guimont and Lawrence Edmund Guimont, Jr. Unlike my parents who had come from different races, religions, backgrounds, and values, and were divorced, both of her parents were Creoles, both had been raised in the same New Orleans parish, and their marriage seemed to be rock solid. And compared to the lifelong rollercoaster ride that had characterized my father's life, Laurie's father had worked for only one employer since his high school graduation: the U.S. Postal Service. And since he was supporting a family of nine, overtime work was normal for him.

But it was what I learned about Laurie herself that was most important. She was smart, headstrong, funny, temperamental, and she loved to laugh. "Growing up, I was Daddy's girl," she said. "They even named me after him. I was a tomboy, and a good athlete. And any time Daddy went to a football game, it was just assumed that he would take me and my brother." I liked the sound of that.

But I felt an unusual empathy when Laurie admitted why

this tomboy role had meant so much to her. "It was very hard for my father to open up, emotionally," she said. "I loved him so much, but he was a reserved, poetic, and intellectual man. So sports events were a way for me to get closer to him, a way for me to have a relationship with my father that was different from the ones that my sisters had with him."

Yet I was also listening as a young man truly in love, and what I heard between the lines was "You're the opposite, Drew. You're an open, gregarious, and fun-loving guy from Brooklyn. There's an easiness about you, and that's the kind of man I need."

In fact, we quickly confessed that we needed one another. I was a guy who needed to be mothered, because I still had a lot of growing up to do, and Laurie was born to that role. Her own mother was a tall, gorgeous woman whom, at the time, most people would mistake for Laurie's older sister. Lynne had a twinkle in her eyes, a kind smile, and a vibrant laugh that made me feel warm all over. But like Laurie's father, Lynne was also hardworking.

"In order to send all of us to Catholic school," Laurie recalls, "Mom worked for Shell Oil Company. That left me, as the oldest child, in charge. So every morning, I gave orders to my younger sisters, Joni and Patrice, to make sure all the little ones were washed, fed, and had clean uniforms for school. My word was law." Because of this, I later learned, the other Guimont children nicknamed Laurie "Bossy the Cow."

But being motherly too soon affected Laurie. "Sometimes I felt as though I were carrying the weight of the world on my shoulders," she recently explained to a friend. "But Drew didn't. He had the appearance of lightness and bounciness about him that was a real complement to the intensity I felt. Also, I had always been fascinated by people from other lands, races, and religions. But I was especially intrigued by Jews. I didn't know very many in New Orleans, so I thought they must be very special people. I've always felt special, too. So meeting Drew, seeing how different he was, and dying to be different, myself, I immediately fell for him."

Laurie's burden, I would discover, came from the childhood pain of losing two siblings—Gerilyn and Suzanne—who died within a year of their births. "I remember Suzanne's death in particular," she told me one night. "My sisters and I were at Aunt Esther's house. We knew that Susie was in the hospital and that our parents were very worried, but that's all. Then my parents returned from the hospital, and we could see the expressions on their faces, so we knew before my mother said, 'Susie died.' Everybody else broke down and cried, and we formed a circle and hugged one another. But I didn't cry. I was six. I was the oldest surviving child, and somehow I knew that I should not cry."

After that, her father, who had been attending SUNO to get his degree, quit school. "He felt that, in some unexplainable way, he was responsible for Suzanne's death, because he had not been with us as much as he could have," Laurie recalled. "After that, I used to practice not showing emotions—just in case anything else devastating ever happened—and like Daddy, to show others that nothing could get me down."

I understood completely. She had two scars, and I had many. Yet both of us remained sensitive people who, though adept at masking our feelings from everyone else, had chosen one another as the person with whom we would, finally, let down our guards. And that, we decided, was love. Suddenly, being a big playboy on campus didn't matter to me anymore. God had given me my wife. So once we made up our minds, I wanted to get married as soon as possible. Laurie agreed, and we set events into motion.

I rented a house on New York Street in New Orleans, though it was actually a broken-down one-bedroom shack that she and I, aided by her mother, brother, and five sisters, would have to transform into a honeymoon palace so that we could move in. Then I found an Episcopalian minister who would marry a Jewish groom and a Catholic bride, and we told our families.

When the day came, Daddy, my friend Craig Allen, and I headed for the church, but we couldn't find the place. By the time we finally reached it, Laurie and her family were furious. They had been waiting for more than an hour. What's more, once we got inside the chapel, the minister asked for the marriage license, and I realized that I had forgotten it.

"If you don't have the papers," he said, "then I can't marry you."

As if no one else were in the chapel, I turned to my father and said, "Daddy, that's not what marriage is about. Marriage is a commitment between two people. It has nothing to do with paper. . . ." The longer my spiel lasted, the more pumped up Daddy got.

To him, this marriage meant that Laurie and I would be the only legitimate members of his immediate family, and he didn't want his marital history repeated in my life. In addition, from the day that I had first phoned him about it, he had been bragging nonstop about us to his friends and associates. He particularly loved, and was proud of, Laurie. He nicknamed her "Angel."

So Daddy's mind was made up when he pulled the minister aside. Minutes passed while the two men chatted—except that my father did most of the talking. Then the minister returned to the altar and, once again, Daddy took his seat. The next thing I knew, the minister was saying, "We are gathered here today . . ." and the wedding proceeded.

It was a small ceremony, attended by my father, Laurie's parents, her brother, and her five sisters. The ceremonial party consisted of the minister, Laurie and me, my friend Craig who was the best man, and one of Laurie's friends, Haidee Morgan, the bridesmaid. And immediately afterward, we all went back to our New York Street house and signed the license before the minister had a heart attack. So the entire wedding was unorthodox, but to me, it symbolized the fact that marriage is not the signing of papers; it's the giving of selves to one another, and we were two very young people who did it our way.

In preparation for our reception, which was to be at the Guimonts' house, they had spent the earlier portion of that same day taking out the wall between their living room and dining room in order to have one large room for partying. Thus, all within a few hours, they decided upon and completed a major undertaking. But by the time guests began arriving for the reception, everything in the house was fixed, painted, in order, and beautiful. That's life in the Big Easy, and I would soon learn that's just how Laurie's parents are. They live to accommodate family and friends. In his own style, Daddy contributed too. He rented a new, sleek, black Thunderbird for Laurie and me to drive, not only that day and night, but for the remainder of our honeymoon.

"It did bother me, though, that Drew's mother wasn't there," Laurie recently told a friend. "But since then I've learned that he's a replica of Rhoda. In essence, he's that little Jewish boy who has such a rapport and such a connection with his mother, but there are also times when his early childhood memories create an inner struggle that's too much for him."

And that was true. In later years, Momma and I have resolved most of our conflicts, and I am deeply indebted to her. Our love has matured and become more accepting. But in those days, we were distant, and there was still so much bitterness between her and my father that I didn't dare to have both of them in the same place at the same time. So I thought I was avoiding trouble by inviting only him. Ironically, that proved *not* to be the case.

Before the reception, we thought Daddy had made arrangements to stay in a hotel. That's what Laurie told her parents, but that started the confusion. The problem was, because Daddy considered them "new members" of the Brown family, he expected to stay with the Guimonts. Meanwhile, once my new in-laws learned that Daddy was staying in a hotel, they became upset. It's a southern reaction. For them, hospitality is an unbreakable commandment. As a result, the stage was set for conflict before the play ever began.

During the reception, I got my first glimpse of how proud and festive and devoted Creoles are as a people. Over the centuries, they have maintained their specialness and distinctive culture by adhering as strictly to Creole traditions as they do to Catholicism. When they party, for example, Creoles dance from the heart—doing unique dances like New Orleans' famed Second Line with as much chutzpah as Jews do the hora. But an equally enduring tradition is membership in a social club, and Creoles maintain as much secrecy about these organizations as they do about the succulent ingredients that give their hot sausage and gumbos such marvelous flavors.

At our reception, then, virtually everyone was linked to the social clubs to which Laurie's parents belonged. "Mother's club is for women, and it's called The Gay Twenties," Laurie had informed me ahead of time, "and my father's club, the Bonjondou, is for men." Each organization, she explained, limits its membership to twelve persons who have basically socialized together throughout their adult lives.

"It's like an extended family," Laurie said. "As children, we couldn't belong to our parents' clubs, but both clubs held several functions each year—such as dances and picnics—to which their families were invited. So these people are like aunts and uncles and cousins to me."

Over centuries, and not unlike Jews, Creoles had avoided persecution by segregating themselves. Creoles socialized exclusively with Creoles, and they only married Creoles. Thus, these clubs sprang up—at first, under the auspices of Roman Catholic parishes—to perpetuate that segregation and self-protection.

"But because of the Black Power movement, color distinction started dismantling when my generation came of age," Laurie emphasized. "I treasure my ancestral history, but I've never really fit into that 'Creoles only' mentality." And our wedding was proof enough of that. She and her family remained solidly devoted to their culture, but they had clearly abandoned its discriminatory traditions, because all of them accepted, with love and open arms, this black Jew into their family.

After the reception, Laurie and I left for a honeymoon at our New York Street home. But at 3 A.M., loud knocks at our door startled us. And when I opened it, there stood my father and Craig Allen.

"They won't let me stay at their house," Daddy babbled, and I had never see him so hurt. It was evident that he had been drinking heavily. But even that didn't lessen the fact that someone had hurt my father, and now, I was incensed. So I put him on the couch, then dressed and drove back to my in-laws' house. And by the time I reached the Guimonts', I was so enraged that, once inside, I started screaming and ramming my fist through the walls that, just hours before, had been freshly painted on my account.

"*Why* did you do that to my father? How *could* you?" I yelled repeatedly. "Just tell me why he can't stay here. . . ."

To their credit, my in-laws made no excuses. Instead, they tried to calm me, and Mr. Guimont agreed to follow me in his car, go to our New York Street house, apologize to my father, and then bring Daddy back with him.

The next day, however, I learned what had triggered the incident. "After Drew and I left the reception, my parents and Bundini remained in the 'new' room and continued partying with the guests," Laurie recalls. "But then Bundini got plastered, and when he was drunk, he had a terrible disposition. He turned on some of the women in Mother's club. He pestered one of them in particular and kept calling her an 'ugly bitch.' Well, these verbal assaults persisted until Mother said, 'Don't you think it's time, Mister Brown, to go to your hotel?' But when Bundini didn't respond, she asked Craig to take him out."

Daddy would never discuss the incident, so I don't know what he was thinking. I can only assume that the differences that had drawn Laurie and me together somehow ignited my father against the sedate guests in the Guimonts' house that night. Or maybe it was just the mixture of booze and loneliness, because these Creoles had such secure and caring lives, while Daddy had known anything but that.

Whatever his motivations, though, Daddy and Craig left, then partied on Bourbon Street, and finally ended up at our honeymoon cottage. "The next day, I still knew none of this," Laurie recalls. "So when I got to my parents' house, I was shocked to discover that both my new father-in-law and my new husband had, the night before, made separate scenes in front of my family. It was humiliating, and I couldn't believe how my marriage was starting off."

And that scene still haunts me. I showed my new in-laws a very ugly side of a Drew. I was ashamed of my actions, but I promised myself that I would make it up to them by loving and taking care of their daughter in the royal fashion that she deserves.

In the midst of all this, I kept going to class and playing basketball. But this season, I played with the fear that Coach

Manego would pull me out of the game. The rub was, he had little confidence in my abilities, and I usually got into foul trouble, so I feared the sound of gametime buzzers, because I always expected the coach to point to me and say, "Drew, you're on the bench!"

In addition, the coach and I didn't get along. He didn't play me often enough, and I didn't play up to my capabilities. But overall, I just wasn't motivated. Then my father returned to New Orleans for the SUNO-Dillard game. He had rented a private jet to fly him into Lakefront Airport, and all the way home, he kept saying how proud he was of me and emphasizing that he had rented this jet just so he could see me play.

Talk about pressure. I didn't dare to explain that Coach Manego might not even start me. But at the game, when the coach learned that *the* Bundini was in the crowd, I started, and the game became a tension-filled contest. At the time, Dillard had an 11-10 record, compared to the dismal 4-13 record that had mounted against us through that year. Plus, even though SUNO and Dillard were longtime crosstown rivals in New Orleans, SUNO had *never* beaten Dillard.

That night, however, we came close. It was as though something came over me during the game. For the first time, I could care less about Coach Manego. All I cared about was playing well for my father. And I did. I made and blocked shots that were amazing. I scored thirty-six points and played the best game of my career. It was as if I couldn't miss—couldn't, that is, until the last ten seconds of the game.

We were down by a point when a teammate fired a pass to me. I dribbled to the top of the key and took a thirty-five-foot jumper. It angled straight toward the basket, and I just knew it was going in. I could feel my daddy's excitement that *his* son was going to sink the winning shot of the game. But the ball spun in and back out of the rim, and Dillard's Billy Ray Hobley got the rebound, giving his team possession. Then they scored a field goal and a foul shot before the final buzzer.

We lost, 107–103, and I failed to become a hero. Yet when I spotted my father, Laurie, and her brother and sisters in the stands, they were all elated. They saw past the loss to the effort that I had put forth, and they couldn't be prouder. I was their hero. On the other hand, Coach Manego's face looked like a ripe melon. He had never believed that I had any talent. So I walked over to him and said, "I told you so."

My SUNO years ended with me garnering *cum laude* distinction in academics, and my third Scholastic Athlete of the Year award from the university. I earned a bachelor's degree in business administration with a minor in economics. But the real prize that I had been hoping for didn't come my way. I was not drafted by an NBA team. A few weeks later, I learned that Daddy had made calls to the Boston Celtics and the New York Knicks, attempting behind the scenes to get NBA tryouts for me. But I didn't want my chance to play in the pros to come because of who he was. I wanted to be chosen on the basis of my abilities, or not at all. So I telephoned him and asked that he stop.

Two days later, however, I received an invitation from the Harlem Globetrotters to come to their summer tryout camp, and I was elated. Finally, this was *my* ticket! I was certain of it, because this opportunity had come to me strictly on the basis of what I had accomplished during my college years. And more specifically, the Dillard game had been a key factor, because a Globetrotter scout at that game had been impressed with both me and my opponent, Billy Ray Hobley. As a result, *both* of us got tryout invitations.

So for the next few months, I worked harder to get in shape than I had ever worked for anything. I practiced and trained, morning, noon, and night, until I was in the best possible physical condition. And I really concentrated on making trick shots—half-court shots, spinning the ball on my finger and then punching it into the basket—the kind of stuff that was proven Globetrotter magic.

Then in June, Billy Ray and I flew to Arizona for the tryout camp, and as in the SUNO-Dillard game, I felt as if I could do no wrong. During my very first practice in front of the Globetrotter coaches, I broke away on a fast break, Billy Ray fired the ball downcourt to me, and since I was solidly positioned under the basket, I had several seconds to act. Dunking the ball would have been the fastest move, but that was too predictable. So I spun the ball on my finger, then punched it up to hit the glass backboard. But it didn't drop. Instead, the ball went straight up, hovered like a spaceship, and then swished into the basket. Nobody could believe that I would risk such a wacky shot at tryouts camp—much less my *first* shot—but that choice made me an immediate star.

From that point on, Billy Ray and I stuck together, and day after day, we excelled. Then one day, I was standing on the half-court line, and for a kick, I started shooting underhanded shots. But after I made the first one, all of a sudden, Meadowlark Lemon ran over. He's the legendary star of the Globetrotters, but he had a frustrated look in his eyes as he said, "Do that again. Do that again."

I was shocked. I thought that he would be delighted to see that one of his potential recruits could do a standard Globetrotter trick, but he wasn't. In fact, he was angry, and that shook me. I tried the same shot about three or four more times, while Meadowlark hovered beside me. With each effort, I did come closer, but I missed them all. Finally, he walked away without saying another word.

That night, however, one of the Globetrotter team members cautioned me, "Stop clowning, Drew. You should start playing *straight* basketball. That's what they want to see in tryouts." So I took the veteran's advice, and the rest of our practices went well.

Then cut time came, and when I went to the board, my name wasn't on it. The next day, they posted final cuts, and by that time I had already played in a couple of scrimmages, and had been funny with the kids and had a good game, as if I were already a Harlem Globetrotter. So when the final cuts were posted, and my name still wasn't on the board, I wasn't surprised. I had been conceived above Sugar Ray's in Harlem. My childhood had been spent just out of camera range for photographers from *Time* and *Sports Illustrated*. In short, I was born to be a Harlem Globetrotter.

I ran to a telephone and told Laurie, "Guess what, guess what? I did it! Our dreams have come true!" And she was so excited that she kept saying, "I knew you could. I knew it."

Two days later, however, I was having lunch in a restaurant with the team and just being one of the guys when Meadowlark and Marcus Haynes came over. Meadowlark asked that I talk to them outside, and being the kind of person I am, I thought they wanted me to be the team's new star, or at least to inquire about the terms of my contract.

But once we got outside, Meadowlark said, "I'm sorry, Drew, but we're going to have to ask you to go home."

Stunned and disbelieving, I said, "What do you mean?"

Meadowlark looked me in the eye and explained that he had been playing this game for twenty years—going back to the days of segregation in America when he had to stay in hotels that were fifty or more miles away from the game sites. But this season was the first time that he expected to make any real money. The team was finally gaining respect and more bookings than it could fulfill. Then he said, "So I can't have a young kid like you, whose famous father trains Muhammad Ali, come and take away my glory."

All I could say was "I don't understand. . . ." Later, though, I learned that both Ali and my father had made phone calls to Meadowlark and had asked the Globetrotters' star to "look after Buddy Drew" and to make certain that I was "taken care of." They thought they were helping. But Meadowlark thought they were interfering at best, and at worst, threatening.

So the combination of their calls and my trick playing got me kicked off the Harlem Globetrotters, two days after I became a member. And the worst part was, I couldn't tell the story. Except for Laurie who loved me, and Billy Ray—who knew the truth (and still remains on the team) but could not jeopardize his job for my ego—nobody would believe that I had been cut under such unusual circumstances.

To me, though, it was just like my earlier disappointments in Israel and New Mexico. But this time, I had not failed because I wasn't good enough. This time, I got cut because I was too good. It wasn't fair, and I knew it. The loss certainly convinced me that real life isn't fair. But it also made me finally understand the power that, by then, Ali and my father were wielding in the sports world.

So while I rebounded from my Globetrotters' rejection by accepting a nine-to-five job at WGNO, an independent television station in New Orleans, I kept pondering. WGNO had hired me to sell advertising, and throughout the rest of 1977 I did that, working hard as a concrete-pounding, cold-call-hustling salesman. I went from storefront to storefront along the streets of the Big Easy, and I got good at selling TV spots. But I wanted more out of life. So I made a deliberate choice, and before the year ended, I entered my father's world.

PART FOUR: Minus Drugs

15

You see, if you don't make it in this country, it ain't my fault. It's your fault. If you don't make it, it's nobody else's fault but yours. I never want to have you blame it on your color. You'll have to blame it on your intelligence.

I'm sorry, but people have been lying to you kids for a long time, and I'm gonna apologize for the adults in this country. Because, you see, when you were born, you knew what I'm about to tell you. You all used to know this.

There is no black and white. There's only ignorance and intelligence. And when your butt gets scared enough, you will always follow intelligence. There is no black and white.

If black and white were so important, blind people would be prejudiced. And if black and white were so important, then handicapped or mentally retarded children would know the difference. But they don't. Black and white have never once crossed their minds. Never!

So you better wake up and tell me who's really blind, handicapped, or mentally retarded in this country, 'cause it's not those kids. They know that there is no black or white. They know that there's only ignorance and intelligence. . . .

Prejudice is a human trait. It has nothing to do with color. Hitler only killed white people. He was white. Idi Amin only killed black *people. He was black. Prejudice simply means you don't like yourself, so you have to put someone else down—because of how they look, feel, or act—in order to make yourself look better. Look in the mirror. If you have any of that garbage in your body, the truth is, you really don't like yourself. . . .*

I focused more on my father and his world because, by August 1977, I had also become a father. Our first child was a beautiful little girl whom we named Taryn Christine Brown. She was bright-eyed and so helpless as an infant that, after I held her for the first time, I no longer felt like the same man. It was as if my experiencing her birth (my first true miracle) had somehow caused a *new* me to come forth as well. My baby girl had not asked to come into this world, and I knew that. So I felt an extraordinary responsibility to secure her place in it, and at the time, the only security I envisioned was financial.

During the final months of that year, then, I began negotiating with a Texas-based firm to produce souvenir programs for championship boxing matches. The idea was a natural, and I was certain that Daddy's influence could help me launch it with promoters and others in the fight game because, at the time, no one outside of New York City consistently produced full-color, quality magazines for the boxing matches that were held elsewhere in America. Occasionally, major events might have a hastily prepared program, but most fights either had none or, at best, a simple brochure-type publication.

Well, the Texas firm liked the idea, offered me $350 per week to start, and agreed to name me as its sales and sports director. Since the money was far more than WGNO was paying, I moved Laurie and Taryn to Richardson, a community near our firm's Dallas headquarters. However, my functional office was to be in Las Vegas, where most championship boxing matches were then being held.

Las Vegas is a city of stars and hustlers, and on my arrival I felt that pressure as soon as I got off the plane. Slot machines lined the walls of the airport, and limousines were everywhere. It was a real star-studded place that got my hormones and body cells bubbling before I ever reached the hotel.

By arrangement, my office and accommodations were at the

infamous Caesars Palace. Major boxing matches were held either there or in the Las Vegas Hilton, and the top fight people usually hung out in that vicinity's lavish bars, restaurants, and casinos. In addition, the Palace offered "RFB status" to me because, like the Texas firm, the hotel's management was enthusiastic about my idea to enhance the quality of fight publications.

RFB meant that I could charge my room, food, and beverages to the house. My luxury suite featured a round bed underneath a ceiling mirror. Each morning, I could roll out into a huge, bedside Jacuzzi. Room service was available twenty-four hours a day, or I could be served at any of the Palace's restaurants or bars by simply signing the check. So here I was, twenty-three years old, living in Vegas like a millionaire, and I didn't have to spend a dollar of my own—meaning that most of my salary would go directly to Laurie in Texas.

My first magazine was for the January 1978 Undisputed World Lightweight Championship bout at the Palace, between Roberto Duran of Panama and Puerto Rico's Esteban DeJesus. In preparation, I sold ads door to door in Las Vegas, just as I had learned to do in New Orleans. And after busting my butt working a few weeks, we produced a sixteen-page publication that was half information, half advertising. It sold very well at the event, and coupled with the ad revenue, it was profitable. But to accomplish this, I also ventured into the backroom realms of boxing—the shadowy part of my father's world that I had not known, and was not prepared for.

Everybody in boxing has an angle, a gimmick. One promoter gives fifty dollars to a guy to start a rumor. Another promoter counters that with a hundred dollars and a different rumor to the same guy-become-mouthpiece. Or a veteran pimp with a lot of money and a lot of girls will offer their services free of charge to young boxers, just to be near the limelight. Or a down-and-out hustler will beg for jobs, just to carry luggage or run errands or hand out autographed pictures for the famous hotel guests, because everybody in Vegas knows that glitter is the only ticket to ride.

It wasn't that I was naive about boxing circles. In fact, Daddy used to tell me, "Put a bunch of crabs in a bucket, son, and then watch. As soon as one crab tries to get out and become free, the other crabs in the bucket will always pull the escaping one back down." And boxing, he warned, suffered heavily from this "bucket-crab syndrome." Yet his advice to me was "Remember the Circle Theory. Never talk about the promoters and the other fight people. Let them be, and they'll leave you alone, too."

So I plunged into this realm with the solid belief that I could succeed within it, while remaining immune to its drawbacks. I was, after all, the son of a prince in the boxing world, and the word quickly spread around Vegas, "Don't mess with Bundini's boy."

In time, my immunity would prove to be more imagined than real, but Laurie worried about that from the start. She resented my leaving her and our infant daughter behind in Texas, but even more, she feared what working in Nevada might do to me. Her staunchly moralistic and Catholic background made her look upon Las Vegas as a fun place to visit, but no place for a husband and father to live and work.

Laurie also understood—better than I did at the time—that I had a lot of unfinished business to deal with, personally. "Drew thinks he bears great shame, as far as his background is concerned," she confided to one of our Texas neighbors. "So he does what he does because of what he came from. To everyone else, he acts as though he had the greatest childhood in the world. But sometimes the truth just gets the best of him. That's when all the pain comes out, and I do mean all the pain. Yet that anguish also motivates him. It's the primary reason Drew holds so dearly to the goals that he wants for our family. It's as if, since the day we got married, he has been trying to fix everything that went wrong in his childhood and mine. This move to Texas, for example, is his way of getting the family away from the crowdedness of city life and into the wide-open spaces. Since he grew up in the projects of New York City, he has always wanted *space*. So he thinks that by giving us a harlequin Great Dane, a Volkswagen van, and a suburban house with a big backyard, then everything at home will be okay—no matter what he endures to make it all possible."

*   *   *

Early in 1978, though, I was more interested in new gain than in old pain, and for good reason. Ali had given our company the rights to produce a fight magazine for his February bout in Vegas against Leon Spinks, a twenty-four-year-old contender with only six professional fights to his credit. So all the odds were on Ali. But anytime the Champ entered a ring, the fight was still major—meaning that our magazine could be a real moneymaker.

Meanwhile, Herbert Muhammad (the nephew of Black Muslim leader Elijah Muhammad) also took a hard look at anticipated profit margins for the Ali enterprises that Herbert managed, and a few days later, I got a call from my father. He was very upset and hurt.

"They want to cut the budget," Daddy said. "They aren't going to ask us to come in until *five* days before the fight."

At the time, the "us" was Ali's veteran training staff that included my father, boxing analyst and trainer Angelo Dundee, assistant trainer Wali "Blood" Muhammad, security chief Pat Patterson, masseur Luis Sarria, technical advisor Gene Kilroy, and Lana Shabazz, the cook. Prior to all of the Champ's earlier fights, these seven people had worked for months with various part-time workers and sparring partners to get Ali into shape. This time, however, Herbert had talked Ali into deciding that five days would be sufficient.

According to my father, Herbert thought the Champ had nothing to fear from Spinks, so why spend the usual amount for preparation time and staff? But Herbert was really trying to pull Ali away from these people who, in the past, had given the Champ strength and advice. That way, if Ali could win without the entourage, then Herbert Muhammad would not only increase profits, but he and the other Muslims would subsequently have Ali all to themselves.

But my father's hurt went deeper. "I'm with Ali because God sent me," he said. Then with a mixture of anger and prophecy in his voice, Daddy suddenly concocted a classic Bundini parable. "The Champ *knows* I'm the nutmeg that makes the cake special," he said. "But the *man* doesn't believe that. So let the big man find flour and sugar and water on his own, but unless he's got the nutmeg, he won't have the cake."

*   *   *

When the entourage finally arrived in Vegas, I just knew that my father would make a scene at Caesars Palace. But he didn't. Instead, he went straight to work, though I could tell that he had a certain distaste about how the prefight situation was being handled, because he spent more than normal time with his souvenir operations and less at Ali's workouts.

The souvenir business was my father's bonus. He never signed contracts with Ali and earned whatever the Champ wanted to give after each fight. But he owned the slogan "Float like a butterfly, sting like a bee . . ." and their verbal agreements also gave Daddy the exclusive rights to sell Muhammad Ali T-shirts, memorabilia, and souvenirs at most event sites, and the arrangement had worked smoothly for years.

Three days before the Ali-Spinks fight, however, Daddy and I were at the entrance to the Las Vegas Hilton when Herbert Muhammad and two lawyers walked up. The three wore fine business suits, and one carried a leather briefcase from which he produced several documents as soon as my father said hello.

"Here's the contract that we agreed upon," Herbert said abruptly. Daddy, it seems, had agreed to sign a contract that waived his legal claim to "Float like a butterfly, sting like a bee" for one fight. This would enable Ali's management to produce and sell all the Champ's paraphernalia, and in return, they were to pay my father twenty-five thousand dollars for that one-fight waiver.

It sounded like a good deal. But Daddy seemed to want to prove something to these men, so he took the contracts and handed them to me. "I want my son to read it," he said and grinned. "He graduated college."

I didn't want to. I knew nothing about contracts. Yet I could see that this mattered to him, so I did. And as I began reading, I felt an uneasy aura surround all five of us. Then I realized, based on what I was reading, that this contract would take "Float like a butterfly, sting like a bee" away from my father forever. It was all in black and white, and since they knew he couldn't read, I assume they thought he would simply sign and that would be it.

Yet I couldn't believe that they were doing this, so I just said it aloud: "Daddy, they're trying to rip you off. If you sign this, they'll take the rights away from you forever."

He looked at me, then he looked at them, and the three men protested at once. "I didn't know that was in there," one said. "Hey, Bundini, it's news to me," said another. And the third one said nervously, "It must be a mistake. We told them to say 'one fight.' "

My father ripped up the documents and threw the pieces in Herbert's face. But instead of unleashing more anger, his honesty and truth stopped them cold when he said, "I don't have to take care of you. Shorty will take care of you all, one day." Then he walked away.

Later that afternoon, Daddy told Ali what had happened, but the Champ didn't seem to understand my father's concern. So Daddy warned, "If they're doing this to me, just imagine what they're doing to you." And three days later, Muhammad Ali would find out for himself.

For the first three or four rounds of the Ali-Spinks bout, the Champ fought well but he tired quickly. He wasn't in shape. Yet he seemed to believe that, since he had such a good start, he could simply outlast Spinks, even though the contender was twelve years younger than Ali.

Fight judges always pick up their pens during the last ten seconds of each round, so my father used to yell, "Close the show," and that always cued Ali to make a good finish. Usually, the plan worked, and the Champ won most of those rounds. But not this time. Spinks had the stamina that Ali lacked, and by the last four rounds, the Champ was weary. Spinks won all of those rounds and the fight itself. As a result, boxing tradition was shattered. For the first time in forty-three years, a reigning champion lost by a judges' decision.[1]

My father was devastated that Ali lost, but I could also see a certain gleam in Daddy's eyes. "You can't beat Shorty," he mumbled as we walked back to the locker room. But he said nothing to the Champ. He felt sorry for Ali, because Herbert Muhammad and his management staff had done something to the Greatest that even Ali's opponents in the ring had been unable to do. They had attempted to defy fate, but Shorty stopped them. "If you don't run the miles, you can't wear the smiles," Daddy always said, and this tragic loss proved it.

*   *   *

Being around all the wealth in Vegas, but not having it myself, I became totally consumed by money, and making money. By selling ads, I did honest work, got a reasonable salary, and enjoyed excellent perks. But drugs, sex, and new talent were the real currency in that marketplace, and I thought no legitimate endeavor could compete, financially, with the Big Three. So even though I figured my job was cool, my magazines were small potatoes to the fight people. In fact, most made it clear that they didn't have time for me, and that was frustrating, because I was pumped up to succeed.

But after our Ali-Spinks program proved to be successful and impressive, Daddy and Ali introduced me around during their time in Vegas. And suddenly, all the fight people started changing their attitudes, as if befriending me could get them closer to the Champ. So when I next called or dropped by their offices, they treated me with deference, asking why I hadn't called sooner—when, in fact, I had been trying for months to get through to them.

Soon, it became clear that, for most fight people, the real devotion was not to boxers themselves and certainly not to the quality of any given promotion, but to the bottom-line dollar. So I immediately abandoned my New Orleans approach—a superpolite, half-apologetic manner of approaching clients with lines like "I hope I'm not getting you at a bad time." Instead, I turned the tables and acted as though the client was privileged to get a couple of minutes with me. To my delight, it worked. Vegas types, I began to realize, only want to do business with busy and important people. If you feel and act like a little guy, they treat you like one, and you get zip.

For clients, I targeted everybody and usually started with the telephone book. Anybody whose picture appeared in the yellow pages was prime, because they obviously enjoyed self-promotion and had huge egos. A similar approach was to visit clients' offices and look at the family photos on display. If a guy had pictures of his attractive daughters or grandchildren, I sold him, not an ad, but a golden opportunity to get that picture in the hands of all the celebrities, sportscasters, and media people who would get our magazines at the next event. That rarely failed. I also went to suppliers for the major hotels and fight events, and if they said no, I would respond, "That's fine. Just tell me how to spell your name. You see, I have to turn in a list of people who don't want to sponsor this event. It's just a quirk that [Insert the name of a hotel promoter] has. He keeps track of such stuff. . . ."

In addition to door-to-door sales, I also went after national accounts like Budweiser and Nike, though our home office in Texas was skeptical. But I knew that—as in life itself—If you want something, you have to ask. So I told my boss, "If they don't want calls, they'd have their phones taken out," and I persisted. Soon, I landed regular ads from a number of national accounts, just because I had the audacity to ask.

While I was enjoying some success and living RFB at the Palace, Laurie was becoming more dissatisfied with each passing month. "I'm clipping coupons, turning off lights to keep down the bills, and watching every penny," she complained during one of a series of phone calls. "I'm living as modestly and as cheaply as I can, Drew. I don't buy any new clothes. Taryn and I eat Rice-A-Roni and Hamburger Helper. . . ."

I tried to explain that what I spent wasn't our money. It was expense-account funds. But she remained unconvinced, and I vaguely understood at the time that money wasn't the real issue. Between my salary and what she earned as the business manager of a dentist's office, she had enough funds on hand. The real problem was that I wasn't coming to Texas. I was staying in Vegas, months at a stretch.

"Things got so tough, but I still wouldn't talk to anybody about my problems," Laurie recalls. "I had this huge mirror in the kitchen, and I'd stand there and cry with large tears streaming down my face, and I'd say, 'Don't you dare let him get you. Don't you do it. Don't you let him break you.' And that's how I kept myself going."

But I didn't know because I wasn't home enough to know. And my excuse—which I solidly believed as well—was "Look, honey. I'm putting out three or four magazines a month, and this is a dog-eat-dog town. If I travel back and forth, we'll have even *less* money. I'll have less time to sell, and we won't make it."

During my first six months in Vegas, I was telling Laurie the truth. But once I got settled in the job, everything got easier.

My clients began buying ads on a regular basis, so the magazines filled up faster. My life fell into a routine.

However, my routine was not an average one. Work in Las Vegas is a party, and partying is work. Alcohol was such a normal tool of my business that I considered it no more harmful than the telephone, and charging three-hundred-dollar bottles of champagne or two-hundred-dollar meals to RFB became so easy that extravagance lost its effect. Soon, even time became meaningless. A Sunday was no different from a Wednesday, because Las Vegas is buzzing twenty-four hours a day, 365 days a year.

It's no coincidence, by the way, that there are no clocks on any wall in the casinos, because Vegas is a Disneyland for adults. They must rely on the sense of timeless euphoria that enhances gambling among the players on their glittering floors.

At first, I started gambling a few dollars at a shot, mainly to combat boredom. But I started getting good, and was gambling with people who had lots of money to throw away. They tossed hundred-dollar and five-hundred-dollar and thousand-dollar chips at a turn—the equivalent of my entire month's salary—and yet those chips had no meaning for them. After a couple of drinks, I felt just as special as anybody else. So instead of sticking with the five- or ten- or twenty-dollar bets that I could afford, I threw down hundred-dollar chips, too.

Then one weekend, Laurie came to Vegas for a visit. We hit the casinos, and she played the slot machines and won. But seeing her win made me hungry for the real thing, so I excused myself and went alone to break the house bank.

"I thought you were probably seeing somebody about business," she recalls. "But after several hours, I got worried. So I went back to our room, and there you were, sprawled across the bed, and crying like a baby."

After about fifteen minutes, I finally admitted, "You can't say anything to me, Laurie. I know it was wrong. But I took some money from the fight. I gambled . . . and I lost."

Horror splashed across her face as she asked, "How much was it, Drew?"

"Thirty-five hundred dollars."

"Jesus," she cried, "*how* much?"

"All the proceeds from the fight. Everything."

While she kept screaming, "What the hell did you do?" I rambled, "I just knew that I could double it. You know, make some money for us. Ease things for you back home. I just knew I could. Baby, I was hot. And you know I would have given the original proceeds back. . . ."

Finally, she stopped me. The joy that always seems to be in her expression had vanished, and her voice was cool, almost indifferent as she said, "Where is your head, Drew? My God, what are you becoming?"

Dreams

Dreams make us live for a better life.
For those who strive toward their dreams, reality is not far away.
For those who don't, dreams are fantasies.
Dreams are made from wants and talents we possess. . . .
Reality and dreams are only separated by hard work. . . .
Dreams and fantasies are divided by pessimism. . . .
If you don't dream, you cease to exist.
So wake up and dream, and may all your dreams come true. . . .[2]

16

And if you really want to get deep, there's never been a great religious book with God's name in it—whether the Torah or the Old Testament or the New Testament or the Koran, the Buddhist or the Hindu books— there's never been a book of God written that's ever spoken about people being black or white. There is no black or white.

Yet I'm not going to lie to you. There is racism in this country. But you know what? The best thing that ever happened to some of you is that some people are prejudiced against you. Because if somebody stops you from becoming a doctor 'cause you're black or white or Jewish or poor or whatever, then you'll have to work twice as hard to be that doctor. And if you work twice as hard, in the end, you will be twice the doctor.

They can't stop you. Ignorance versus intelligence—You see?—so I don't want to hear your funky excuses. "I'm black." "I'm white." "I'm from Mississippi." I don't ever want to hear that. I come from New York. I am all of you, and if you don't make it, then you better look in the mirror, because there will be only one reason: You. . . .

In the following months, I rarely called home. By replacing what I had lost, we were broke. My salary still went to Laurie, and for my own survival, I learned how to barter in Vegas. One client would give me the use of a car, another some clothes, and in return I gave their ads better placement in the magazines or allowed them some other promotional benefit. Otherwise, I kept up appearances, since the worst that could happen to me in Vegas was for the word to get around that Drew T. Brown III had hit rock bottom.

Because Laurie and I weren't communicating, I didn't know how miserable she was. I couldn't see past my troubles to consider hers. Recently, however, she recounted how she felt during those months. "It was clear that your life was in Vegas, and not with us in Texas. I really thought that you had gone off and wouldn't be coming back. And it had gotten to the point that if you came back, I didn't even know if I wanted you anymore. Because the guy I married would not have chosen the Vegas life over us."

So Laurie hated the strain on our marriage, but even more, she saw that I was becoming just like the sleazy types with whom I was doing business. Today, with the perspective of time, I know she was right. But I couldn't see it then. Somehow, I had forgotten how, years earlier, I had called out in vain for Daddy, only to have him simply send money to me or to Bubba, as if that would right his wrongs. But at the time, I couldn't see that I was now doing the same things.

The climax of this period came as I began work on the publication for Ali's "Third Comeback." If he beat Spinks in this return bout and regained the championship title, Ali would become the first heavyweight ever to win it three times.[1] So the Champ had shattered boxing history by his loss to Spinks in February, but Ali now had a chance to get a new world record in the September rematch.

That prospect made this comeback highly promotable, and I viewed it as a godsend. We had handled the February program so well that Ali showed no hesitation in granting me the rights to do the September event, too. And this time, the fight was to be in New Orleans. For me, it was a perfect arrangement. I knew the Big Easy. I knew Ali. The only question seemed to be, how big a magazine could we produce before the costs became prohibitive—because I knew that we would sell this one with ease.

But unknown to me, there *was* another question. Ali's management sold the rights for the "Third Comeback" to Louisiana Sports, Inc., a New Orleans–based firm. They paid three million dollars for the fight's overall promotion, and their contract reportedly included "the right to sell and market, worldwide, and without limitation, programs and other souvenirs relating to and pertaining to the event."[2]

Meanwhile, I was in New Orleans, operating on Ali's word, and selling ads like crazy. I never once considered getting the Champ's permission in writing. My daddy had never needed it, we didn't need it for the first Ali-Spinks fight, and everything had gone smoothly. Why would this be any different?

A month before the fight, we completed production on a seventy-four-page magazine. The first printing was twenty-thousand copies. Its full-color cover featured a LeRoy Neiman painting (that he had given to me) of Ali and Spinks from the last fight, and we immediately got the edition into the city's drugstores, supermarkets, and newsstands. But that same week, LSI officials contacted me and said, "Hey, you can't do this book unless you give us twenty-five thousand dollars."

I didn't know what they were talking about, so I told them, "Wrong answer. I'm doing the book anyway, 'cause Ali told me I could."

In response, they filed suit in federal court, seeking to prevent the magazine's distribution in New Orleans prior to the fight. And they subcontracted the official fight program to a New York firm.[3]

When the story hit the *Times-Picayune,* Daddy stormed into Ali's suite and intervened. "These people ain't suin' my boy for nothin'," my father said. "He started this a long time ago, back when nobody else was interested in it, and nobody else was doing it. But now that it's hot, here they come, tryin' to rip my son off for twenty-five grand."

However, what neither of us could see was that, as first evidenced in Daddy's own contract dispute back at Vegas in February, Ali's management was rapidly changing business as usual. Verbal agreements—the backbone of the fight game for decades—were being sidelined in deference to teams of lawyers and stacks of contracts. And with us on one side, while his management was legally bound to the other, Ali was caught in the middle.

In reaction, the Champ sided with LSI. His statements and mine contradicted one another,[4] and the whole affair resulted in hurts that affected me for a long time. A few days later, attorneys for both sides negotiated a settlement that allowed us to proceed with our publication. We just couldn't sell it in the Superdome. So LSI won and lost. They kept control of the official program at the fight, but they couldn't put us out of business in New Orleans.

Minutes before the actual fight began in the Superdome, Daddy and Ali were in one corner and the lonely-looking Spinks was across the ring in his. Suddenly, my father reached around the Champ's left shoulder and held up two fingers. The gesture looked like a peace sign or a prediction of victory, but it was neither. It simply meant: *This time, Leon, you can't beat* both *of us.*

In an eerie way, this gesture was a silent echo of what Spinks's manager, George Benton, had warned a few days earlier. "I've said this many times before about Ali," he commented about the same time that Spinks had dropped out of training and disappeared into the seedy bars of New Orleans. "Liston. Foreman. Frazier. The draft thing. Ali always comes up on his feet. It's like there's some mystical force guiding his life, making him not like other men. When I think of that . . . it's scary."[5]

Nutmeg in the cake. The two-fingered gesture. The same message seemed to surround the Superdome that night. Then through fifteen merciless rounds, Ali beat that message into Spinks's body. It was a masterful demonstration of boxing skills, and because of them, the Champ became the undisputed world heavyweight champion for a historic third time.[6]

Afterward, my father leaned over to me and whispered, "Everyone sees, but only a few know. Everyone sees the glitter and glamor of winning a championship, or anything else in life. But only a few know what it really takes to make a champ, or to be successful."

I nodded silently, as if to say that I understood how his wise words applied to boxing. But I didn't realize, that night, how many years it would take before I discovered their real meaning for my own life.

In the months that followed, it became apparent that LSI's legal battle with our Texas firm had more lasting effects than we had anticipated. After they succeeded in keeping our magazines out of the Superdome, other fight promoters like Don King and Bob Arum became interested in the percentages that they could get from our publications. And if we didn't cut them in, they threatened to repeat LSI's maneuver and bar our magazines from other boxing events.

But we didn't make enough profits on the magazines to start buying rights or cutting others in, so we found ourselves boxed in a corner. Fortunately, this dilemma did not immediately shut us down, but it did make everything much harder—including my job.

During the next few months, I began feeling as though I were viewing everything in Vegas through new eyeglasses. The glitter had gone dull. I noticed dirt in the rugs at the casinos and the Palace, and smudges on all of their mirrors. And the only happy people in sight were those who were in Vegas for just two or three days.

Also, circumstances had stymied my progress. Since, like my father, I had refused to sign contracts with the Texas firm, I had no pull with them. They had the business's financial backing and its connections with printers and distributors. All I had were contacts in the fight game, and that was precisely where our strength was eroding.

Depressed and without options, I devoted more and more expense-account lunches to the beverages instead of the food. I drank booze for courage and consolation. And I began confusing clients with pals.

One night, I was hanging out with a client whom I considered a close friend. We went to his house, and while I drank, he started cooking up, and smoking, crack cocaine.

With a bottle in my hand, I warned him that when you smoke crack, all you live for is the next high. "Because the first one is a ten-second high," I said. "And after that, the only thing you want is another hit off the pipe to duplicate the first one. But it never happens. You just start chasing the high. You lose control."

When I finished my comment, he laughed at me. But soon, all of his based cocaine was gone, so my friend said, "I don't have money. Lend me fifty dollars." And seeing that he was doped up and wired, I gave him the fifty and he left.

In about fifteen minutes, he returned with more cocaine. Again, he cooked it and smoked it, but by then, I was getting antsy.

"You got fifty more?" my friend asked.

"Yeah," I said, "but I'm not giving it to you. I want to go out."

"I'm serious, man. I *need* fifty bills."

"I'm serious, too," I said, "and I'm sliding."

At that, this guy—who wasn't as big as I am—grabbed my arm, pulled me and said, "Well, then, I'll kill you. Because until I get fifty dollars, you're not leaving my house." Then he flashed a pistol, and I realized that for what little cash I had, he would blow me away.

I threw him aside and ran like hell. But I knew that I wasn't really running from *him*. Instead, I was fleeing the horrifying control that crack cocaine can hold over one man's mind; because this guy wasn't some mugger out to kill me for crack. Until that moment, I thought he had been my friend.

The next day, I saw the same dude in Caesars lobby, and a more frightening thing occurred. He approached me as if nothing had happened between us the night before; and it was clear by our conversation that, as far as crack allowed his mind to know, nothing had.

Even though I could see the cause of my friend's problems and the shams of Vegas itself, I remained blind to myself. Then my father came to Vegas during the early months of 1979. He was living in Los Angeles but frequently stopped in to visit me, anytime there was a major fight in Nevada. After this particular visit, though, he returned to L.A. and immediately telephoned Laurie.

"Angel," he said, as soon as she picked up the receiver, "what's wrong with that boy? I think he's gone real crazy this time."

"Listen, Daddy," she responded, "I don't know what it is. He's just having a time of it. He shouldn't be where he is, but there's really nothing I can do about it. I'm just trying to deal with the situation as best I can."

"But when I hung up," Laurie recalls, "I thought: What kind of man *is* Bundini Brown? He says all the right things, but *he* doesn't even live what he talks. So how is he going to persuade his son to do anything different from what Bundini does?"

What Laurie didn't understand was that my father was prophetic. He spoke the truth, whether he lived it or not. The man that he seemed, based on the life that he lived, was vastly different from the inner man that he was.

In addition to being a prophet and a master motivator, though, Daddy was also a devastating critic. So on his next visit to Las Vegas, he asked me how things were going. I said that I had been working one fight after another for more than a year, and that soon, we would have produced twenty-eight editions for championship events.

"You know what, son?" he said, looking directly into my eyes. "I don't care how many championship fights you work. You're a bum. And you're a bum because you're doing the same thing I'm doing. You're hustlin'. But you, boy—you've got a college education. So don't bullshit a pro. You're not a real Drew, boy, because a real Drew would *use* his education. . . ."

I began protesting, but he fired straight back. "If you *ever* think of doing anything to hurt your family," he said, "you'll not only end your relationships with them, but you won't have me as a father anymore. I will *disown* you. Because the most important thing in life, Buddy Drew, is your family."

17

The funny thing about drugs is, you're gonna stop. You ain't so bad. Anybody in here who's gettin' high is gonna stop. One day, you're gonna stop, and either you stop now, when I tell you to stop, or you stop when they send your butt to jail.

They have those big brothers in jail—dudes with hair growin' out their ears and up their neck—and when those boys tell you, "Come here!" they don't wanna dance.

Or you can stop when you go cryin' to your mother, your father, your doctor, your lawyer, your rabbi, your priest, or your teacher, and you say, "Please, please, help me get off this stuff. I'm killin' myself. Help me!"

Or you can just stop like this. Everybody, please close your eyes. Even the cool ones way in the back, close your eyes. You ain't so bad, and don't worry. I'm not gonna hit you. So close your eyes.

Or you can stop like this, and this will be the last time that you ever hear this sound, CREEEEAK-UH-THUD. That's the exact sound it makes when they shut your coffin. You see, all of you are gonna stop gettin' high, if you're gettin' high on drugs. Either you can stop now, or you will stop when you hear that sound. 'Cause if you take drugs, you're gonna die. Why do you think they call it dope, DOPE? . . .

Our second child, a son, was born in July 1979. We named him Drew Jacques Brown IV; of course, "Drew" extended that

Brown tradition into a fourth generation, and "Jacques" provided a name that honored both Laurie's Creole ancestry and
the memory of my Poppa Jack. But being responsible for yet
another *Drew* made it imperative for me to abandon Vegas and
the boxing world. Never again did I want to give my father a
reason to call me "a bum." So I escaped cold turkey, the way
many people free themselves of addictions. I simply packed up,
left Caesars Palace in the middle of the night, and without
giving notice or a forwarding address, severed all ties with the
Texas firm.

A few days later, I arrived in New Orleans and phoned Laurie. I explained what I had done and asked that she and the
kids remain in Texas until I was settled, had some money coming in, and could lease an apartment for the four of us. Being
called "a bum" was one thing, but having my wife and children
bumming around was too much. So I didn't want them with me
until I was a winner again.

Next, I moved in with my college friend Craig Allen and
immediately started searching for opportunities. But I purposefully ignored the classifieds in the *Times-Picayune*, because
I didn't want to work for anybody else. I was determined to
start something of my own. Then after cruising around town
for several days, I decided that New Orleans lacked a high-class
entertainment spot that catered primarily to blacks. The challenge, though, was how to launch a million-dollar nightclub
with only a handful of dollars in my pocket.

The answer was my "Cinderella Theory," which asks, *Who
says the ball* must *end at midnight?* And to demonstrate my argument, I found a handsomely furnished, multimillion dollar restaurant, The Old Spaghetti Factory, on St. Charles Avenue. It
was adorned with antiques, Tiffany lamps, chandeliers, Orien-
tal rugs, wall tapestries, and lots of mirrors in gilded frames.
Seven days a week, it enjoyed a terrific business, yet it was only
open from 10 A.M. until 10 P.M.

So I spoke to the owner, Dale Michael. "What about the other
twelve hours each night when your restaurant is closed?" I
asked. "After all, like Las Vegas, New Orleans has a twenty-
four-hour liquor law, and I've got a plan that will make 'round-
the-clock money for you."

From that discussion I developed *Bundini's*—a classy after-hours nightclub that would use the restaurant's facilities from midnight until dawn, but only on Friday and Saturday nights. A few days later, Dale bought my idea, and he particularly liked the part about limiting the club's access to two nights a week. He understood that when people can't get enough of a good thing, they keep coming back for more.

"It's *New Orleans,* Drew," Laurie said, when I telephoned with what I thought was good news—that within only a few days, I had launched something that could solve our financial problems. "But I married you because you promised to show me the *world.*"

I knew what was coming, and I tried to nip it by reminding Laurie of all the good times that we had enjoyed here in her hometown. But in my haste, I hadn't considered Laurie's needs. To me, New Orleans was a fallback position. Here, I could get my head straight. I could catch up, emotionally and financially. Yet no matter how much she loved the Big Easy—and in spite of what she was saying, I knew that she did—Laurie simply wasn't ready to return. Not yet, anyway.

Then, in a subsequent phone call, her real concerns came out, and they were rooted in how our marriage had affected her.

"As a child in New Orleans, I was always 'first banana' in my family," she said. "But since we've been married, I've become 'second banana.' Admittedly, I chose that. I pushed you forward because I was tired of leading. I needed to follow for a while. That's why, when we've disagreed, I've battled and battled as best I can. But you're a powerful, relentless person, Drew. In the end, you always get your way, and that intimidates me. So I've given in and become the marshmallow wife, believing that everything you say or do is right."

Then Laurie paused, and her voice began to quiver. "But when it comes to moving back home," she said, "I've got to draw the line. Coming back means that I'll have to explain what's happened to me. My family and friends will *see* how unhappy I am and how drastically my personality has changed. And the truth is, Drew, I don't want them to see what I've become. On top of all the other problems in our marriage, I just can't deal with that, too."

There were more phone calls and more arguments, but nothing I said would convince Laurie. So she and the kids remained in Texas. I stayed in New Orleans, and our fate seemed to rest in whatever I could, or could not, accomplish with my new gimmick.

We opened Bundini's in November 1979, on the cusp of the disco era, so we employed two deejays to keep the music pumping. The entire staff was uniformed. The men wore tuxedoes. The women wore coats with tails and fishnet pantyhose. We looked superbad, and we gave free roses and champagne to women patrons. The entire atmosphere was classy and stylish, and from that first weekend on, patrons flocked to the club. Outside, lines of others hoping to get in usually stretched around the block, and the word that rapidly spread among young blacks in the Big Easy was "Bundini's is the hottest thing going."

After the first few weekends proved so successful, the restaurant's owner and I became partners. We set my salary at five hundred dollars a week, plus a percentage of profits, and I was beaming. But when I telephoned Laurie with this news, she didn't get excited. Instead, we launched into another long-distance argument.

"I've still got mixed emotions about coming back," Laurie said. "A part of me is happy that the kids could be raised around my family. I know that. I do. But at the same time, we've got serious problems, Drew. For starters, you've done all of this without even consulting me."

I was so furious that I hung up. But five minutes later, I called back, and this time, I tried to be polite and persuasive. I emphasized how much more money I was making compared to the Vegas job. And I tried to explain how different Bundini's was from the fight-game world.

"But of all things, Drew, why the *bar* business?" she said.

"You're right," I snapped, losing my cool. "I am running a bar. Oh, it may be the classiest spot in town, but it's still a bar. You're right. I'm only after the money. Is that clear enough?"

Clear, yes. But not persuasive. She wouldn't budge from Texas. Meanwhile, I was now locked into a Louisiana venture, and something much wider than the Mississippi was pushing Laurie farther and farther away from me.

* * *

In the early morning hours of Christmas Eve, I phoned a buddy, "Jefferson Street" Joe Gilliam, who used to play pro football with the Pittsburgh Steelers, and asked him to ride with me to Texas. He agreed and we kept my Cadillac humming the highway for ten straight hours in order to reach Dallas–Fort Worth before the stores closed.

At Sears, I bought a set of no-stick pots and pans for Laurie, some crib toys for Drew Jacques, and a bicycle for Taryn. Then I raced the Caddy toward Richardson, pulled it into my driveway, and when Laurie came to the door, Joey and I roared in. Our arms were loaded with packages.

Laurie didn't hide the fact that she was still furious with me, and her expression got worse once she opened her gift and saw the kitchenware. Obviously, a bad choice! But she had the house beautifully decorated. Taryn loved the bike. Little Drew Jacques was a bundle of energy. Mascara, our harlequin Great Dane, wrestled all day with Joey. And all of us adults did our best to make the day happy for the kids.

Yet driving back to New Orleans, I didn't feel happy. Being a "Christmas father" actually left me lonesome inside, and not joyful, as I had imagined it would. So in the next few weeks, I searched the Big Easy for my own apartment. There was no other option. Without Laurie and the kids living with me again, everything else would be meaningless.

And the place I rented on Trapier Street was spectacular. It had two bedrooms, a nice kitchen, and a sunken living room with a big fireplace. It rarely got cold enough in New Orleans to use a hearth. But I figured that we could use the air conditioning to make it cold enough inside for us to build a fire. After all, it was the feeling of warmth and closeness and family that the four of us needed to recreate, and this fireplace was the perfect symbol to show Laurie how badly I wanted all of that with her.

Meanwhile, during the early months of 1980, Bundini's appeal grew at a phenomenal pace. The Big Easy understands partying the way Wall Street knows business, and mine was a *good* party business. The big boost came when Ali and my father made appearances at the club. That brought lots of media attention. Over the club's twelve months of operations, Bundini's would gross $250,000, or about $2,500 for each of the one hundred nights that we were open. The place was jumpin'. It also meant that I finally had enough financial security to convince Laurie to bring the kids and join me.

"But my parents didn't like the setup a bit," she recalls. "They didn't want me in the nightclub business, and they were unhappy that you were doing this for a living."

On the other hand, Laurie and her sisters fell in love with Bundini's. At first, those nights at the club were good times for her and me, because we were sharing New Orleans in ways that we could never have done in Vegas. Partying in Las Vegas had been business, while some innocence still existed in what went on in the Big Easy.

Laurie and her sisters saw only the innocence, and my wife was the most gorgeous woman in the place. Yet I knew the type of men who hung out at Bundini's, and she didn't belong there. The innocence that she and her sisters exuded was not what those dudes lived for. And with my marriage to Laurie still not on solid ground, jealousy was another factor, so one night I asked that she stop coming to Bundini's so often.

"What you did was make it sound like the club was your thing," she recalls. "You wanted to have fun, to get down and party, but without my scrutiny. And I resented that a lot."

Looking back, I guess some of what Laurie said was the case. From my perspective, though, I just wanted to make money, keep the family with me, and somehow prevent anything from rocking the boat. Yet Laurie's presence at Bundini's threatened to unravel all of that, because the closer she got to me, the more likely I was to tell her what was really troubling me. And as would soon become evident to everybody, I was a troubled man.

So to avoid her, or anyone else I would have to be emotionally honest with, I began losing myself in New Orleanian nights. I somehow hoped that my hurt would disappear in the alcohol that I consumed, side by side with the patrons in my bar. And when I wasn't there, I hit the other night spots in New Orleans. My excuse was that I had to keep up with the competition. But I was actually staying out night after night, and heading toward the kind of alcoholism that I had so abhorred in my parents' lives. Ironically, I was twenty-four years old—the same age that Momma had been—the year I was born—and at least one of my reasons for drinking was similar to hers: *My father had another son.*

My hurt didn't come from having just learned that fact. Twenty years earlier when I was a child in Spanish Harlem, my parents told me about the boy. But the story back then was that a married couple who were my father's friends had been unable to have children. The husband, according to that version, was sterile; yet because this couple thought so much of my father, they asked him to impregnate the man's wife. Momma said that Daddy had done so, and then nine months later—the day before I was born—the woman gave birth to a son.

Upon first hearing this, I was thrilled. "Then I've got a *twin!*" I said. "When can I meet my new brother?"

But my parents said that could never happen, because the boy had his own life and family, and he had not been told about Daddy being his father. The boy thought that his father was the husband still married to the boy's mother. Besides, the woman was also a famous jazz and blues singer, and it was the fifties. If anyone found out about this, my parents cautioned, it might hurt her career.

So for the next two decades, this mysterious half-brother remained a secret that only his parents, my parents, and I knew. Often, I had wondered about him—imagining that somewhere I had this twin who looked like me and felt the same way that I did about things. But throughout, I faithfully kept the secret. Even Laurie didn't know.

After Drew Jacques was born, however, I became preoccupied once again with that other link to *Drewism,* my secret half-brother. So when Daddy came to New Orleans and appeared at Bundini's, I asked him about the boy.

My father told me his name and said, matter-of-factly, "He's in L.A."

Daddy was also living in Los Angeles, so I asked if he and the boy had met.

"We may, soon," my father said. "His mother's giving a concert next month, and he's going to be her warmup act. And after the gig, she has invited me backstage. That way, if she sees that the boy doesn't object, she'll introduce us."

My voice sounded like a five-year-old's as I asked, "Can I come, too?"

"Not now," Daddy said. "Stop speeding."

"I didn't know why, but we were living separate lives," Laurie recalls. "If you chose to be around, that was fine. Otherwise, I just pretended that you didn't exist and found other ways to stay busy."

But Laurie and I did spend some good times together during this period, and most of them were when her parents invited us to their clubs' social events. One that I particularly recall was at the Autocrat Club, a black-owned hall used for weddings and other social events in New Orleans's Seventh Ward.

At this party, as at other club functions of that era in New Orleans, the evening began with the guys on one side of the room, the girls on the other. It wasn't southern just to walk over to some babe and start your rap. You had to catch her eye first, or maybe bump into her in the food line, and then go apart for a while longer, in order to play the game.

It was very romantic. So romantic, in fact, that I decided to play the game with Laurie. She was busy, helping the other married women arrange the array of delicious finger foods at the tables. I stood with the men. And though it was difficult, because Laurie had gotten very good at ignoring me, I finally caught her glance. I flirted, and she looked away. Ten minutes later, however, I got her attention once more. Again, I flirted, and this time she smiled. So I headed for the food line. We chatted casually over the gumbo, and a little later, I asked her to dance, and it accomplished what all of our arguing and talking could not. There, dancing without inhibitions, and in an atmosphere sanctioned by family and friends, Laurie and I broke through the barriers. We didn't erase our problems, but we got back some of our romance. And that night, as we slept in each other's arms, we were in heaven. But it sure was a trip through hell to get there.

A few weeks later, Daddy was in L.A. and went to the concert where he expected to meet my brother. The theater was nearly filled to capacity—as my father subsequently described the event to me—and he emphasized how impressed he was by the appeal that this world-class singer still had, more than two decades after she first became famous. Then the band took their places, performed an introductory number, and a young black man ran onstage.

Daddy was seated in the center section, a few rows from the stage; and as he explained it to me, when he looked into the young man's face, my father saw the resemblance: The young man was shorter and darker-skinned than I, but he was still my father's son. That was unmistakable. Daddy said that, in response, he felt excited and scared all wrapped into one, because he couldn't take his eyes off the young man.

For a while, my brother sang without any noticeable reactions toward Daddy. Then suddenly, according to my father's account, it was as if a giant spotlight focused on Daddy, making everyone else in the audience fade into the shadows, because the young performer looked at him and the singer's voice cracked. He quickly recovered and finished the number. But for that single moment, the two of them knew. The secret was out. God told.

Afterward, they sat around the dressing room and made small talk. But as my father recounted to me, in particular describing how charming and pretty the woman was, I knew by the way he spoke that there had been no "arrangement" for the birth of this boy. In 1954, Momma was Daddy's wife, and I would become the legitimate son that they conceived. Yet during those same months, Daddy and this woman had been lovers. And they, too, had conceived a son.

Then my father said that the three of them discussed the truth but that the young man was obviously displeased. Unlike me, he had not spent the intervening years imagining the lost joys of having a twin. He had not wondered where I was or what I was doing. The truth was, he had not even *known* that I existed. And when he found out, it brought no joy into his life. If anything, he seemed disappointed, as if everyone he knew had betrayed him.

Then a couple of months later, I also met my brother, and what I felt in those moments rekindled all of my feelings about the "twin" that I never had. But I could tell that the feelings weren't mutual. So for weeks after that visit, I felt numb. I couldn't really blame anyone for what had happened. Daddy and the famous singer were nearly my age when they had been in lust, and I knew firsthand how confusing life in one's twenties could be. Moreover, I couldn't blame my half-brother (whom I had always called "David") for not sharing my enthusiasm at what he and I might be to one another. Our childhoods were long gone. Anything that we might have had was, for all practical purposes, lost. But still, it hurt. It penetrated deep inside me, down into the realm of blood and genes—those inaccessible niches that doctors still don't fully understand.

And my initial response was to get drunk and stay drunk. The spree lasted for days. I got so drunk that I lost track of everything until, early one morning, I ended up back at our apartment.

"You woke me up," Laurie recalls, "and to my shock, the personality coming through you was Bundini's. The tone of voice and the facial expressions were ones that I had seen in your father, and you repeatedly moaned, 'Laurie, I'm somebody. Me! Me! Me! I *am* somebody.'

"At the time, I didn't know about the incident in L.A. But even if you had told me, I couldn't take this. You were scaring the hell out of me. So I punched you in the face—hoping either to knock you sober, or fend you off—and then I screamed, 'Don't you *ever* try to be that man to me. Don't do that to me, Drew Brown. You are *not* your father, and don't ever do that to me again.'

"At that, you caught yourself and calmed down, but it was like you *had* to be that man. He was in your eyes, in your voice. It was as if the entire love/hate relationship between the two of you had suddenly come to life. But because it happened in front of me, the horror was unbearable."

In the months that followed, I acquired a new nickname, *Boodanno,* and started hanging around the hustlers and drug dealers who gravitated to my club. Soon, a woman known as the "Angel Dust Queen" became a distinctive regular at Bundini's. She was there most Sunday nights, and once she realized that I wasn't paying the attention that I should to the business, she set up regular operations. Working straight from my bar, she wandered from guy to guy, negotiated deals, and then met them one at a time in the back restrooms. It didn't take me long to catch on, but I didn't really care. By then, all signals indicated that this venture would end soon, and badly.

Then about five o'clock one morning, the Angel Dust Queen was plying her trade with the last few customers in the place, and I realized how futile everything was. Bundini's was closing. I was out of control. And nothing could change anything. So I went to the back room with her, paid, and snorted her stuff.

Hours later, I awoke in the restaurant's meat locker. Apparently, I had freaked out on the angel dust, locked myself inside the frigid room, and then passed out. One hit had strung me out alongside the frozen meat parts and bags of vegetables. Had I not come to, the Sunday manager would have found me, iced out and dead, by the time the day crew arrived for work.

"The man is a hell of a man," my father had been quoted as saying, a few months earlier, when he and Ali had launched the Champ's "Fourth Comeback." No one knew then how ill-fated this campaign would be. Instead, the Muhammad Ali momentum started all over again. "We were born to be together," Daddy reminded reporters. "God is my employer. . . . I went in the wash Drew Bundini Brown, and I came out Drew Bundini Brown. He went in the wash as Cassius Clay and came out Muhammad Ali. Remember, you didn't know Jesus 'til he died."[1]

As outrageous as these comments were, most people assumed that my father was just revving his hype toward new levels of intentional controversy. But I knew better. This was drug talk, because Daddy had become an everyday cocaine user. Snow was no longer recreational to him. It was his only means of becoming introspective enough to talk about God.

But given how confused I was at the time, I wondered: *Can drugs really help men reach God?* So the next time I was in New York City, where he had temporarily returned in order to work with Ali, I asked Daddy, "Can I get high with you?"

He said no, and did so very quickly.

But I kept bothering him about it. "You never talk about God and life when you're straight, Daddy. So how else are we gonna have such discussions?"

Well, he said no, once more, and we just continued riding in his black Cadillac along the streets of New York. Just the two of us, and the Caddy weaving in and out of traffic, even though we weren't headed anywhere in particular. All at once, he pulled out a folded dollar bill and said, "Do you want some?"

When I saw that it might be cocaine, I said, "Sure," even though my mind was going, *This is great! Me and Dad gonna get high!*

But after about five or ten minutes had passed, I asked, "Can I finally have some back?"

"This is what you want?" he asked, looking straight at me, even though the car kept speeding down a crowded Manhattan street. "Is *this* what it's really all about?"

I stared at the dollar bill, and while my gaze was fixed on it, my father rolled down the window of his Cadillac and threw out the folded dollar bill. Then he glared back at me and said, "Don't you ever, *ever* let a drug rule your life, boy. Don't you ever lie for white powder, or for a bottle. 'Cause if that's what you live for, you're not livin'."

Whether there was any coke in that dollar bill or not, I had never seen anybody throw drugs away like that, and Daddy's only apparent reason was to show me that if drugs and money were all that my quest was about, then I was already dead, whether I knew it or not.

That's when I realized that, in a sense, my life had come full circle—back to the day when I was bar mitzvahed, back to the day when I was sitting with a drink in my hand, and beside my father, under the sign behind us that stated, TODAY, I AM A MAN. But I didn't truly become a man that day. Instead, when my father threw those drugs out the window—because he saw that cocaine was what I really wanted, and not just to talk to him about God or life—*that* was the day I truly became a man.

That was the day I understand that my father had refused to glamorize the bad things in his life. Oh, I had certainly glamorized them, but he never did. He hated the way he was, but he was a survivor. If he had to con, he would. Winning the game of life was more important to him than the rules. And that's what made him the best man I've ever met, because he dealt with the truth—whether he lived it or not.

Yet my daddy never wanted me to walk in his shoes. He

always wanted his boy to be better than he was. My father often said that I would be a rabbi, a teacher of God's will, so he insisted that I only be allowed to play by the rules—God's rules—or I would never live up to being a real Drew.

Daddy knew that all my life I had been struggling to get high, and he hoped that I would ultimately find the way through means other than drugs or alcohol. And I finally did.

I became a man when my highs no longer threatened to destroy me. I became a man when I discovered God's natural high: *the opportunities within my own drug-free mind.* And in so doing, I became what my father always wanted—the new Drew.

Drugs could have killed me, just as they are doing to people today. Drugs poison your mind, corrupt your soul, and finally destroy your body.

If you use drugs, you're gonna die!

18

Why do you think I'm a pilot? Do you think my father and mother had a little plane in the back of the projects, and they'd say, "Come on, son. Let's take a little spin today"?

I never wanted to fly an airplane, not one day in my life. So why do you think I'm a pilot? Because I have something that each and every one of you sitting in here has. It's called your "commonsense computer." All of you have it. All of you use it every day. But whether you use it to your advantage is not up to me. It's up to you. Remember: Garbage goin' in makes garbage comin' out. But all of you have the computer.

However, I entered information into my computer like this: "I WANT TO MAKE A LOT OF MONEY." ENTER. "I DON'T WANT TO WORK REAL HARD." ENTER.

Don't you dare be lookin' at me funny. You all have been doin' that every day: "LOT OF MONEY." ENTER. "LITTLE WORK." ENTER. "GOOD GRADES." ENTER. "I DON'T WANNA STUDY." ENTER.

But a little light started flashin' on my computer screen. A little tiny light! And you know what that light said? I thought they'd sent me the wrong software 'cause the little light said, "AIRLINE PILOT." Airline pilot? What's an airline pilot? They don't have no airline pilots in the projects.

216

Well, I looked it up in the library, 'cause I graduated from Southern University in New Orleans and I learned how to use a library. And what I found out was: An airline pilot can make $175,000 a year, workin' twelve to fourteen days a month.

Guess what? I WANNA BE AN AIRLINE PILOT! I WANNA BE AN AIRPLANE PILOT!

But the street brother in my mind tapped me on the shoulder and said, "Yo, Drew."

I said, "What?"

And he said, "You don't know how to fly."

"Oh, yeah," I admitted. "That's right." But I didn't quit. Instead, I put it in my computer like this: "DON'T KNOW HOW TO FLY." ENTER. "HAVE NO MONEY." ENTER. "WANNA LEARN." ENTER.

Then another little light came on the screen, and it said, "JOIN THE MILITARY. . . ."

An old wise man from the Louisiana delta once told me, "Anything that grows fast dies fast," in reference to upstarts who ventured too quickly into politics or business or romance. So when Bundini's started to fade in the autumn of 1980, I wasn't surprised. I had lost a Cinderella business because of ignorance and alcohol—the same mistakes that had sunk my parents' bar business in Manhattan more than a dozen years earlier.

Also like my parents, I had failed to learn from the past. My New Orleans errors were, in many ways, the same ones that had hurt me in Las Vegas. And I had grown tired of disappointing my wife. Everything that I had promised her I would do I had failed at. So even though I was only twenty-five when I left Bundini's, I felt like a loser. That's what I saw when I looked in the bathroom mirror, and that's what I saw in the eyes of my wife, her family, and my own parents.

But whether I was a loser or not, we still had children to feed, so I combed through the *Times-Picayune* in search of a job. I had not abandoned my dream of starting another venture of my own, but it was time to face reality. I had no money to invest, and Bundini's had been too public a failure for me to persuade another New Orleans investor to back one of my ideas anytime soon. So something had to give, and that something was me.

* * *

One day I went looking for a job with the Offshore Drilling and Exploration Company. There's no glamor in oil-rig work, but it's honest labor and, at the time, it paid better than most occupations in New Orleans. ODECO offered me a job on the spot, and because I had a college degree, they wanted to make me an industrial engineer, or a "safety man" in offshore drilling who maintains safety requirements, conducts safety classes, and is in charge of emergency procedures on a rig. The pay was seven hundred dollars a week.

For that sum I would work seven days straight, forty miles out in the Gulf of Mexico, before being brought back ashore for a solid week of leave time; and the cycle would repeat itself twice a month. However, counting that pair of off-duty weeks, this meant that my monthly income would drop about 25 percent from what I had been earning at Bundini's. It also meant that Laurie, the kids, and I would have to give up our classy apartment and move into more affordable quarters.

It was a negative choice, and nobody likes to take a step backward, financially. But at least the oil-rig pay would be steady money, which meant a lot to Laurie, and I *had* to prove to her that I could rebound from Bundini's. So I took the ODECO job.

"Maybe the difficulties in Drew's childhood make him so resilient," she recently told a friend. "He's able to take a 'no' and let it appear to roll right off of him—when in fact, he pursues that negative, and just pursues it and pursues it until he turns it into a positive."

And transforming a negative *was* my goal for the ODECO job. I needed the radical change in lifestyle that it offered, because just getting to the rig promised that my life *would* be different. First, I would have to leave home in the wee hours of delta mornings and drive to the Louisiana shore. That eliminated the all-night drinking and partying I had been doing. Then once I reached the gulf, I would have to ride by helicopter for over an hour to reach the rig itself. That ensured complete isolation from the world I had known. There are no phones, no nightclubs, no booze, no drugs, and no women on an oil rig. It's a manmade island devoid of anything that doesn't contribute to hard manual labor.

*   *   *

Laurie and my parents knew that oil-rig work was dangerous, so they worried about me. But beyond that, Laurie knew
that having her husband out to sea also solved some of her
problems. "I actually welcomed the time to myself," she recalls.
"I missed you, but it had been very hard living with you. So I
felt relieved when you were gone. Those absences gave me
great inner time, and for once, I could pick up my life again
and start moving forward."

Laurie had resumed working with D. H. Holmes, and about
the time I went on the oil rig, the department store made her
a trainee/assistant buyer. And that had a real impact on me. I
saw Laurie growing, exclusive of me, and it was scary. She was
developing into her own person, and I didn't really want to
remain the type of person that I had become. I *did* want to be
a good husband to her and a good father to the kids. But I just
didn't know how. . . .

Even though the Gulf Coast beauty of water and sky surrounded the *Ocean Traveler*—the ODECO oil rig to which I was
assigned—it was actually an emotional desert. The *Traveler* had
been constructed of metal and steel, and designed for only one
purpose: to pump mud and pull oil from the ocean floor. Nothing had been built for comfort. Everything on it merely stored
something, dug something, or was there for safety; and every
piece of metal and steel was coated with a deep gray paint
because that color showed the least amount of dirt.

There were no *other* facilities—nothing for physical fitness,
recreation, or entertainment—so life was a hollow existence on
a dingy, dull, and very lonely place. I'm talking a total, dark,
deep, do-nothing boredom out on the gulf.

What kept everybody else sane out there was that they worked
their butts off, drilling for twelve hours straight. After enduring
that kind of shift, all they wanted to do was take a shower, eat,
and go to sleep. In addition, though, their work/sleep routine
was made worse by the fact that they had to share only one bunk-
house. We called it "swapping sheets"—meaning that while one
shift worked twelve hours, the other shift slept, and yet both
shifts shared the same bunks, just at alternate times.

But I didn't have a physically demanding job. I checked safety lines, fire extinguishers, and other regulated devices, or I conducted a few classes, and was on call for emergencies. Otherwise, the hardest part of my job was to look busy. Over a seven-day shift, I probably had about half a day of actual physical labor that I had to spread over the entire seven-day haul.

The good part, though, was that as safety officer I got single-bunk quarters that I didn't have to share. My ten-by-fifteen-foot room had a metal bed, a cabinet, and a closet. The only decorations were my pictures of Laurie, Taryn, and Drew Jacques that I kept in plastic frames. I also had a small black-and-white television set, but it couldn't pick up more than a couple of stations. So once I did my job, I really didn't have anything to do. And since I roomed alone, that down time forced me to think.

In October 1980, during one of my weeks off the oil rig, I returned to Las Vegas, because Ali was fighting his old sparring partner Larry Holmes. I had seen them fight many times at the Deer Lake training camp, but in those days, the Champ always held court on his younger employee. I distinctly remember one time when the sparring session turned into a street fight. Ali and Larry battled with such fire in their eyes and fists that my daddy had to jump in the ring to stop the war.

But years later, on this chilly October night, millions witnessed something center stage in Caesars Palace that I had never seen. During ten agonizing rounds, Larry Holmes whipped the king as if he were a peasant. And instead of jumping into the ring to stop this war, my father was in shock. Angelo Dundee stopped the fight, and the king was dethroned. He would never hold court again.

That night, Ali demonstrated that he was, at last, too old for heavyweight competition. He never should have fought Holmes. But I knew why he did it. Over the years, people had mistaken the Champ's kindness for weakness and had taken most of his millions. So Ali *had* to fight Holmes for the money. Even more, though, Muhammad Ali—like so many other fighters at the end of their careers—needed to hear the addictive sound of fans calling out his name.

Holmes, on the other hand, fought at Caesars that night for the respect of the world. He did beat his hero, but it was Holmes's misfortune to be the great fighter who followed in the wake of the Greatest of all time. Standing at ringside when the bout ended, I could see in Holmes's eyes that he felt, *I didn't want my respect this way—not beating Ali.* Yet that expression earned Holmes my respect. It told me, Ali, and the world: *I'm sorry, Champ. You'll always be my idol.*

This tragic end to the mythical era that had lasted most of my life had an enormous effect on me. It was sobering. It forced me to reevaluate my views on age and life and values. And for a while, I withdrew from everyone.

"You were never home, even when you weren't on the rig," Laurie recalls. "And when you did come home, you always seemed very distant and indifferent."

I used my *aloneness* at sea to rethink my life, and I had a lot to consider. After just over three years of marriage, Laurie and I were living completely separate lives. Unlike my father, I had always made certain that my wife and kids had money. But I had established no presence in their lives. So approaching my twenty-sixth birthday—the same age that my father had been when I was born—I could claim little more in my personal life than he had attained, even though I had the education and the advantages that he had never been allowed.

And as Ali had just proven, life's evergreen years don't last. I, too, was getting older, but I had never held down a job longer than a year. I had not stuck with any venture longer than my initial enthusiasm for it, because I couldn't remain interested in anything that lasted longer than a year. So I had no viable work record, and nothing to prove that I could be counted on. Basically, the problem was that I still hadn't discovered what I wanted to be. I knew that doctors dedicated years of training after college, and lawyers did, too. I also knew that anything worth becoming is worth working for. So if I wanted a professional career, I was going to have to head directly toward that goal. My youth was fading fast.

But what goal? What profession? And how could I be sure that it was for me? Years later, I would write a poem about all these disconcerting feelings:

Funny thing about decisions, if you don't make one,
     you do.
Our life is put in front of us with many to choose.
Some think luck and destiny are in the cards. I believe
     you must play the right ones.
We make some fast, others we ponder.
Some good, some bad. . . .
But it's your decision, even if you don't.[1]

Then one day a tragic accident happened on the *Ocean Traveler*. I was walking along the rig, and the crew was "slinging mud"—meaning that they were making sludge for the drilling hole from hundred-pound bags.

Periodically, rigs over the workers' heads hauled in more bags on pallets. But suddenly one of the pallets broke, and before anyone could react, this guy got pummeled by sixteen or seventeen of the hundred-pound bags falling one at a time on top of him. I thought he was crushed to death, but once we cleared away enough bags for me to examine him, I saw he was alive but his spine was broken and he had multiple internal injuries. He could not move his neck, and he was bleeding from his ears, nose, and mouth.

We finished unearthing him from the mound of bags, and an emergency helicopter rushed him shoreside to a hospital. Fortunately, the man would recover, but his recuperation would be long and painful.

That day, however, I watched the helicopter carry him away from the lonely rig, and I prayed to myself, "Dear God, I want to live too. I don't want to die. So please help me get off this thing, because I've accomplished too little in life to lose it all, out here in the gulf."

"After that incident," Laurie recalls, "I could see real changes in you. More and more, I caught glimpses of that *earlier* guy. And I could tell that you were soul-searching, digging deeper, and trying to decide what you were going to do with the rest of your life. That made me like you again, and like the person you were becoming."

One reason for my change in attitude was that, each time I came ashore, I had been gradually collecting brochures and booklets about professional career opportunities. And when I took these back to the oil rig, the stuff actually brightened the dullness of my work existence. I carefully read material about lawyers, doctors, architects, and engineers, and I knew that I was capable of becoming a professional, too. But none of these seemed right for me.

Meanwhile, Daddy had begun advising me along the same lines. "Get a profession, son," he kept saying. "Find a way to use your education in a field that requires talent. And when you do that, you'll have something that no man can take away from you."

I knew that his experience was talking. Since Ali had retired, my father was left unemployed with no real options, even though Daddy was only fifty-two years old. If I was to avoid his fate, I had to secure a profession that did not depend upon the success or failure of someone else. And I needed to join a team that had lifetime staying power.

During the spring of 1981, I kept noticing military jets flying missions in the crystal blue sky above the *Ocean Traveler*. They looked superbad and reminded me of the fighters that I had seen flying over Israel when I was a boy. Ironically, when I went ashore the next week, a friend told me how airline pilots form "a type of hidden country club in America," because of the amount of money that they made and the kind of lifestyle that they lived. They only worked a few days each month.

That sounded great. By then, I knew I wanted a career that would allow me to make a lot of money but that wouldn't consume all of my time. I still had inklings of things, outside of work, that I wanted to do with my life. The only problem was, how could I be trained as a pilot? I certainly couldn't afford private lessons.

On my next shore leave, therefore, I visited recruiting offices in New Orleans, and I was surprised at how enthusiastic the military was about me. At the time, I had no idea that there were very few black pilots in the air force or marines, and even fewer in the navy. What I did learn, though, was that the military offered both career training and boundaries. With its training, I could gain access to airplanes and new skills. And because I would have to commit for a period longer than a year, the military offered discipline that, so far, I had been unable to develop on my own. So all of that excited me.

"Then the next time you came to visit," Laurie recalls, "you announced that you were going to be a pilot. You looked determined, and I knew that once you put your mind to it, you could do anything. I thought, 'Finally, I'll have my husband again. He'll earn a regular salary that we can live on, and he won't have the outside influences that had separated us.' It also meant getting out of New Orleans, and leaving all the past behind. It meant starting over, so I gladly jumped into it."

PART FIVE: Equal Success and the American Dream

19

Now when you come from New York City, you got to look good. That's what you think it's all about. So when I went to join the military, I figured airplanes/air force, and that's where I went first.

I was gettin' ready to sign up—except that I noticed their uniforms— and all those boys looked like a bunch of Greyhound bus drivers. So then I went to the army and the marines. But all them dudes looked like G.I. Joes.

Finally, I went to the navy, and I saw them pretty white uniforms and blue flight suits with gold wings. So that's why I decided to join the United States Navy. I saw their uniforms and said, "ANCHORS AWEIGH. Here I come."

But don't ever forget this: Before I joined the navy, I had never been inside an airplane cockpit. I hardly even knew how to spell aerodynamics, and I knew nothing about airplanes.

But you know what I did? I worked hard and worked hard. I studied and studied. I worked hard and studied. . . .

From the beginning of its history until only recently, the United States Navy was known to be racially discriminating. It was the last branch of the U.S. military services to integrate. But because of this history of bias, once the navy did integrate, its push for black pilots became an obsession.

However, I knew none of this when, in April 1981, I telephoned my father and told him that I wanted to join the navy. But he knew, and that moment was the first time I ever found him to be speechless. Daddy truly thought I was losing my mind. He had watched me go from Vegas to Bundini's—all the while nearly losing my family and my own reputation—and he didn't really understand the navy officer program, so he thought a naval career was my final act of stupidity. But he was also intrigued.

So after some discussion, he decided that I was not mentally disturbed, but that I was running away to sea, the way he had done decades before. I could almost hear his mind working— *The navy will straighten my boy out. And his checks coming home will take care of Angel and the babies. So why not? I can live with that, if he can*—and after another long pause, Daddy said he approved and would help.

A few days later, I discovered in my mail that my father had obtained a letter of recommendation for me from his author friend George Plimpton, who wrote that I was "a most engaging young man—bright, a fine athlete . . . and it gives me great pleasure to recommend him for your branch of the service." Meanwhile, I had also asked my favorite SUNO professor, Dr. Norman Wilson, to endorse my application, and his letter arrived a few days after Plimpton's. "I am recommending to you for service as a Navy pilot," wrote Dr. Wilson, "Drew T. Brown III, a most pleasant, likable, intelligent, brave young man who works well with everyone and who very much wants to serve his country whether in peace or war. . . . As a student, young Drew showed flashes of brilliance. It is a pleasure to recommend him."[1]

Then I began taking physical exams and a series of tests that gauged my motivation, aptitudes, and skills for several branches of the military. But what actually sealed my decision to choose the navy was a discussion that I had with Lieutenant Dennis Franklin, a naval recruiter at New Orleans's Dauphine Street station.

"Imagine taking your car and going to the Lakefront Shopping Center," he said, "and then parking that car in one of those mall parking spaces on a dreary Sunday afternoon when no other cars are there."

"It would be pretty easy," I said.

"Now imagine doing that same thing on Christmas Eve, when there are no spots available, but you *have* to find a certain spot because your life depends on it," he said. "Or better yet, imagine driving at a hundred miles an hour into your garage, but stopping before you ever hit the back wall."

I nodded, somehow understanding that I was being told something important.

"The point is, Drew, anybody can park a car on an open lot with acres of available space," he explained, "but it's a lot different when you *must* put that car in just that one particular spot."

Then he showed me the film *Sea Legs,* where navy jets fly on and off an aircraft carrier. But when he told me these unforgettable words, I knew that I *had* to be a naval aviator. "They got two kinds of pilots," he said, "ones who are navy jet carrier pilots, and all the others who wished they could be."

In order to become a navy jet pilot, however, inductees must first become naval officers. So my next step was to enter officer candidate school. The following year, when the producer of *An Officer and a Gentleman* sought a consultant to aid actor Louis Gossett, Jr., in making his gunnery-sergeant role of Foley as authentic as possible, the United States Navy assigned a topnotch gunny from the Naval Air Station in Pensacola. That Florida NAS is *the* legendary officer candidate school. So I was overwhelmed when I secured a spot in the Pensacola program.

"The day you left for the navy," Laurie recalls, "you had on a loud yellow-nylon running suit with matching jacket and pants. Your Afro was big and unruly. Your face was virtually hidden underneath a haphazard beard and mustache, and you were thirty pounds overweight. So I was really worried about you."

She called it worry, but I considered it nagging. Our marriage seemed so near its end that, at any moment, I expected my wedding band to start spinning and then launch from my left hand like a flying saucer that would hurl into space and take our relationship with it, beyond the point of no return.

So I only halfway listened as Laurie cautioned, "Remember, this navy training is just a mind game. They're going to try to mess with you, Drew, but just ignore it. Do what you have to do to get through this program. And then you'll get what you want."

I didn't listen and I had no fears, because I truly had no idea what I was doing. If my marriage was about to be over, I was twenty-six years old, but my life was about to be over, too. I had no direction and no purpose. Yet with the navy, I at least had one more dream left.

If, on the other hand, I stayed in New Orleans and returned to the hustling game, then I would really become an authentic imitation of my father. I would lose my family, and never be anything. I would simply spend the rest of my life being "Mister Excuse."

By heading out to the navy, however, there was a chance that I could become somebody. The navy was the first time that I would be doing anything society's way. Even in college, I had made the system work for me, instead of me working within the system. Yet the navy was a straight line to success, the way everybody else does it, but the one way that I had *never* tried.

When I arrived at Pensacola's Aviation Officer Candidate School, I told myself, "Just keep your mouth shut. Say nothin' and do what you're told." For more than a quarter of a century, I had survived by mouthing my way in and out of trouble. This time, however, I intended to try a new tactic. *Cool silence.* And sure enough, I would need that defense within a matter of minutes.

I walked into a classroom to join the other civilian candidates, and I saw that all of us had long hair, but the common links stopped there. The other guys were much younger than I, and the moment everybody realized that I was the only black guy in the class, the entire atmosphere in the room changed to a very *white* feeling. You know. Guys sitting up straight, clearing their throats while their eyes glaze over—as if everybody is suddenly thinking some common thought on some wavelength that I, the black guy, couldn't possibly understand.

So while they played white, I just chilled out. It was obvious that I was bigger than these guys, and I could tell by their expressions that none of them had graduated from the streets of Harlem, Brooklyn, New York, Las Vegas, and New Orleans. So nobody here posed a threat to me. I was in control of this situation.

After the introductory session got started, we listened to a series of speeches from the base captain, a medical doctor, the lieutenant in charge of our academic program, and on and on. It all felt like summer camp back when I was a boy, and I thought, *Man this is* great. *I have come to camp, and I'm going to get paid for it. This. Is. A. Breeze.*

Then the lieutenant said calmly, "Now I'm going to bring somebody who you'll become very intimate with. Your drill instructor, who's a marine—"

Well, that really pumped me up, the idea of me being trained by one of those guys in a Smokey the Bear hat!

"—so I want you men to meet Gunnery Sergeant Stephen W. Clark."

From the back of the room walked a man whose stride could part a traffic jam in Manhattan. He was white, six feet four, 205 pounds, wearing corny black government-issue eyeglasses, carrying his hat in his arm, and when he reached the front, he turned about face, and—*wham*—he looked like Moses. I had never seen a bigger, stronger, meaner, more serious person in my life, and my street brother whispered within my mind, "I think *this* is where the problems begin."

"My name is Gunnery Sergeant Clark, United States Marine Corps," he snapped. His eyes looked at no one else's while he spoke. "You *will* be with me for the next sixteen weeks. During those sixteen weeks, I'll make all the women go home and all the men become naval aviators. There are no questions, 'cause I don't answer any questions." Then he turned, walked out, and I was tripping.

I wondered: *When does this guy shake your hand and tell you what the curriculum is going to be like?* All of the other officers had reminded me of college professors, explaining what they expected from us, so I knew what to give back to them. But Gunny Clark was an alien from Atmosphere Seven. I had never encountered a man with such presence, not on the streets of Harlem nor in the back alleys of Vegas or New Orleans, not from my father nor Muhammad Ali nor anybody else. I couldn't believe that his man was so straight, so forthright, and so calculating. He seemed perfect in every sense, and that made me feel as though I wasn't good enough in any sense. No wonder he hadn't looked at us when he spoke. Compared to him, we were street slime!

Later that day—after we had been issued fatigues called "poopie suits," and silver-painted helmets called "chrome domes"—we all went to our assigned rooms. Everybody else started playing cards, reading books, or just hanging out, but I freaked. These guys were talking about F-14s and A-6s—except I didn't even know what a DC-9 was. I swear, the only plane I had heard about was a 747—just because it came out when I was growing up, and the media had raised such a fuss over it. So listening to these guys made me feel stupid.

What's more, when we talked about where we were from, I found out that some of these guys hailed from Cornell, Yale, Dartmouth, Embry-Riddle, and other big universities, and that they had never heard of SUNO. My only consolation was that the rooms were plain with dingy brown paint on the walls. That reminded me of the projects and made me relax. So I fell asleep, feeling right at home and thinking that, just maybe, everything in the navy was going to be all right.

At four the next morning, however, my life changes radically and forever. Mister Cool Brown who had his stuff together and knew how to talk his way in and out of problems is jarred into another dimension by—*bang, crash, bang*—the sounds of a large metal garbage can being flailed against the hallway walls.

Then a scream: "Get up, you sonuvabitches, get-up-get-up-get-up!"

I am scared to death. I think that there's a war happening or a fire breaking out, so I jump out of bed.

Another scream: "Get all your brown-stained underwear off, and get out here in the hallway. Now!"

What the—

Within three minutes, however, I am standing naked, alongside fifty other guys, and shivering in the cold. Then when all of us guys are naked, confused, and out in the hallway, Gunny Sergeant Clark screams, "You didn't do it fast enough. Get your slimy asses back in bed. Go to sleep. And get back out here like *real* men. I'm telling you: Half you sissies ain't makin' it, *today*. Now, move!"

This is not summer camp anymore. We all run back inside, and I wonder: *How do I make believe I'm sleeping?* But I try and am trying very hard when the gunny screams again, "Ready? Begin. Up-up-up-up. Up-up-up-up. . . ."

But back outside, we are greeted with "You bunch of slime balls. Everybody get down on-your-face, on-your-face, on-your-face!" And every man falls.

Once we're down, though, the gunny yells, "Get on your feet!" And we jump back up.

"On your face. . . ."

"On your feet. . . ."

And so it goes, face to feet, over and over like a joke that's not getting funny. Then Gunny Clark orders us to start the whole thing over. "Get back in your beds," he screams like a banshee, "and I want you to do it *right* this time! Like *men*. NOOOW-UH!"

As we run back, it strikes me that even though I'm the only black guy in sight, everybody is being treated the same. Like scum. So I tell myself: *I get it. We're all being psyched into acting like one, like brothers. And I can handle that.*

So as we jump back in our beds, I ease up. The seconds pass, and I wait. I *know* the screaming will resume. And when it does—"Right now, get-up, get-up-you-bunch-of-slime-balls, you'll-never-get-it-right. *Get* dressed!"—I feel a little cooler. "You have *seven* minutes to get dressed and out on the marks. . . ." This is not that threatening to me, because I am not losing it. I'm maintaining cool silence.

Back outside, it's pushup time. Gunny bellows, "Up. Down. Up. Down," and we do pushups until we're weakened from exhaustion and fully primed for intense humiliation. That's when Gunny Clark orders us back on our feet and unleashs a barrage of insults, none of which are printable. Then we are herded into a small shop where, one by one, barbers peel hair from our heads like so many potatoes, and I watch my big Afro fall to the floor, its thick black beautiful rolls lying right alongside the smooth blond, red, and brown waves of the white boys' hair. It is five o'clock, dawn is nowhere to be seen, but equality is upon us. We are now even *less* than slime. We are "poopies."

Then we are rushed back to our marks—which are actually

big "feet" painted on the floor—and the gunny's voice turns
into a trumpet. "All right, you pukes," he screams. "Now we're
going to show you what pain *really* means. I'm sorry your fathers ain't helpin' you no more. You think you're gonna get
keys to jets out here? Well, you're not, boys. You *ain't* gonna
make it. None of you. I'm gonna D-O-R this whole class."

D-O-R, as we would learn, means "drop on request," and the
only way that a poopie can get out of the aviation program in
the United States Navy is to D-O-R. From this moment on, if
anybody wants out, all that person has to do is ask, and he *is* out,
nothing is held against him, and he owes the navy no time.

Just then, however, the gunny bellows, "Come here, you big,
black sonuvabitch."

Now, there is no doubt who he means. But at the same instant, I cannot believe that this man is talking *color,* because I
know the military can't use racial discrimination. Yet I immediately rush forward, face him, and stand at attention.

Gunny Clark catches the confusion in my eyes, and he says in
sarcastic, catlike whines, "*Ooooh,* are you mad that I called you
'black'? Well, I'll tell you what. I'll go and call Martin Luther
King for ya. Nah, he's dead. Well, maybe I'll call Jesse Jackson
or the NAACP. 'Cause *you* don't like what I said—right, boy?"

I am totally freaking out. Gunny Clark is ridiculing me—the
only black poopie in front of an otherwise all-white class—and
even though I'm as tall as he is, I now I feel three inches high.
Yet he is eyeing me hard. So I eye him back, and he screams,
"Don't ever eyeball me, boy. Get back in line, you big ugly
dirtbag."

I do it. His is the voice of Moses, the fury of a cyclone, and my
life stops on a dime. I have no future, no past. And somehow I
sense that for weeks on end, Gunnery Sergeant Stephen W.
Clark will be ripping me apart and hurling the pieces back
together—recreating me into a new breed—and for the first
time ever, not a single maxim from the streets of New York will
pop into my mind. Nothing from my past will guide me. I am
caught up in total helplessness. . . .

Those first seven days of AOCS training turned out to be the
hardest 168 straight hours of my life. By comparison, practice
in college athletics now seemed like a picnic, and hazing with

the Alpha Phi Omegas at SUNO, a mere game. The pressure of Globetrotter tryouts, or the beatings that I got on the streets of Harlem—all of that was erased from my memory—because the hell of living under Gunny Clark's boot heels was, by far, the worst. We dug ditches. We ran miles. The gunny stomped on the tables while we ate, and we couldn't laugh or cry or think one thought unless he told us to.

We dug more ditches. And we ran more miles on the beach, all the while carrying our heavy, antiquated M-1 rifles until they felt like a third arm. But no matter what we did, Gunny Clark remained true to form. He didn't just order us to run. He ran right alongside us. And while we wore shorts, chrome domes, and T-shirts, he was always in full Marine uniform. And whenever we were sweating to death and dying, not a bead of sweat ever appeared on him. Even the pleats in his perfectly starched shirt seemed undisturbed. So we couldn't complain, because the gunny always did exactly what we did—only he did everything better. Every time.

Within four days, half of that class of poppies quit, and everything that we endured was a physical, academic, or psychological nightmare. The only reason I didn't quit was because, deep down, I knew that I was as good as or better than any man in my class. Yet none of them were slouches. Everybody was top-notch.

Our class—"2081, We Kill Commies Just for Fun"—had poopies who had been educated as aeronautical engineers, while I had never seen the inside of an airplane. Other poopies had fathers, uncles, and grandfathers who had been admirals and pilots, and these poopies had never considered any option other than becoming naval officers, too. All they had ever wanted to do, their entire lives, was fly. They were the cream of America's crop, and yet even these guys were quitting.

Throughout the first four weeks of AOCS, we had been allowed no communications with the outside world. This meant no letters to Laurie and the kids. No Sunday phone calls to Momma. And no communications from them, either. But even after the ban was lifted, whenever I thought about my family, I still had no more time or energy to do anything about it. So I could tell no one what I was going through, and I could get no sympathy or encouragement from anyone, because I could not show the guys in my class that there was a chink in my armor. As in my weeks on the oil rig, therefore, I was alone with a demon of my own choosing.

"We were separated, not only by you being in AOCS," Laurie recalls, "but we were still in a trial separation as far as our marriage was concerned. I made myself happy with work and dancing classes and the kids. And since you and I were banned from communicating anyway, I just put it all out of my mind."

When I finally did telephone Laurie, I had too much to say, but too little time to get it all said. How do you pour your soul into a single long-distance call and explain how your life has been shaken from its very foundations?

"You were so different. So military and official," she recalls. "I remember that you kept saying things like, 'Laurie, you're really going to love being an officer's wife.' And you said the captain's wife, Mrs. Rasmussen, kept asking when I would be coming down to visit. But I liked the trial separation, and I just wanted to keep my distance. To see how everything with the navy turned out. You were asking, but I wasn't responding, because for the first time in years, I could breathe emotionally and psychologically. I didn't have to worry about you. At that point, you were beyond my control. The navy had you, and you were either going to make it or not."

When I hung up the receiver, I didn't know what to do. Laurie had never expressed this much independence with me, and with that added to my own problems in AOCS, I was a wreck. Here I was in a world where orders were carried out, without comment or question. But my own wife wouldn't come to visit me, not if I begged, pleaded, or commanded. So I left the pay phone and wondered if my marriage was ever going to work out at all.

Then AOCS itself changed. We were issued khakis instead of poopie suits, and in measuring for the new uniforms, it was obvious that I had lost a lot of weight. I had grown stronger by the day, but I was dying inside too. Nothing let up. Everything in the program escalated, becoming harder and harder, in order to make us tough individuals but even tougher as a class. And it was at this point in AOCS that I found out how stupid I was. I found out how weak and ugly I was. And I really found out how uncool I had always been.

One day we were carrying our rifles while we ran on the beach, and after we had run so hard for so long, I just couldn't do it anymore. So I prayed, "God, please give me a heart attack. Because if you give me a *small* one, I'll be able to fall to the ground and still have an excuse for Gunny about why I am stopping."

Years before, when I had played "Fifty-two" in the projects, I knew not to quit anything. But nothing had ever hurt like this. Yet the real quitters in our class had already gone home. Only the strong had survived. So even though I was praying for a heart attack, I knew that I couldn't drop without one. If God didn't answer my prayer—and He didn't—I would not drop, because that meant an immediate D-O-R. And I had no intention of quitting.

That's also when I realized that, without my noticing, my gunnery sergeant's voice had miraculously changed. Its strange mixture of animal screams laced with an odd British accent had gradually become music to my ears. It now brought out melodies to the cadences when we marched, and inspiration when we suffered. My daddy had told me many times, "Son, you'll have many fathers in your life," and I had always hated hearing that. But in Gunny Clark, I was discovering the father figure that my daddy had predicted. Gunny was becoming my father, my grandfather, my Bubba, my rabbi, and my mother—all wrapped into one comforting terror.

Another day we were marching along the seawall in Pensacola, and since I was the tallest guy in class, Gunny Clark yelled, "Come here, you big puke." Then he positioned me at the front of the class, and he barked, "I want you to march down this seawall and tell me how deep it is. And if you drown, boy, I'll know it's too *deep*!"

We never answered the gunny. We didn't even dare look at him. We just did what he said, so I awaited his command. "Ready? Begin. Lehf. Rye. Lehf. Rye . . ." and I started marching. But the ocean wall was covered with algae slime, and after my first few steps, I slipped. In one motion, my knee twisted and I fell.

"Get up, you big stupid fool. What are doin', fallin? I didn't *tell* you to fall. If I tell you to fall, *fall*. But I told you to *march*. Get right back up here. Right-now, right-now, right-now."

I ran back up, and my knee was killing me, but the gunny's voice kept ringing in my ears. "When I tell you to march, I want you to march. I don't want you to fall, you big dope. Ready? *March*. Lehf. Rye. Lehf. . . ."

I hit the seawall and—*bam*—I dropped again, which sent the gunny into a fit. "Are you so stupid you can't walk?" he hollered. "I'm tellin' you right now boy, you are *not* gonna make it. Why don't you just D-O-R on the spot?"

And for the third time, I was ordered back to the line, then back down the seawall, marching as if I were headed nonstop to China. But when I fell this third time, I felt a sharp pain shoot up my right arm. When I looked down, I could see that my hand had been split open by a razor-sharp oyster shell. Blood was gushing out like a scene in a horror movie.

I grabbed my hand and tried not to scream, because I knew Gunny Clark would be furious. But a weak moan escaped my lips, anyway.

"What's *wrong* with you, boy?"

As I climbed back up the seawall, he saw the blood spurting from my hand, but he showed no signs of panic. Instead, he yelled at one of the other guys, "Get over here, you puke," and he ripped off the man's T-shirt. But while the gunny wrapped my hand in it, he yelled in my face, "Don't you dare scream, you big sissy. Don't you make a sound!"

Then Gunny Clark hailed down a telephone truck that was passing by, sent all the other guys marching back to our barracks, and then rode with me in the phone truck to the infirmary.

During the entire ride, Gunny Clark never said a word to me or the driver. But inside the infirmary, while we were waiting, ole Rosie the Witch emerged from within my gunny. It was just like the day back in Brighton Beach when Rosie had opened up to me and—just once—had talked instead of chasing me away as she usually did. Well, Gunny Clark did the same thing.

"How are you feeling, son?" he asked, and at the sound of caring words coming from his mouth, I really tripped out. Was it possible that he could be an ordinary man? "Is everything okay?" he continued. "I think your hand will be okay. Let me look at it." Gunny Clark was talking to me as if he were a real human being, and I had no idea how to react.

"Yeah, it's pretty nasty, but don't worry," he said. "Things like this happened in Nam all the time and guys turned out okay." He was not only a real person, but he had a past, too. Until that moment, Gunny Clark had never revealed a second's worth of his personal or professional history to any of us.

Finally, the doctor arrived and examined my hand. I could see in his expression that he was appalled. But when Gunny asked in an unbelievably sincere tone, "Is he going to be okay?" the doctor said, "Yeah, I think we can fix him up."

At that, Gunny turned to me and spoke in that same tone, "Then good luck to you. I'll see you back at the barracks." But suddenly, his voice snapped and he screamed, "And don't you *ever* say I spoke to you, you piece of shit!" Then he spun on his heels and strode out the door.

In the days that followed, I had to do everything that the other candidates did, except for pushups. My bandaged hand got me out of that portion of PT, or physical training.

After a week, though, I noticed that my hand was giving off an odor like dead fish. So I went to the man. "Gunnery Sergeant Clark, United States Marine Corps," I said, "my hand doesn't feel right. I think there's something wrong."

"What are you talkin' about? Of course your hand doesn't feel right. You have thirty-six stitches in it," he screamed. "You're just tryin' to get out of PT-PT-boy-PT. That's all. You just want outta PT."

I didn't argue with my mouth, but I guess he saw the expression in my eyes because he snapped, "Then go the infirmary." He said it as if I were three years old.

Back in the doctor's office, they removed the bandages and immediately saw that my hand had become gangrenous. After closer examination, they found that the doctor's assistant who had sewed me up the week before had failed to clean out the wound properly. So they had to remove the stitches, reopen the wound, remove some shell particles that had been left inside, and then every day for the next two weeks, they cleaned the wound with alcohol and large wooden Q-tips.

At first, they used eight staffers to hold me down so they could scrub out my hand. *No painkillers. Twice a day. Every day. The worst pain imaginable.* Gradually, the number went down to six, then four, and finally two guys holding me. But after the first time, I just started crying even before I got to the infirmary. And throughout, they warned me that I might lose my hand. So the only motivation I had, forcing me to go back for guaranteed torture twice a day, was that I wanted to keep my hand. There are no one-handed jet pilots.

But in a strange sense—explainable only in the context of AOCS—I kept going back to the infirmary, and back to PT, because I was damn certain that I would not D-O-R. By then, nothing could make me quit.

The Power
Don't listen to those fools who tell you to fight the power; the truth is, you need to get the power.

And that power is the power to determine your own destiny.

Your power comes from education, the belief in yourself, and hard work.

Let nothing take your power away. Drugs, alcohol, ignorance, racism, and low self-esteem suck the power from your very soul.

Power is freedom and freedom is life; but don't confuse freedom with responsibility.

You are responsible to God.

You are responsible to yourself, to do the best you can with what you have.

You are responsible to your family, your true friends, your neighbors, your environment, and to the enrichment of all mankind.

Get the power; don't fight it.

20

You see, the man who has been speaking to you for the past forty-five minutes hasn't been me. It's been my daddy. I'm too young to tell you the things I've just said. Only an older, wiser person could tell you that. So for the past forty-five minutes, my father has been speaking to you.

My father was the greatest man in my entire life, and my best friend. My daddy! He died four years ago. But before my father died, he gave me the greatest gift a man or woman will ever receive. Before my daddy, died, I sat on his hospital bed, and he looked in my eyes and said, "Boy, I am proud of you. And I'm ready to die, 'cause I got a son like you to carry on."

You see, now, it's time for you to grow up because, one day, every one of your parents will die. But if you want to receive the greatest gift you'll ever get, then it's time to grow up. Because the greatest gift you'll ever receive is when your parents look you in the eyes, one day before they die, and say that they are proud of you, too. My father gave me, and my mother continues to give me, that special gift.

You ain't so bad! Bein' bad is having your parents be proud of you. And that's the real reason why I'm so bad. . . .

Midway through AOCS, I had abandoned any hope that Laurie might bring the kids and live in Pensacola. By then it was too late anyway, because once I received my bars and became a navy ensign, I would be transferred somewhere else for flight training. But Laurie did decide at least to come for a visit. And these are her memories of the Naval Air Station, Pensacola:

> Drew had bought us a little black 1966 Mercedes, and I had driven down with the kids and two of my sisters. But I was intimidated when we pulled onto the base. I had never been on a military base before, and this one was beautiful, grand, very immaculately kept and spotless, but also kind of monotonous, because everything looked so official.
>
> Well, we parked and went walking to get information when suddenly I see this tall, lean, mean, and very handsome guy with excellent posture coming out of a building and walking toward us.
>
> "Laurie," my sister Andie whispered in a small, frightened voice, "I think that's Drew."
>
> "No way," I responded, though I could feel my blood rising and tears swelling up in my eyes, because I thought that the man *did* resemble you.
>
> "No, it is!" she insisted. "That's Drew."
>
> That's when I see that it really is you, so I say, "Kids, it's your daddy!" and immédiately, Taryn and Drew Jacques sprint toward you. So do Andie and my youngest sister Leslie.
>
> But I proceed more slowly, because I cannot believe my eyes. You look like you've lost about thirty pounds, and you seem taller than ever—a totally different person. There is a glow around you, everything about you is marvelous, and yet I am stunned. Has it happened? I can't be certain—but from everything that I can see, you've become the kind of man that I definitely did *not* want to be having a trial separation from! At least not for much longer. . . .[1]

While we exchanged hugs, I could see the pride and amazement in my family's eyes, and that pumped me up. Then we went to the base cafeteria, and Laurie observed a new class of poopies who provided her with a glimpse of what I had just been through. They marched in and sat at the tables, but not until they received commands from their gunny, and the poopies then waited for other commands to do everything else, like "Ready? *Pray*," and "Ready? *Eat*."

"Maybe it was because I had been so leery of the whole thing before I got there," Laurie recalls, "but you seemed too good to

be true. And yet everything on the base appeared so regi-
mented that I had to believe, if anybody could change you,
these marine sergeants would."

Because the base captain's wife, Phyliss Rasmussen, had
asked, I had arranged for Laurie, her sisters, and the kids to
use the captain's private guest house. But later than night, after
the six of us had enjoyed a relaxing afternoon and early evening
at the guest house, the captain's wife dropped by.

"Well, Andie," said Mrs. Rasmussen, "why don't you take
Leslie and the kids, and you all come and stay with the captain
and me. We've got extra bedrooms in the main house."

"Oh, no," Andie said. "That's okay. We couldn't do that. We
can all stay here. It's *real* comfortable!"

"No, Andie," Mrs. Rasmussen repeated. "I think you should
come with me."

"No, no, no, no," Andie protested. "We haven't seen Drew in
a long time, so we all want to stay here. We'll just spread blan-
kets on the floor—"

At that point, Laurie interrupted her sister and whispered,
"Andie, maybe Drew and I should be *alone*. . . ."

"Ooooh," Andie said. "Now I understand." Then Laurie's
sisters exited with the kids and Mrs. Rasmussen, leaving my
wife and me to ourselves for the first time in ages.

It was wonderful, that night with Laurie, and we rekindled
the hopes that I had of keeping our dreams alive. I tried to be
a perfect gentleman, and it was almost as if we were dating
again. Romance was in the air, I *was* a new guy, and once Laurie
understood that, she seemed to like the new me.

So a few days later, after my family had returned to New
Orleans, I wrote this letter:

Dear Laurie, Taryn, and Drew,

How are all of you doing? . . . I passed my seapower final with
an above-average grade. I'm doing pretty good in academics,
knock on wood. We have only four more weeks of school, and
next week, we start with the big three: Aerodynamics, navigation, and engines. They are the hardest, but they will probably
be the most interesting, and they will all relate directly to flying,
so I will get a taste of what we'll study in flight school.
For some bad news, we had our third inspection yesterday,

and the class failed. So they took those white tapes back from us, and we are back in an unsecured status. Also, that takes all hopes of me coming to New Orleans for the July 4th weekend. The class is not together. A few people . . . are really pulling us apart.

Today, another candidate woke up and just left. He was an ex-Marine. Another one bites the dust. But I'm feeling pretty good because I had the opportunity to be with you, Laurie. And I had a supergreat time. You guys made me feel really great. I hope you all had an equally good time.

I think the way things were, we (Prince Charming and Cinderella!!) have a fighting good chance of living happily ever after, Laurie. I hope visiting down here, seeing that navy life is really doing me some good, and having a lot of fun together has made the difference. . . .

I really feel good about the whole thing. So start making plans for the ball. It's only two weeks away.

By the way, guess where my dog tags were, and guess who found them? The captain himself. Yesterday, I was called down to the office and was given a little black box, all taped up with DREW BROWN written on the outside. The captain had sent the tags with specific instructions that they would only be given to me, and not the drill instructor, so I wouldn't get into trouble. . . . Please write back ASAP.

I will love you always,
Drew[2]

Yes, the dog-tag story. Early on the morning after our romantic evening in the captain's guest quarters, I had to race from Laurie's arms and back to be with my class. Yet once I got to the barracks, I couldn't find my dog tags, and since Gunny Clark checked dog tags every morning, this was no game.

During inspection, he meticulously looked every man up and down, and then patted each guy on the chest to feel for the metal tags. Without mine, therefore, I was dead. A future naval warrior can't lose his dog tags. I'd rather have lost my underwear and pants, and stood naked once again at inspection, than to lose my dog tags. So I didn't know what to do. I certainly couldn't make up dog tags, and nobody could lend me his.

Then the inspection began, and while I stood anxiously in line, Gunny Clark started down the row, eyeballing every guy and tapping for tags. He didn't miss tapping a single guy, and

I knew that I was dead. It was over. No military ball. No bars. Nothing. I was finished.

But when he got to my bunk, suddenly Harlem resurfaced within me. He looked me up and down, then reached to touch my chest. But at that exact moment, I let out a painful cry.

"What's wrong, you big dope?" he responded.

"Nothing," I said, then dropped my voice. "Uh, the stitches just opened in my hand."

"Goddamnit, Drew," he screamed, "take your butt down to the infirmary." And I was out of there, missing the dog-tag check by one beat shy of the gunny's tap.

In a few weeks, Laurie returned to the base for the formal Military Ball, and this time, she left the kids back in New Orleans with her parents. Since the two of us had few chances like this, I made every effort to court my wife again. I wanted to convince her that I intended to continue wearing my wedding band long after I earned my navy bars.

"Things were much more relaxed between us," she recalls. "I got my first taste of shopping at a commissary exchange. Big, clean stores where all the merchandise is half price with no taxes! It's one of the greatest benefits to military life." We also spent our days on the beach and our nights down by the Strip, where Laurie fell in love with a Kentucky bluegrass band that was playing at Seville Quarters—a club where all the navy guys hung out.

On the night of the Military Ball itself, however, my Laurie looked like a movie star. She wore a purple dress, and because she had spent too much time in the sun that day, her beautiful tanned complexion was beaming with a constant rosy blush. This was also the first formal affair—complete with a receiving line—that the two of us had ever attended.

"I liked what I saw," she recalls. "You seemed to be very happy, and a perfect gentleman. You were also real responsive, and you hadn't been that way in years. It was as though you had been out on a limb for a long, long time, but you were finally coming back in. So I really hated to leave the next morning, and the drive back to New Orleans was very frustrating. For the first time in months, I didn't want to be away from you."

*   *   *

During the final weeks of AOCS, when only the program survivors were left among our class's candidates, I encountered some very hard academics. And what really frightened me was that guys started using terms that I didn't know and couldn't seem to understand. Like *vector*.

A vector quantity, according to the dictionary, is that which "requires for its complete specification a magnitude, direction, and sense and that is commonly represented by a line segment the length of which designates the magnitude of the vector, the orientation of which designates the direction of the vector, and the sense of which is designated by an arrowhead at one end of the segment. . . ."[3]

But once some of the guys saw how words and definitions like this confused me, they kept using them in conversations, in and out of class, as if to trip me up. Peer competition is commonplace in naval aviation, and it's always keenest as one nears a goal. Yet struggle with the word *vector* as hard as I could, it somehow remained the most impenetrable term I had ever encountered. It was such an aerodynamic word that I started doubting my academic abilities.

Years later, I would tell kids in my speeches, "The reason some of you don't dream of becoming a doctor is that, when you go to one, they use strings of big words that you can't understand. And right on the spot, your mind says, 'I got no chance at being a doc. I can't even understand what they say.' Yet the tragedy is, the dream dies before you ever even dream it."

Back in AOCS, though, when I finally learned what a *vector* meant, it was so simple. I had been terrified of nothing, because a vector is merely a direction used to navigate in the air. But not everything in AOCS academics was that easy.

We had a saying, "Thirty-five and fly," which meant that since a 35 was the minimum grade, all you really had to do was get a 35 in order to pass. On my navigation final, however, I got a failing grade of 34, and no officer candidate could get his bars unless he passed every course. So my only chance was to restudy the course on my own, and retake the test. Meanwhile, the 34 was put on my permanent record.

The second time around, I earned a 50 on the navigation

final, which was a perfect score. But they never put that on my record. Instead, it retained the 34 mark of failure, followed only by a "P" for the second test score.

This meant that in the future, whenever an officer looked at my records and saw the navigation scores, he wouldn't know how perfectly I had passed. He would only know how low I had gone in failing the first test. And in the navy, passing the first time is imperative.

While I was recovering from this blow, however, another gauntlet came hurling at me in the form of a letter from Laurie that stated in nonnegotiable terms:

Dear Drew,

. . . I've been doing some heavy thinking. I really don't know how to say this, but I'm willing to give our marriage a solid try. Things will have to be different, though.

First and foremost, the children need to be brought up in a safe, sound, loving, and secure surrounding. There can be no liquor, drugs, or any mind-altering substances in our lives. [The children] are most important, and I'm sure you as well as I would like to have them be as wholesome and clean living as possible.

Secondly, we will both contribute to the household chores. I am a working woman and always will be. I will not have everything dumped on my shoulders. . . .

Thirdly, decisions must be mutual—especially MONEY MATTERS. Things are too tight right now to go on spending sprees, the way things were done in the past. We have to get ourselves established and start building for the future. . . .

And everything has to be done in the open. I never want to feel shady again. I don't care how you were brought up, or what was in the past, I'm talking about *now*. Our children will never experience anything shameful. They will learn the respectful way to do everything—honesty, righteousness—not just how to get over. Getting over is a loser's way, and sooner or later, everyone knows your game. . . .[4]

Just as my gunny always did, my honey nailed me too. These were her rules, and either we were going to have to play by the rules, or we weren't going to play at all. Because if I was to remain a changed man, she cautioned, then those changes had to penetrate inside me and become permanent. Simply donning a navy uniform had not made me worthy of the American Dream. My heart had to change, too.

But I accepted the truth in Laurie's letter, because I was also finding out how much of a real man I had become. Manliness, I realized, had nothing to do with overpowering my wife. It had nothing to do with being a drunken fool. It did, however, have something to do with marching in time, running side by side with Gunny Clark, and passing these tests at AOCS. Real men know when to live by the rules, instead of always following the beat of a different drummer as I had been doing for so many years.

What I could not accept, however, had nothing to do with Laurie. Instead, it was resentment toward me from the guys in the AOCS program who had been brought up strait-laced, white, and so-called perfect all their lives. They resented me not so much because I was black, though that was definitely a part of it, but because I was black *and* had a vibrant personality *and* was a born leader. I was everything that the *old* country-club atmosphere wanted from white navy jet pilots, but never from a black one. Yet the irony was, the system itself has nothing to do with racism, because the modern naval system was designed for all men and women to enjoy equality and fairness.

This meant, however, that the old values and the new system were often in conflict back then—making racism surface when it was least expected. My first real hints of this, for example, came in such strenuous tests as the Dilbert and Helo dunkers.

These tests teach the underwater survival techniques that all military jet pilots must master, because most real-life mission flying is off of aircraft carriers and over the world's enormous oceans. And if, God forbid, a pilot downs a jet at sea, the impact of an AOCS dunker into a swimming pool is nothing by comparison. So we took these dunker tests very seriously and spent a lot of time in the pools.

But my first day in the water, a white navy petty officer who was our swimming instructor came right over to me and said, "Look, Brown, I'll help you learn how to swim, 'cause I know *y'all* can't swim that good. You sink when you get in the water—right?"

Now, I love it when my southern wife or friends say "y'all."

This instructor, though, was using that same phrase to avoid saying "you blacks," and he was also revealing what the expectations of blacks in this otherwise all-white country club really were.

That's why I didn't protest. Instead, I blew the man's mind, because I swim like a fish, and I did so that day with an unwavering grin on my face. By the end of the session he confessed, "I've never seen a black guy swim like you!"

"But," I responded, "I *have* seen too many white guys who think like you, and I hope this day will change your thoughts."

One of my last survival tests, however, was not as easy to conquer. The Helo dunker is an enormous device that simulates the interior of a helicopter. It contains six seats, though at any one time only four guys are placed inside while undergoing a series of four tests. But the experience of these tests is the same: It's the equivalent of being strapped by seat belts into a death trap while it plunges into twenty feet of water.

For our first test, the Helo went straight down into the pool, and once submerged, we had to count to five, unbuckle, and then everybody had to escape through the Helo's windows. For the second test, it took us straight down again, and once submerged, we had to count, unbuckle, and then exit with everybody else through the same door. Both tests demonstrated teamwork and the ability to orient ourselves under ideal crash simulations.

The third time down, however, the Helo flipped upside down—and this was very scary, because the Helo could flip rapidly in either direction, making us very disoriented—but once submerged, we still had to count to five and unbuckle, and then everybody had to get out through the windows. The fourth time down, though, was the pass-or-fail test on the Helo dunker. In it, we wore goggles that had been blacked out and the Helo flipped upside down. So once it submerged, we couldn't see, we were totally disoriented, but everybody still had to unbuckle and exit through the same door.

I did fine during the first three tests, but when I saw a demonstration of the fourth one, my mind immediately snapped back to when I was sixteen and scuba diving along The Cut. So before I ever entered the water for the fourth Helo test, survival became my primary objective. And as soon as the Helo flipped us upside down, with us blinded and strapped inside, I could *not* count to five or wait on the other guys. Surviving was my only motivation, because no matter what the navy's rules were, my street brother's voice kept nagging within my mind, "Remember Harlem, remember the projects, remember The Cut, and save your life, Drew."

Consequently, I had to do the Helo dunker sixteen times, with the last try being the only one where I actually counted before I escaped. By then, however, I was so psyched out that I stayed under for a full forty counts before I resurfaced—just to show the instructors that it wasn't fear that had driven me earlier, but in fact, a primal instinct. "I will survive. I will never die in a navy accident," I kept saying to myself during that long forty count. "I will always survive."

That same commitment would stick with me through the rest of my naval aviator's career. Years later, for example, when our jetattack squadron from the U.S.S. *Nimitz* was preparing for the raid over Libya, all of the other pilots spent the night before that planned attack writing letters to their wives, their parents, and their children. These were the traditional farewell letters, saying that if the pilots died the next day, their deaths would not be in vain. . . .

But I walked in, asked what they were doing, and then said, "Damn, just give the letters to me, man. I'll deliver them personally, 'cause *I'm* coming back!" It had never crossed my mind to write letters to Laurie, my parents, or the kids, because I had no intention of dying—not in a jet-bombing raid, nor during a stormy night carrier landing, nor earlier in a Helo dunker at AOCS, nor years earlier, while I wandered underwater along The Cut. Death *is* a mystery, but life is far too mysterious and wonderful in its own right. It's heaven right here on earth, and I can't imagine giving it up for death. I have to live first, before I can even think about dying.

During our last weeks of AOCS training, things got much better. We gained a little freedom and got to go into town on weekends. And by the last week, we were also allowed to wear either our khakis or the whites, the navy's sharp-looking dress uniforms. Each of my class was also assigned to a different gunnery sergeant to help indoctrinate the newest classes of poopies. My assignment was with Gunnery Sergeant Buck Welcher, who would serve during the next year as a consultant for the film *An Officer and a Gentleman*. But this real-life gunny made that movie's Foley look like a social worker.

One time, for example, Gunny Welcher took a new crop of poopies into the barbershop and said, "Look, you pukes, one of you children is going home. Right now! Every class that I've had in Pensacola, a guy goes home the first half hour. Now you have two choices, you bunch of worms. You guys ain't gonna be jet pilots anyway. So here are your choices. Either you can go home, looking the way you look, or you can wait until they shave your heads and then leave looking like a real dickhead. But one of you *has* to quit, or we're going to PT until one of you dies."

Then from the corner of the room, a kid raised his hand, said, "That's it for me, sir!" and the twelve-hour poopie D-O-R-ed on the spot. It was amazing.

But working with this new GS also meant that I was no longer under Gunny Clark's command. So he and I started hanging out together, and one night we agreed to meet at a bar near the base.

However, when I showed up wearing my whites, instead of the khakis, Gunny Clark gave me a hard time.

"My *black* skin just looks better in whites than the white guys do," I quipped. "But you knew that from the first day. Right?" And we laughed, because Gunny Clark and I both knew that he had not used color against me throughout the remainder of my sixteen weeks—not since that first predawn jab.

Then we downed a couple of beers and were chatting about the new poopies when, suddenly, Gunny Clark said, "You wouldn't be wearing whites because the other guys are wearing their class stripes? That wouldn't be it, now, Drew? Huh?"

I looked down in my drink. During the last week of AOCS, a lot of guys were wearing the khakis because navy regulations allowed us to wear our performance bars, or "stripes," on the khaki shirt collars. Particularly the guys who had four bars, which meant that they had been voted by our peers as tops in the class. But I hadn't been voted four stripes. I only received one, and that hurt me.

"No, Gunny," I said, "I just love *whites*. Don't you know that by now?" But the truth was, I purposefully wore my whites every hour of that last week because we could *not* put stripes on the whites' collars. That way, I let nobody see me in stripes, so nobody knew exactly how I had finished in the peer-voted rankings.

"Drew, you're going to go through a lot, being black in the navy," Gunny Clark said, interrupting my thoughts. "And that racism is the nature of the beasts you'll be around. You'll always have to work twice as hard. That's why I called you a 'big black sonuvabitch' that first morning. Right from the start, I wanted to know if that prejudice garbage would turn you away. And if it would, then I wanted your ass out! There's no sense putting a guy through hell unless he's going to be the kind who can take blows and use them as motivators to succeed."

I didn't know that night how prophetic Gunny Clark was. But my next seven years on active duty in the navy, plus my subsequent years in the reserves and flying for Federal Express, have proven that my gunny did right by me.

August 21, 1981, was the first time in my life, other than my graduation from SUNO, that I completed something I had started. In five months, I would be twenty-seven years old, but until that moment, everything in my past had been a string of aborted missions: *See Buddy Drew hustle success, see Buddy Drew run from failure.* But no more. On that day, I was commissioned Ensign Drew T. Brown III, an officer in the United States Navy.

It was gorgeous Pensacola weather. Laurie and the kids had their pictures taken with me in my whites, complete with white ceremonial gloves. And I could see in my wife's eyes that our trial separation would end. It did, by the way, and we've been happily together ever since.

Later that day, however, our class marched onto the parade grounds. We heard speeches, bands, and more speeches. Then Captain Rasmussen presented us with our certificates, and we put on our new ensign shoulder boards. Everything was grand.

But I had an even grander secret that sustained me. Earlier in the day, I had received a telegram from my father. In 1942, Daddy had served in the navy, and his duties on board ship had been as a ship's porter. But one day, while he was shining a lieutenant's shoes, the white officer slapped him and called him a "nigger." My father responded by throwing the man overboard. After that incident, the only thing that saved my father from being jailed and court-martialed was that he had lied about his age in order to join. His records confirmed that he was only thirteen years old.

Because of that incident, however, he would not come to my AOCS ceremony. Daddy feared that the navy would somehow discover his tainted record and deny me my commission. But he did send a telegram, and its succinct message was unforgettable:

TO; DREW TIMOTHY BROWN III, ENSIGN, U.S. NAVY
FROM: DREW BUNDINI BROWN, JR.

CONGRATULATIONS, SON. I'D BE PROUD TO SHINE YOUR SHOES.[5]

So throughout the commencement, I thought about my daddy, and nothing that happened seemed as wonderful as his telegram tucked into my back pocket.

After we became ensigns, our class and guests were escorted into the base chapel. It was a very solemn moment, and throughout the worship service I kept looking at Gunny Clark and thinking about my own father. These two men were the exact opposites of one another, yet somehow the same, too. Then I reached into my pants pocket and felt the tokens I had brought. It's a naval tradition to present your GS with one silver dollar, and when you do, he salutes you for the first time and calls you "sir."

Moments later, our class stood and began to file one by one past Gunny Clark, but I made sure that I was last. Each ensign gave him a silver dollar, received the GS's salute, and exchanged handshakes. But when my time came, Gunny Clark popped me his finest marine salute, almost sending shock waves through the atmosphere, and I handed him two silver dollars—one from me and one from my daddy—and I returned his salute.

Then tears swelled up in our eyes when he called me "sir." Technically, I was now his superior in navy rank, but I knew that I could never be better than this man. My father had been right—"You'll have many fathers in your life, son"—and in sixteen short, horrible, but wonderful weeks, my gunny had become the most influential of those other fathers. In four months, he had given me all the things that my real daddy could not. But because of those sixteen weeks, Gunny Clark had also prepared me for the rest of my life.

. . . You remember this, and you take it with you always: You may not get what you want, when you want it, but I promise you one thing. God is never ever late.

Epilogue

My years in the United States Navy could be a book in themselves (and maybe the full story will be, someday). But the following summarizes that story and culminates with my present mission that I've accepted in America. During military service, I put my life on the line overseas for this country, and now I'm devoting much of my life to it at home.

Just after Labor Day in 1981, I entered primary flight training at the Naval Air Station in Corpus Christi, Texas. During the next three years, I would undergo various types of jet-aviator training before being assigned as an aviator on an aircraft carrier. But primary training was my first hands-on experience with airplanes.

My initial task was to complete several months of intense, self-directed study. After that, I could begin flying the navy's warhorse of a propeller-driven airplane, the T-28 Trojan. These planes were like the ones that John Wayne piloted in those dramatic war movies—complete with Spanish subtitles—that I had watched back in theaters near the projects.

But two weeks into primary training I was confronted by a nightmare. A Drug Enforcement Administration official arrested me on the base. The charges were conspiracy to obtain, possess, and distribute twenty-five grams of cocaine, and they stemmed from an innocent car ride I had taken with some so-called friends while operating Bundini's in New Orleans. I remembered that ride only because, at the time, I had a gut feeling that I was in the wrong place at the wrong time. And with this arrest, my earlier instincts proved to be correct.

The DEA agent took me to jail, where I was fingerprinted, stripped of my bars and uniform, hosed down with disinfectant, then tossed an inmate's uniform and a pair of flip-flops. Thus, less than a month after my naval commissioning, I was once again being transformed. This time, however, an officer and a gentleman had become a drug defendant, and another one of society's incarcerated animals.

I was innocent of the charges. But I *was* guilty of having associated with the other New Orleans defendants whom the DEA's investigations had linked to alleged drug deals. Big Easy lowlifes like the Angel Dust Queen were taking another payment on the debts I had incurred while operating Bundini's. During the next two months, therefore, I had to work with the public defender in New Orleans to prepare for my trial, while I also continued struggling to complete ground studies in Corpus Christi.

And when my case finally went to trial, as the *Times-Picayune* subsequently reported, a jury in the court of U.S. District Judge Veronica D. Wicker deliberated for an hour and found me innocent.[1]

Afterward, Judge Wicker told me, "You should not have even been in my courtroom. Forget that this happened, and go protect our country."

Exonerated of these charges, I was finally able to concentrate on flight school. And with Laurie's help, I soon caught up with my class. By December, Lieutenant Craig Luigart supervised my first successful flight behind the controls, and in March 1982 I completed basic flight training.

The most memorable aspect of this milestone was that I got

to fly with a black pilot, Lieutenant Chuck Nesby. His call sign was "Sneakers," and for my sign, my AOCS class had chosen "Dark Gable" (a nickname that, earlier, Momma had coined for me as a boy). We flew an F-14 Tomcat—my first experience with jets—and immediately, I became addicted to G-forces. Subsequently, since my grades were high enough, I requested that my next training be as a jet pilot.

But when orders came down, sending me to the Naval Air Station in Meridian Mississippi, one of my friends cautioned, "What's the matter with you, Drew? Are you crazy? Black guys don't make it out of Meridian."

Yet I was so fired up about jets that I ignored the warning. I was convinced that, one day, I would get my wings of gold. So no matter how long and dark the tunnel might be, I was optimistic as I headed toward the heart of Old Dixie.

The Meridian NAS is actually miles from the small Mississippi town for which it is named. So the base is surrounded by fields of cotton and soybeans, and by tiny black communities, as far as the eye can see. What first impressed me there was that the grounds were meticulously kept but every officer's face was white—reminding me of New Orleans's Pontchartrain Park golf course which, for decades, had operated for "whites only," even though it was located in the solidly black neighborhood where Laurie grew up.

Then a month later, an old black man confirmed that I was not just being paranoid about racism. He was Cholly Davis, a retired navy man who lived in a trailer near the back of the base. His lot was infested with junked vehicles that he used for spare parts while repairing cars for naval personnel on the base. And even though he had never climbed higher in the ranks than second-class petty officer, he knew the score at Meridian because he also worked on base as an NAS civil servant. So I took seriously his warning one afternoon: "Never forget that you're a black pilot because *they'll* always treat you like a black pilot."

By mid-August, Cholly proved to be prophetic. During my first five months of training at Meridian, I had received a series of "downs," or unsatisfactory evaluations, for my flights in a

T-2 Buckeye. So that month, when I got my fourth one, I was heartsick. Guys had gotten kicked out of flight school with as few as three downs.

In addition, all personal signs during that same period indicated that I was being targeted. Laurie had been snubbed by wives of the white naval officers. And I experienced several humiliating moments—like the night at a club called Bonnie & Clyde's when a white woman from a party of couples from the base refused my invitation to dance by politely saying, "I don't dance with niggers!" In an effort to save face, I retaliated, "Then I guess having sex is out of the question?" but the damage was done.

I got my fifth down in early September while on detachment to the U.S.S. *Lexington.* So I had to fly back to Meridian and face the Long Green Table—a board of three officers who would decide my fate as a jet pilot. To my surprise, they decided to give me one more try.

Suddenly, it seemed that Cholly had been wrong. What's more, my daddy counseled me to view the entire ordeal as constructive. "Since you have to re-fly each test twice, every time you get a down, what's the problem?" he said. "Now you'll be better than everybody else who just slid through."

For the next twelve weeks, then, I perfected my flying skills, outscored most pilots as I redid each down, and the hard work culminated in my second attempt to qualify on an aircraft carrier. In late November, I circled the U.S.S. *Constellation,* then slowed my jet to 110 miles per hour before landing five times on the ship's surface as it rolled in the Pacific. Most pilots describe these landings as "controlled crashes," and they are. But after my sixth trip, I heard the magic words through my headphones, "Buckeye 502, you're a *qual.*"

Yet even qualifying paled by comparison to what happened next. As I taxied from the runway at the Naval Air Station in San Diego, California, I first saw a long black Cadillac parked under a C-130 Hercules. Then I spotted a civilian waving his hands in the air while MPs encircled him, their rifles at rest across their chests.

I knew it was my daddy, so I slid back my canopy and returned his wave. But immediately, Daddy's hands flapped madly, and I could tell that he was screaming that unrivaled

Bundini scream. When I landed, he explained how he had forced his way onto the tarmac and persuaded the MPs that he had a right to watch his boy fly a jet.

"But what were you yelling when I waved back?" I asked.

"You fool, keep your hands on the wheel!" he said with a grin.

Back in Meridian during the early months of 1983, I trained in the TA-4J Skyhawk. It's the dazzling jet that Vietnam and the Blue Angels made famous, and in it, I learned the intricacies of air combat maneuvers (ACMs)—the flight techniques that enthrall air show audiences but are actually the warfare skills for dogfights in the sky.

Yet there were problems. The most persistent was that, at six-five, I could barely fit into an A-4 cockpit. However, I was determined to earn my wings of gold, so I refused to admit the problem while on duty. But when I returned home every night, Laurie knew. Working the cockpit pedals routinely resulted in serious problems with my knees and cuts along my shins.

Then in mid-April, eleventh-hour racism surfaced. I was too close to earning my wings, and the all-white inner circle of instructors in Meridian was hating every minute of it.

My proof? During eyesight drills one day, slides were rapidly shown to us, and we were tested on how quickly we could spot a particular image on the screen. But as I raced through the test, a bizarre image appeared: a cartoon of eight Ku Klux Klansmen in white robes who had a beleaguered Harlem Globetrotter surrounded. Then the instructor yelled, "Pick out the basketball player." Of course, I was the only former Globetrotter in the room of grinning white pilots.

A few days later, I had a solo flight. But the weather was bad, and under such conditions, regulations required that an instructor ride in the backseat and function only as an observer. So Marine Captain Hammond Snake, who had a bitter reputation, was assigned as my observer.

But during my landing—even though it had clearly been a perfect flight—he said that I had landed too fast, and he issued my sixth down.

I appealed to the commander on the basis of unfair treat-

44

ment, and he allowed me to redo the landing. But when I passed, he refused to remove the down from my jacket.

Then in May, while I was being evaluated during night landings off the U.S.S. *Lexington,* I got my seventh down. Emotionally, I hit the bottom. I was sent back to the Long Green Table, and at that dreaded hearing, they attrited me—or kicked me out of jet training.

Afterward, as I walked around the base at Meridian, I saw on the faces of young black enlisted men, of guys like Cholly, and of the few who were also naval officers, that I had let them down. Obviously, Cholly had been right about black pilots at Meridian. And because I had not heeded his warning, Dark Gable also failed to accomplish what only a handful of black jet pilots had ever done up until that point—i.e., earn the wings of gold.

When I asked the commander about an appeal, he said with finality, "Nobody has ever beaten attrition."

But if I had learned nothing else in Harlem and Las Vegas, the word *no* ignites me; and if I had learned nothing else from the rest of my rollercoaster life up until that point, I knew and believed that The System still works in America. So I spent the next five weeks moving up the chain of command and seeking redress for the discrimination that had enabled Meridian instructors to attrite me.

Finally, through the help of my first flight instructor, Lieutenant Craig Luigart, I got a hearing with Admiral Peter B. Booth, the CNATRA (pronounced like *Sinatra*) or Chief of Naval Air Training. The admiral seemed convinced by my documentation and determination (I told him, among other things, "I'm here because I can prove that I've been discriminated against. And I won't stop appealing this along the chain of command until I get to the President of the United States."), so the admiral instigated an investigation.

Then, during the week of July Fourth, the CNATRA confirmed racism in Meridian. And his postinvestigation orders allowed me to make history: I beat an attrition. It was truly Independence Week for Buddy Drew, because the admiral also transferred me to the Naval Air Station in Beeville, Texas, where I could resume my jet training.

During the next two months, the Beeville squadron tested

me to the limits. Then, realizing that I was a damn good pilot, they embraced and cheered me on through every evaluation. Finally, on August 25, Captain David A. Page, USN, the base commander at Beeville NAS, announced that I had finally earned my wings of gold.

By year's end, *JET* magazine ran this report about my wings ceremony: "Drew 'Bundini' Brown . . . says that although he's proud of the title, 'trainer of champions,' for having been Muhammad Ali's number-one man from start to finish, the thing that swells his chest the most is talking about his son, Drew III. 'From the root to the fruit is what I call it,' said the veteran trainer."[2]

By January 1984, Laurie, the kids, and I had settled into a new home in Virginia Beach, Virginia. I was stationed at the Oceana Naval Air Station, and my orders placed me with the Replacement Air Group (RAG) at VA-42 in Oceana to receive a year of training on an all-weather attack bomber, the A-6E (TRAM) Intruder.

This jet—manned by a pilot and a bombardier/navigator—was the *baddest* version of attack aircraft used by both the navy and the marines. Manufactured by Grumman Aerospace, the Intruder was designed to carry bombs, rockets, missiles, naval mines, gun pods, and special weapons. It is equally effective on both support and deep-strike missions.

And as an all-weather jet, the Intruder is equipped with cockpit displays that show targets and geographical features on the land above which you're flying at speeds of up to 550 miles per hour. But for all its intricacies, nothing compares to the experience of landing an Intruder on an aircraft carrier. "At night, it's even crazier," I was quoted as telling a navy reporter about the "black hole" into which we had to fly. "There's nothing out there. The cat-shots [catapults] are even more exhilarating. It's like [playing] a [video] game when you're up there using your instruments. The only difference is that you don't just lose your quarter if you play bad."[3]

During the next three years, I would spend over twenty-four months at sea as a naval attack aviator, and during that time, I got over three hundred traps, or landings.

Our squadron, the VA-35 "Black Panthers," is the oldest attack squadron in naval aviation history, and at the time, we were assigned to the nuclear carrier U.S.S. *Nimitz*. That carrier is most popularly known as the on-site location for the Kirk Douglas film *The Final Countdown*. And during my tours of duty, our squadron would operate off the *Nimitz* during several international crises, including those of Libya and Beirut. But historically, the Black Panthers were no strangers to crises.

In World War II, the squadron had served in the escort group for the B-25C Mitchell bombers that launched the Doolittle Raid against Tokyo. During the fifties, the VA-35 again saw significant action in both the Korean and Lebanon conflicts, and in Vietnam, Black Panthers flew A-6s in four deployments before participating in the last U.S. air strike in South Vietnam against the North Vietnamese near the DMZ. In addition, VA-35 pilots responded to the *Pueblo* crisis in 1968 and, in 1980, spent 144 continuous days aboard the *Nimitz* in response to the hostage crisis in Iran.[4] So I was proud to be a Black Panther. Ours is a heritage of being warriors, and I am a warrior.

After my first cruise at sea in 1986, however, Laurie and I began to understand the negative implications of navy life. The cruises separated me from my family for up to seven months at a time. This eliminated telephone conversations, and it made letters from home sacred, more valuable than gold. Yet these separations also made my sea duty much worse than the months I had spent on the oil rig in the Gulf of Mexico. "Channel fever" was the naval term for the homesickness that seamen experience, and I had it bad. So each cruise became harder for me to endure.

So I devised a plan. Back in primary training, I had been invited to speak about flying to a class of elementary students in Corpus Christi, and I had loved the experience. Then, years later in Norfolk, I met John F. Lehman, who was then the U.S. secretary of the navy. So in September, I sent him a formal proposal which contained these observations:

—I was the only black pilot on board [the *Nimitz*] in a flying status.
—I was the only black medium-attack pilot attached to any Air Wing in a flying status in the Atlantic Fleet.

—I was the only black pilot in the RAG at VA-42 during my
  training period.
—I was the only black student in Advance Jets (VT-7) and Basic
  Jets (VT-9) in Meridian, Mississippi, during my training.
—I was the only black student at Basic Flight Training (VT-27)
  in Corpus Christi, Texas, to be selected for the jet pipeline.
—I was the only black candidate in my class at AOCS Pensacola,
  Florida.

   These facts along with the *CNO*'s [Chief of Naval Opera-
tions] recently released minority-manning percentages indi-
cate that the percentage of black aviators in the navy is well
below an acceptable level. Personally and professionally, I feel
that it would be a positive step in the right direction for Naval
Aviation to increase the percentage of black aviators.[5]

That letter also contained my proposal for combining fly-ins
and lectures at various black colleges and universities—all
aimed at enticing more blacks to enter the navy. But during the
next eight months, I got no response.

In December, the *Nimitz* made its farewell departure from
Norfolk harbor. After having its base in that historic seaport for
eleven years, the carrier was headed for six months in the Mediterranean Sea before moving to a new home in Bremerton,
Washington.

The Washington Post covered that event, and the next day,
Laurie and the kids woke up to find that our pictures were on
the front of the "Metro" section. The cutline read, "Lt. Drew T.
Brown bids an affectionate good-bye to son Drew, wife Laurie,
and daughter Taryn."[6]

My father died on September 24, 1987, in Los Angeles, but
we returned his body to be buried alongside his father in Sanford, Florida. "After the funeral," Momma recalls, "you and I
were standing outside the garage at Cousin Pocket Brown's
house, and the question was: *What next?* And I encouraged you
to start speaking to young people. I knew that you had written
to the secretary of the navy, and that the first letter had been
disregarded, but I knew you could do it.

"Not long after that, you started the program on your own.
I just knew it would all work out. For centuries before you were
born, black children in America had no real reason to dream
about an education. And then the year before you were born,

Brown versus the Board of Education opened the doors. So yours is the first generation to have always known the doors to be open. They were closed to your father, and to his father, too. But you, son, are of a new era, and you embody that era."

Those were difficult but challenging days for me. My own naval career was drawing to an end, and losing Daddy made me realize how much I had yet to accomplish. I was thirty-two and had such powerful hopes of making a difference in mankind.

During the spring of 1988, several amazing opportunities came my way. Fred Francis, a correspondent for NBC, did a series on blacks in the military for the *Nightly News,* and one of his segments featured me as a black jet pilot. Then on the *Today* show, former cohost Jane Pauley interviewed me and another naval officer about my special recruiting program, and that summer, NBC correspondent Connie Chung did a profile covering my life from Harlem to the navy for the *Summer Showcase.*

The immediate effect of this concentrated media exposure was that requests for me to do speaking engagements seemed to skyrocket. Throughout the year, I would speak to more than 350,000 students, teachers, and principals in a score of cities.[7]

And that's when I made a crucial decision. I began applying for jobs as a commercial pilot, with the aim that by doing so, I would also have enough time to become a professional motivational speaker to junior high, high school, college, and other institutional audiences. I had something to say about drugs, education, and opportunities in America, and the time had come to say it.

Then in September, I was featured in *Fortune,* following my participation in a conference that the magazine sponsored in Washington, D.C., on the topic "Saving the Schools." The magazine described me as a "powerful persuader"—noting that a week after another recruiter and I spoke to fifteen thousand students in Baltimore, "participation in student government and other school organizations rose 15 percent."[8] I had found my niche.

After I entered the United States Naval Reserves in 1989, Federal Express hired me as a pilot, so my family and I moved to Memphis, Tennessee. Also that spring, the U.S. Chamber of Commerce honored me with one of its Special Salutes. According to the medal's citation, these salutes are given each year "to outstanding individuals and organizations for their contributions to the quality of American life, and to the advancement of the nation's system of free enterprise and private initiative."[9]

Today, Laurie and I are able to do what, for years, we could only hope for. We now operate The American Dream—a program designed to combat drugs and address education issues in this country. Each month, I visit various cities and speak to audiences of young people, parents, teachers, business leaders, and politicians. My basic message is the text excerpted at the beginning of each chapter in this book, but the meaning comes from the life detailed in this book's chapters.

Through the support of corporate America and private contributions, my goal is to establish a foundation whose purpose will be to motivate its clients to further their education and reverse the drug-abuse trend among primary and secondary students, while promoting family values, morality, and a strong work ethic as they become proud and productive citizens of the United States of America.

For corporations and individuals who want to help in these efforts, our address is: The American Dream, P.O. Box 17403, Memphis, Tennessee 38187–0403.

You can lead a horse to water,
but you can't make him drink.
I make him thirsty.
God bless America.

Acknowledgments

The people you have just read about and the following people have made my life and this book special. They are not listed in order of importance, since each has been number one in his or her own way:

Muhammad Ali, for showing me the Greatest is just a man; Brad and Erna Butler, for making my daddy's prophecy that I would have another father who would look after his boy come true; Uncle Herbert and Aunt Myrna Palestine, and cousins Josh, Tracey, and Beth, John, Lisa, Jennifer-Kim, and Charlegmagne Palestine, and Ely and Lillian Levowitz and Al and Ruth Levine, as well as Uncle Elbert for being my blood; Ellen Brown for being my big sister; Lawrence and Lynne Guimont for making me see what a real *Brady Bunch* family looks like; Joni, Patrice, Larry, Andrea, Cesily, and Leslie, for giving me my dream of having the best sisters and brother a man could ask for; Eric Dozier, Ronald Goodman, Joe Holsten, and Keith Roberts, plus Papa and Grandmother for making the brother/sister family category even bigger.

Grandaddy Drew Sr., Uncles Willy, Alonzo, Coley, Johnny,

Aunt Sadie, Cousin Pocket and Julia Brown, Aunt Sane, Sister, Freida, Keith, Kenny, Larry, Johnny, David, Jimmy, Cedric, Ronnie, Jefferson Jr., Billy Boy, Dallas, Beverly, Claudia, Diane, Phyllis, Julie, Coley III, Bruce, Frederick, Punkin, Earl C., Aunt Bee, Uncle Coley Jr., Altameese, Betty, Bernard, Bob, Willette, Cynthia, Anthony, Juanita, Michelle, Jeanette, Maude and the other Browns, for being my roots; Aunt Fannie and Uncle Al, Butch, Larry, Mona Nealy, Mary and Jane Arroyo for being my home away from home; Ronald Jackson, for being my brother; Gene Kilroy, for teaching me "That is why"; Sugar Ray Robinson, Wali "Youngblood" Muhammad, Pat Patterson, Shelton, Specky, and Pal, for loving me and being my very much needed uncles while I was growing up; Mr. Garcia, Mrs. Wilson, Mrs. Prescott, Dr. Walter Austin, Dr. Norman Wilson, Craig Luigart and every other teacher I've had, thank you.

Carl "Footie" Fuller, Harold "Bud" Doleman, David Rivera, Jeff Hoffstein, Glen Almos, Eddie Paris, Richard Stephen "Cubby" Katz, Gary Prince, Danny Rappaport, Alfredo Garcia, Scotty Camer, Craig Allen, Cornell Charles, Bobby Johnson, Benny Guidry, David Clark, Mark "Benny" Adams, Joe and Sonia Gilliam, John Michael, Doc Richardson, Mark "Killer" Kinnane, Tom Simon, Scott Ripley, Welch Fair, Frank Chukes, Jim Gray, David Pry, Beverly and Terry Davis, Terry and Linda Guy, Mark and Cathy White for being my friends; Mazel, Zvi, Yossi, Shlomo, and Ofra Rauch, for being my beloved Israeli family; Coach Tayer, Coach Al Lopez, Coach Joe N. Hornbeak, Jr., Coach Cirilo Manego, Coach Blitz, and Coach Dave Gotkin, for putting up with me; Richard and Suzanne Tonn, thank you for helping us start off; my commanding officers Commander Steve Richmond and Captain Lou Lalli, the last of the true warriors; Leslie Franklin, Admiral Peter Cressy, Admiral Walter Davis, Captain Frank Horne, Howard and Gerona Fowler, Jack Finley, Harry Wiley, Fred Francis, Naomi Spinrad, Alelia Bundles, Cathy Bennett, Gerry Holmes, Roxanne Spillette, Al Messina, Joe Lapenta, Marcia Perday, Linda Tucker, Barbara Reese, Julie Keller, Marge LaBarge, Daisy Lynum, Jesse Luxton, Emerey Waters, Fred Allen, Byron Hogue, and Eleanor, Naomi, Evelyn, and Rob from Providence, Rhode Island, and Ramon Sanchez, who all believe in me and are helping the Dream come alive.

The United States Navy, Fred Smith and Federal Express, John Hall and Ashland Oil, Gary Tooker and Motorola, Inc., Joe Anderson and Southern Bell, Jim Hayes and *Fortune* magazine, Tom Garth and the Boys and Girls Clubs of America, General Motors and all of my other sponsors of The American Dream who really care about the future of our children.

Thank you Carol Dyrek, for being nice to my daddy, Don King for helping during my father's funeral; Aunt Rinnie, Charles Cleaves, and Cholly Davis, for being the nicest and most honest people I've met; Joe and Paula Adams, for being the best neighbors a man could have; Haidee Morgan, Joann Boisdore Smith, Jean Simon, and Trish Raschid, for being Laurie's best friends; and especially to Lisa Drew and Randall Elisha Greene, who were sent to me by God so the message could be given.

Drew Timothy Brown III

Notes

Chapter Two
1. For this quote, and for some details in scenes prior to it, Budd Schulberg, *Loser and Still Champion: Muhammad Ali* (New York: Doubleday, 1972), pp. 26–27. Reprinted by permission of the publisher.

Chapter Three
1. Muhammad Ali with Richard Durham, *Muhammad Ali: My Own Story* (New York: Random House, 1975), pp. 108–109.

Chapter Four
1. Scene from *Shaft*. Copyright © 1971 by Metro-Goldwyn-Mayer, Inc. Screenplay by Ernest Tidyman and John D. F. Black. Directed by Gordon Parks. Scene enacted by Drew Bundini Brown as Willy; Moses Gunn as Bumpy; and Richard Roundtree as Shaft. Reprinted by permission of MGM.

Chapter Five
1. From *The Color Purple*. Copyright © 1985 by Warner Bros., Inc. Based on the novel by Alice Walker. Screenplay by Menno Meyjes. Directed by Steven Spielberg. Music by Quincy Jones.
2. Ibid.
3. Ali with Durham, *My Own Story*, pp. 108–109.

Chapter Six
1. Compare Schulberg, *Loser and Still Champion*, p. 41.
2. Compare Ibid., pp 40–41; and John Cottrell, *Muhammad Ali, Who Once Was Cassius Clay* (New York: Funk and Wagnalls, 1967), p. 130. Reprinted by permission of HarperCollins Publishers, Inc.
3. Compare Cottrell, *Who Once Was Cassius Clay*, p. 126.
4. Schulberg, *Loser and Still Champion*, p. 41.
5. Compare Ibid., p. 131; for photos, see Jack Rummel, *Muhammad Ali* (New York: Chelsea House, 1988), pp. 48–49.
6. Ibid., p. 49
7. Schulberg, *Loser and Still Champion*, pp. 41–42.

Chapter Seven
1. Cottrell, *Who Once Was Cassius Clay*, p. 198.
2. Ibid., pp. 215–218.
3. Schulberg, *Loser and Still Champion*, p. 48.
4. Rummel, *Muhammad Ali*, pp. 65–66.
5. Schulberg, *Loser and Still Champion*, p. 49

Chapter Eight
1. My mother wrote this speech for my bar mitzvah, and I recited it on February 17, 1968, at the Ocean View Synagogue in Brighton Beach, New York.
2. Rummell, *Muhammad Ali*, p. 59–67.

Chapter Nine
1. See also Ali with Durham, *My Own Story,* p. 264.
2. Taken from a clipping of Malcolm Nash, "Young Drew Brown Gets Israeli Grant," *New York Post;* exact issue, page number, and column were not on the clipping.
3. *Esquire,* November 1969, cover and p. 121; see also Schulberg, *Loser and Still Champion,* illustration no. 16.
4. Ali with Durham, *My Own Story,* pp. 264–267.
5. Rummel, *Muhammad Ali,* p. 75.
6. Ibid., p. 71.

Chapter Ten
1. Rummel, *Muhammad Ali,* p. 77.
2. Ali with Durham, *My Own Story,* p. 281.
3. Ibid, pp. 307–318.
4. Schulberg, *Loser and Still Champion,* p. 69.
5. Rummel, *Muhammad Ali,* p. 83

Chapter Eleven
1. Compare poem in Ali with Durham, *My Own Story,* p. 349.
2. Schulberg, *Loser and Still Champion,* p. 139.
3. Rummel, *Muhammad Ali,* pp. 84, 88.
4. Ali with Durham, *My Own Story,* p. 356.
5. Rummel, *Muhammad Ali,* p. 88

Chapter Twelve
1. Letter, Louis R. Henson, director of athletics and head basketball coach at New Mexico State University at Las Cruces, to Chuck Taylor, basketball coach at Abraham Lincoln High School, Brooklyn, February 25, 1972. Reprinted by permission of Mr. Henson.
2. Rummel, *Muhammad Ali,* pp. 82–83.
3. B. Peter Carry, "Basketball," *1974 Year Book Covering the Year 1973: Annual Supplement to Collier's Encyclopedia* (New York: Macmillan Educational Corporation, 1973), p. 490.

Chapter Thirteen
1. Gene Ward, "Boxing," *1974 Year Book Covering the Year 1973: Annual Supplement to Collier's Encyclopedia* (New York: Macmillan Educational Corporation, 1973), pp. 493–494.
2. Ali with Durham, *My Own Story,* p. 20.
3. Ward, "Boxing," p. 493.
4. Ibid.
5. "Drew Brown Takes on New York," Kingsborough Community College *Scepter,* April 17, 1974. Reprinted by permission of the publisher.
6. Letter, Joe N. Hornbeak, head basketball coach at Southern University in New Orleans, to Drew Brown, March 25, 1974. Reprinted by permission of Dr. Hornbeak.
7. Rummel, *Muhammad Ali,* pp. 96–97.
8. Ibid.
9. Ibid.
10. Frank Litsky, "Boxing: The Champ," *1976 Year Book Covering the Year 1975; Annual Supplement to Collier's Encyclopedia* (New York: Macmillan Educational Corporation, 1975), pp. 403, 497.

Chapter Fifteen
1. Rummel, *Muhammad Ali,* p. 113.
2. An unpublished poem by the author, "Dreams," written April 21, 1985.

Chapter Sixteen
1. Rummel, *Muhammad Ali,* p. 113.
2. Dan Bennett, "Fight Promoter Sues to Halt Publication," New Orleans (La.) *Times-Picayune,* August 3, 1978.
3. Ibid.
4. Ibid.
5. Rummel, *Muhammad Ali,* p. 114.
6. Ibid, pp. 114–115.

Chapter Seventeen
1. "The ALI Forum," New York *Daily News,* July 1, 1979, p. 6.

Chapter Eighteen
1. An unpublished poem by the author, "Decisions," written April 22, 1985.

Chapter Nineteen
1. Letter, George Plimpton to a Dauphine Street recruiter, Major Simon, April 21, 1981; Letter, Dr. Norman Wilson to a navy recruiter, Lt. Dennis Franklin, April 29, 1981. Both letters reprinted by permission of the authors.

Chapter Twenty
1. Written by Laurie Guimont Brown, and reprinted by permission of Mrs. Brown.
2. Letter, Drew T. Brown III to Laurie Guimont Brown, June 25, 1981.
3. Definition of "vector," *Webster's Third New International Directory* (Springfield Mass.: Merriam-Webster Inc., 1986), p. 2537.
4. Letter, Laurie Guimont Brown to Drew T. Brown III, July 28, 1981.
5. Telegram, Drew Bundini Brown, Jr., to Drew Timothy Brown III, Ensign, U.S. Navy, August 21, 1981.

Epilogue
1. Ed Anderson, "Two Men Are Acquitted of Cocaine Sales Charges," New Orleans (La.) *Times-Picayune,* November 25, 1981.
2. "Navy 'A Family Affair' for Ali's Ex-Aide Bundini Brown and Jet Pilot Son," *Jet,* December 26, 1983, pp. 30–31. Reprinted by permission of the publisher.
3. PH2 Chris Holmes, "VA-35 Pilot Is Son of Ali's Trainer," *Jet Observer,* March 13, 1984, p. 3, col. 2.
4. "*Navy Times* Squadron in the Spotlight," *Navy Times,* December 17, 1984, p. 19.
5. Letter, Lt. Drew T. Brown III, to The Honorable John F. Lehman, Secretary of the Navy, September 19, 1986.
6. Photo and outline by Dayna Smith, accompanying Leah Y. Latimer, "Farewell to the *Nimitz,*" *The Washington Post,* December 30, 1986, p. B1, cols.1 and 2.
7. Karlyn Barker, "Shoot for the Moon, Pilot Urges City Students," *The Washington Post,* December 10, 1988, front page, col. 3.
8. Nancy J. Perry, Alan Farnham, and Susan E. Kuhn, "Saving the Schools: How Business Can Help," *Fortune,* November 7, 1988, p. 56, col. 1.
9. Memorandum, Capt. F. G. Horn, USN, Commander, Naval Military Personnel Command, to Lt. Drew T. Brown III, USNR, April 5, 1989.